Principles of
Computer Architecture

Principles of Computer Architecture

Edited by
Earl Bermann

www.willfordpress.com

Published by Willford Press,
118-35 Queens Blvd., Suite 400,
Forest Hills, NY 11375, USA

ISBN: 978-1-68285-480-8

Cataloging-in-Publication Data

Principles of computer architecture / edited by Earl Bermann.
    p. cm.
Includes bibliographical references and index.
ISBN 978-1-68285-480-8
1. Computer architecture. 2. Computer science. I. Bermann, Earl.
QA76.9.A73 P75 2018
004.22--dc23

For information on all Willford Press publications
visit our website at www.willfordpress.com

Contents

Preface

Computer architecture refers to the rules and methods that explain the implementation, functioning and organization of computer systems. It is concerned with the programming and modeling of computers. The different topics included in this subject are logic design, instruction set architecture design, implementation, microarchitecture design etc. This text is a compilation of chapters that discuss the most vital concepts in the field of computer architecture. Most of the topics introduced in it cover new techniques and the applications of this field. As this field is emerging at a rapid pace, the contents of this textbook will help the readers understand the modern concepts of this subject.

To facilitate a deeper understanding of the contents of this book a short introduction of every chapter is written below:

Chapter 1- Computer architecture is a conceptual model that deals with organization and application of computer systems. It also involves microarchitecture design, instruction set architecture design and logic design. The chapter strategically encompasses and incorporates the major components and key concepts of computer architecture, providing a complete understanding.

Chapter 2- Pipeline in a computing system means a set of data which is connected to one another in such a way that one output is another's input. Some of the examples of computer related pipelines are graphics pipelines, pipelining in software, instruction pipelines and HTTP pipelining. This section is an overview of the subject matter incorporating all the major aspects of pipelining.

Chapter 3- Virtual memory is a method of managing the memory of a hardware and software system. Virtual memory is very beneficial as it includes freeing application from sharing space, increases security and can use more memory than a physical system. The following chapter will help the readers in developing a better understanding of virtual memory and caches.

Chapter 4- Synchronization can be of two types, synchronization of processes and of data. The two concepts of synchronization are linked. Synchronization is important for both multi-processor systems and simple processor systems. This chapter provides a plethora of interdisciplinary topics for better comprehension of synchronization.

Chapter 5- A directory is a system used for cataloging files on the computer. They can also be known as folders or drawers. Some of the topics discussed in this chapter are virtual networks, replacement of S blocks and Sequent NUMA-Q. The aspects elucidated in this chapter are of vital importance, and provide a better understanding of computer architecture.

Chapter 6- Parallel computing ensures various computer processes can be run concurrently. There are various forms of parallel computing. Some of these are bit-level, task parallelism and instruction level. The chapter on parallel computing offers an insightful focus, keeping in mind the complex subject matter.

I owe the completion of this book to the never-ending support of my family, who supported me throughout the project.

Editor

Understanding Computer Architecture

Computer architecture is a conceptual model that deals with organization and application of computer systems. It also involves microarchitecture design, instruction set architecture design and logic design. The chapter strategically encompasses and incorporates the major components and key concepts of computer architecture, providing a complete understanding.

Computer Architecture

In computer engineering, computer architecture is a set of rules and methods that describe the functionality, organization, and implementation of computer systems. Some definitions of architecture define it as describing the capabilities and programming model of a computer but not a particular implementation. In other definitions computer architecture involves instruction set architecture design, microarchitecture design, logic design, and implementation.

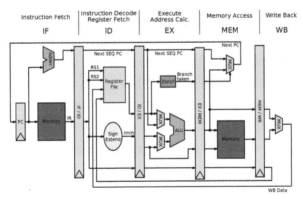

A pipelined implementation of the MIPS architecture. Pipelining is a key concept in computer architecture.

History

The first documented computer architecture was in the correspondence between Charles Babbage and Ada Lovelace, describing the analytical engine. When building the computer Z1 in 1936, Konrad Zuse described in two patent applications for his future projects that machine instructions could be stored in the same storage used for data, i.e. the stored-program concept. Two other early and important examples are:

- John von Neumann's 1945 paper, First Draft of a Report on the EDVAC, which described an organization of logical elements; and

- Alan Turing's more detailed *Proposed Electronic Calculator* for the Automatic Computing Engine, also 1945 and which cited John von Neumann's paper.

The term "architecture" in computer literature can be traced to the work of Lyle R. Johnson, Frederick P. Brooks, Jr., and Mohammad Usman Khan. All of which were members of the Machine Organization department in IBM's main research center in 1959. Johnson had the opportunity to write a proprietary research communication about the Stretch, an IBM-developed supercomputer for Los Alamos National Laboratory (at the time known as Los Alamos Scientific Laboratory). To describe the level of detail for discussing the luxuriously embellished computer, he noted that his description of formats, instruction types, hardware parameters, and speed enhancements were at the level of "system architecture" – a term that seemed more useful than "machine organization."

Subsequently, Brooks, a Stretch designer, started Chapter 2 of a book (Planning a Computer System: Project Stretch, ed. W. Buchholz, 1962) by writing,

Computer architecture, like other architecture, is the art of determining the needs of the user of a structure and then designing to meet those needs as effectively as possible within economic and technological constraints.

Brooks went on to help develop the IBM System/360 (now called the IBM zSeries) line of computers, in which "architecture" became a noun defining "what the user needs to know". Later, computer users came to use the term in many less-explicit ways.

The earliest computer architectures were designed on paper and then directly built into the final hardware form. Later, computer architecture prototypes were physically built in the form of a transistor–transistor logic (TTL) computer—such as the prototypes of the 6800 and the PA-RISC—tested, and tweaked, before committing to the final hardware form. As of the 1990's, new computer architectures are typically "built", tested, and tweaked—inside some other computer architecture in a computer architecture simulator; or inside a FPGA as a soft microprocessor; or both—before committing to the final hardware form.

Subcategories

The discipline of computer architecture has three main subcategories:

1. *Instruction Set Architecture*, or ISA. The ISA defines the machine code that a processor reads and acts upon as well as the word size, memory address modes, processor registers, and data type.

2. *Microarchitecture*, or *computer organization* describes how a particular processor will implement the ISA. The size of a computer's CPU cache for instance, is an issue that generally has nothing to do with the ISA.

3. *System Design* includes all of the other hardware components within a computing system. These include:

    i.   Data processing other than the CPU, such as direct memory access (DMA).

    ii. Other issues such as virtualization, multiprocessing, and software features.

There are other types of computer architecture. The following types are used in bigger companies like Intel, and count for 1% of all of computer architecture.

- Macroarchitecture: architectural layers more abstract than microarchitecture.

- Assembly Instruction Set Architecture (ISA): A smart assembler may convert an abstract assembly language common to a group of machines into slightly different machine language for different implementations.

- Programmer Visible Macroarchitecture: higher level language tools such as compilers may define a consistent interface or contract to programmers using them, abstracting differences between underlying ISA, UISA, and microarchitectures. E.g. the C, C++, or Java standards define different Programmer Visible Macroarchitecture.

- UISA (Microcode Instruction Set Architecture)—a group of machines with different hardware level microarchitectures may share a common microcode architecture, and hence a UISA.

- Pin Architecture: The hardware functions that a microprocessor should provide to a hardware platform, e.g., the x86 pins A20M, FERR/IGNNE or FLUSH. Also, messages that the processor should emit so that external caches can be invalidated (emptied). Pin architecture functions are more flexible than ISA functions because external hardware can adapt to new encodings, or change from a pin to a message. The term "architecture" fits, because the functions must be provided for compatible systems, even if the detailed method changes.

Roles

Definition

The purpose is to design a computer that maximizes performance while keeping power consumption in check, costs low relative to the amount of expected performance, and is also very reliable. For this, many aspects are to be considered which includes instruction set design, functional organization, logic design, and implementation. The implementation involves integrated circuit design, packaging, power, and cooling. Optimization of the design requires familiarity with compilers, operating systems to logic design, and packaging.

Instruction Set Architecture

An instruction set architecture (ISA) is the interface between the computer's software and hardware and also can be viewed as the programmer's view of the machine. Computers do not understand high level languages such as Java, C++, or most programming languages used. A processor only understands instructions encoded in some numerical fashion, usually as binary numbers. Software tools, such as compilers, translate those high level languages into instructions that the processor can understand.

Besides instructions, the ISA defines items in the computer that are available to a program—e.g. data types, registers, addressing modes, and memory. Instructions locate these available items with register indexes (or names) and memory addressing modes.

The ISA of a computer is usually described in a small instruction manual, which describes how the instructions are encoded. Also, it may define short (vaguely) mnemonic names for the instructions.

The names can be recognized by a software development tool called an assembler. An assembler is a computer program that translates a human-readable form of the ISA into a computer-readable form. Disassemblers are also widely available, usually in debuggers and software programs to isolate and correct malfunctions in binary computer programs.

ISAs vary in quality and completeness. A good ISA compromises between programmer convenience (how easy the code is to understand), size of the code (how much code is required to do a specific action), cost of the computer to interpret the instructions (more complexity means more space needed to disassemble the instructions), and speed of the computer (with larger disassemblers comes longer disassemble time). For example, single-instruction ISAs like an ISA that subtracts one from a value and if the value is zero then the value returns to a higher value are both inexpensive, and fast, however ISAs like that are not convenient or helpful when looking at the size of the ISA. Memory organization defines how instructions interact with the memory, and how memory interacts with itself.

During design emulation software (emulators) can run programs written in a proposed instruction set. Modern emulators can measure size, cost, and speed to determine if a particular ISA is meeting its goals.

Computer Organization

Computer organization helps optimize performance-based products. For example, software engineers need to know the processing power of processors. They may need to optimize software in order to gain the most performance for the lowest price. This can require quite detailed analysis of the computer's organization. For example, in a SD card, the designers might need to arrange the card so that the most data can be processed in the fastest possible way.

Computer organization also helps plan the selection of a processor for a particular project. Multimedia projects may need very rapid data access, while virtual machines may need fast interrupts. Sometimes certain tasks need additional components as well. For example, a computer capable of running a virtual machine needs virtual memory hardware so that the memory of different virtual computers can be kept separated. Computer organization and features also affect power consumption and processor cost.

Implementation

Once an instruction set and micro-architecture are designed, a practical machine must be developed. This design process is called the *implementation*. Implementation is usually not considered architectural design, but rather hardware design engineering. Implementation can be further broken down into several steps:

- Logic Implementation designs the circuits required at a logic gate level.

- Circuit Implementation does transistor-level designs of basic elements (gates, multiplexers, latches etc.) as well as of some larger blocks (ALUs, caches etc.) that may be implemented at the log gate level, or even at the physical level if the design calls for it.

- Physical Implementation draws physical circuits. The different circuit components are placed in a chip floorplan or on a board and the wires connecting them are created.

- Design Validation tests the computer as a whole to see if it works in all situations and all timings. Once the design validation process starts, the design at the logic level are tested using logic emulators. However, this is usually too slow to run realistic test. So, after making corrections based on the first test, prototypes are constructed using Field-Programmable Gate-Arrays (FPGAs). Most hobby projects stop at this stage. The final step is to test prototype integrated circuits. Integrated circuits may require several redesigns to fix problems.

For CPUs, the entire implementation process is organized differently and is often referred to as CPU design.

Design Goals

The exact form of a computer system depends on the constraints and goals. Computer architectures usually trade off standards, power versus performance, cost, memory capacity, latency (latency is the amount of time that it takes for information from one node to travel to the source) and throughput. Sometimes other considerations, such as features, size, weight, reliability, and expandability are also factors.

The most common scheme does an in depth power analysis and figures out how to keep power consumption low, while maintaining adequate performance.

Performance

Modern computer performance is often described in IPC (instructions per cycle). This measures the efficiency of the architecture at any clock frequency. Since a faster rate can make a faster computer, this is a useful measurement. Older computers had IPC counts as low as 0.1 instructions per cycle. Simple modern processors easily reach near 1. Superscalar processors may reach three to five IPC by executing several instructions per clock cycle.

Counting machine language instructions would be misleading because they can do varying amounts of work in different ISAs. The "instruction" in the standard measurements is not a count of the ISA's actual machine language instructions, but a unit of measurement, usually based on the speed of the VAX computer architecture.

Many people used to measure a computer's speed by the clock rate (usually in MHz or GHz). This refers to the cycles per second of the main clock of the CPU. However, this metric is somewhat misleading, as a machine with a higher clock rate may not necessarily have greater performance. As a result, manufacturers have moved away from clock speed as a measure of performance.

Other factors influence speed, such as the mix of functional units, bus speeds, available memory, and the type and order of instructions in the programs.

There are two main types of speed: latency and throughput. Latency is the time between the start of a process and its completion. Throughput is the amount of work done per unit time. Interrupt latency is the guaranteed maximum response time of the system to an electronic event (like when the disk drive finishes moving some data).

Performance is affected by a very wide range of design choices — for example, pipelining a processor usually makes latency worse, but makes throughput better. Computers that control machinery usually need low interrupt latencies. These computers operate in a real-time environment and fail if an operation is not completed in a specified amount of time. For example, computer-controlled anti-lock brakes must begin braking within a predictable, short time after the brake pedal is sensed or else failure of the brake will occur.

Benchmarking takes all these factors into account by measuring the time a computer takes to run through a series of test programs. Although benchmarking shows strengths, it shouldn't be how you choose a computer. Often the measured machines split on different measures. For example, one system might handle scientific applications quickly, while another might render video games more smoothly. Furthermore, designers may target and add special features to their products, through hardware or software, that permit a specific benchmark to execute quickly but don't offer similar advantages to general tasks.

Power Efficiency

Power efficiency is another important measurement in modern computers. A higher power efficiency can often be traded for lower speed or higher cost. The typical measurement when referring to power consumption in computer architecture is MIPS/W (millions of instructions per second per watt).

Modern circuits have less power required per transistor as the number of transistors per chip grows. This is because each transistor that is put in a new chip requires its own power supply and requires new pathways to be built to power it. However the number of transistors per chip is starting to increase at a slower rate. Therefore, power efficiency is starting to become as important, if not more important than fitting more and more transistors into a single chip. Recent processor designs have shown this emphasis as they put more focus on power efficiency rather than cramming as many transistors into a single chip as possible. In the world of embedded computers, power efficiency has long been an important goal next to throughput and latency.

Shifts in Market Demand

Increases in publicly released refresh rates have grown slowly over the past few years, with respect to vast leaps in power consumption reduction and miniaturization demand. This has led to a new demand for longer battery life and reductions in size due to the mobile technology being produced at a greater rate. This change in focus from greater refresh rates to power consumption and miniturization can be shown by the significant reductions in power consumption, as much as 50%, that were reported by Intel in their release of the Haswell (microarchitecture); where they dropped their power consumption benchmark from 30-40 watts down to 10-20 watts. Comparing this to the processing speed increase of 3 GHz to 4 GHz (2002 to 2006) it can be seen that the focus in research and development are shifting away from refresh rates and moving towards consuming less power and taking up less space.

Architect's Job

- Design and engineer various parts of a computer system to maximize performance and programmability within the technology limits and cost budget

- Technology limit could mean process/circuit technology in case of microprocessor architecture

- For bigger systems technology limit could mean interconnect technology (how one component talks to another at macro level)

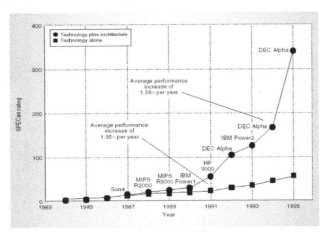

Slightly outdated data

58% Growth Rate

- Two major architectural reasons

  - Advent of RISC (Reduced Instruction Set Computer) made it easy to implement many aggressive architectural techniques for extracting parallelism

  - Introduction of caches

- Made easy by Moore's law

- Two major impacts

  - Highest performance microprocessors today outperform supercomputers designed less than 10 years ago

  - Microprocessor-based products have dominated all sectors of computing: desktops, workstations, minicomputers are replaced by servers, mainframes are replaced by multiprocessors, supercomputers are built out of commodity microprocessors (also a cost factor dictated this trend)

The Computer Market

- Three major sectors

  - Desktop: ranges from low-end PCs to high-end workstations; market trend is very sensitive to price-performance ratio

  - Server: used in large-scale computing or service-oriented market such as heavy-weight scientific computing, databases, web services, etc; reliability, availability and scalability are very important; servers are normally designed for high throughput

- o Embedded: fast growing sector; very price-sensitive; present in most day-to-day appliances such as microwave ovens, washing machines, printers, network switches, palmtops, cell phones, smart cards, game engines; software is usually specialized/tuned for one particular system

The Applications

- Very different in three sectors

  - o This difference is the main reason for different design styles in these three areas

  - o Desktop market demands leading-edge microprocessors, high-performance graphics engines; must offer balanced performance for a wide range of applications; customers are happy to spend a reasonable amount of money for high performance i.e. the metric is price-performance

  - o Server market integrates high-end microprocessors into scalable multiprocessors; throughput is very important; could be floating-point or graphics or transaction throughput

  - o Embedded market adopts high-end microprocessor techniques paying immense attention to low price and low power; processors are either general purpose (to some extent) or application-specific

Parallel Architecture

- Collection of processing elements that co-operate to solve large problems fast

- Design questions that need to be answered

  - o How many processing elements (scalability)?

  - o How capable is each processor (computing power)?

  - o How to address memory (shared or distributed)?

  - o How much addressable memory (address bit allocation)?

  - o How do the processors communicate (through memory or by messages)?

  - o How do the processors avoid data races (synchronization)?

  - o How do you answer all these to achieve highest performance within your cost envelope?

Why Parallel Arch?

- Parallelism helps

- There are applications that can be parallelized easily

- There are important applications that require enormous amount of computation (10 GFLOPS to 1 TFLOPS)

- NASA taps SGI, Intel for Supercomputers: 20 512p SGI Altix using Itanium 2
- There are important applications that need to deliver high throughput

Why study it?

- Parallelism is ubiquitous
  - Need to understand the design trade-offs
  - Microprocessors are now multiprocessors (more later)
  - Today a computer architect's primary job is to find out how to efficiently extract parallelism
- Get involved in interesting research projects
  - Make an impact
  - Shape the future development
  - Have fun

Performance Metrics

- Need benchmark applications
  - SPLASH (Stanford ParalleL Applications for SHared memory)
  - SPEC (Standard Performance Evaluation Corp.) OMP
  - ScaLAPACK (Scalable Linear Algebra PACKage) for message-passing machines
  - TPC (Transaction Processing Performance Council) for database/transaction processing performance
  - NAS (Numerical Aerodynamic Simulation) for aerophysics applications
    - ◊ NPB2 port to MPI for message-passing only
    - ◊ PARKBENCH (PARallel Kernels and BENCHmarks) for message-passing only
- Comparing two different parallel computers
  - Execution time is the most reliable metric
  - Sometimes MFLOPS, GFLOPS, TFLOPS are used, but could be misleading
- Evaluating a particular machine
  - Use speedup to gauge scalability of the machine (provided the application itself scales)
  - Speedup(P) = Uniprocessor time/Time on P processors
  - Normally the input data set is kept constant when measuring speedup

Throughput Metrics

- Sometimes metrics like jobs/hour may be more important than just the turn-around time of a job

  o This is the case for transaction processing (the biggest commercial application for servers)

  o Needs to serve as many transactions as possible in a given time provided time per transaction is reasonable

  o Transactions are largely independent; so throw in as many hardware threads as possible

  o Known as throughput computing

Application Trends

- Equal to or below 1 GFLOPS requirements

  o 2D airfoil, oil reservoir modeling, 3D plasma modeling, 48-hour weather

- Below 100 GFLOPS requirements

  o Chemical dynamics, structural biology, 72-hour weather

- Tomorrow's applications (beyond 100 GFLOPS)

  o Human genome, protein folding, superconductor modeling, quantum chromodynamics, molecular geometry, real-time vision and speech recognition, graphics, CAD, space exploration, global-warming etc.

- Demand for insatiable CPU cycles (need large-scale supercomputers)

Commercial Sector

- Slightly different story

  o Transactions per minute (tpm)

- Scale of computers is much smaller

  o 4P machines to maybe 32P servers

- But use of parallelism is tremendous

  o Need to serve as many transaction threads as possible (maximize the number of database users)

  o Need to handle large data footprint and offer massive parallelism (also economics kicks in: should be low-cost)

Desktop Market

- Demand to improve throughput for sequential multi-programmed workload

- o   I want to run as many simulations as I can and want them to finish before I come back next morning

- o   Possibly the biggest application for small-scale multiprocessors (e.g. 2 or 4-way SMPs)

- Even on a uniprocessor machine I would be happy if I could play AOE without affecting the performance of my simulation running in background (simultaneous multi-threading and chip multi-processing; more later)

Microarchitecture

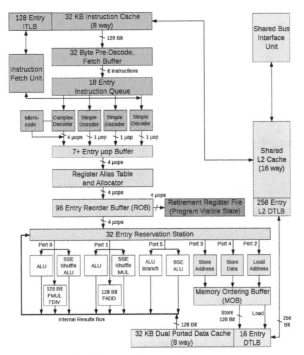

Intel Core microarchitecture

In electronics engineering and computer engineering, microarchitecture, also called computer organization and sometimes abbreviated as µarch or uarch, is the way a given instruction set architecture (ISA) is implemented in a particular processor. A given ISA may be implemented with different microarchitectures; implementations may vary due to different goals of a given design or due to shifts in technology.

Computer architecture is the combination of microarchitecture and instruction set.

Relation to Instruction Set Architecture

The ISA is roughly the same as the programming model of a processor as seen by an assembly language programmer or compiler writer. The ISA includes the execution model, processor registers, address and data formats among other things. The microarchitecture includes the constituent parts of the processor and how these interconnect and interoperate to implement the ISA.

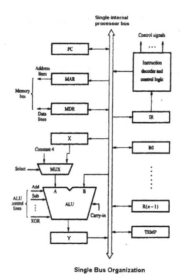

Single Bus Organization

A microarchitecture organized around a single bus

The microarchitecture of a machine is usually represented as (more or less detailed) diagrams that describe the interconnections of the various microarchitectural elements of the machine, which may be anything from single gates and registers, to complete arithmetic logic units (ALUs) and even larger elements. These diagrams generally separate the datapath (where data is placed) and the control path (which can be said to steer the data).

The person designing a system usually draws the specific microarchitecture as a kind of data flow diagram. Like a block diagram, the microarchitecture diagram shows microarchitectural elements such as the arithmetic and logic unit and the register file as a single schematic symbol. Typically, the diagram connects those elements with arrows, thick lines and thin lines to distinguish between three-state buses (which require a three-state buffer for each device that drives the bus), unidirectional buses (always driven by a single source, such as the way the address bus on simpler computers is always driven by the memory address register), and individual control lines. Very simple computers have a single data bus organization – they have a single three-state bus. The diagram of more complex computers usually shows multiple three-state buses, which help the machine do more operations simultaneously.

Each microarchitectural element is in turn represented by a schematic describing the interconnections of logic gates used to implement it. Each logic gate is in turn represented by a circuit diagram describing the connections of the transistors used to implement it in some particular logic family. Machines with different microarchitectures may have the same instruction set architecture, and thus be capable of executing the same programs. New microarchitectures and/or circuitry solutions, along with advances in semiconductor manufacturing, are what allows newer generations of processors to achieve higher performance while using the same ISA.

In principle, a single microarchitecture could execute several different ISAs with only minor changes to the microcode.

Aspects of Microarchitecture

The pipelined datapath is the most commonly used datapath design in microarchitecture today. This technique is used in most modern microprocessors, microcontrollers, and DSPs. The pipelined architecture allows multiple instructions to overlap in execution, much like an assembly line. The pipeline includes several different stages which are fundamental in microarchitecture designs. Some of these stages include instruction fetch, instruction decode, execute, and write back. Some architectures include other stages such as memory access. The design of pipelines is one of the central microarchitectural tasks.

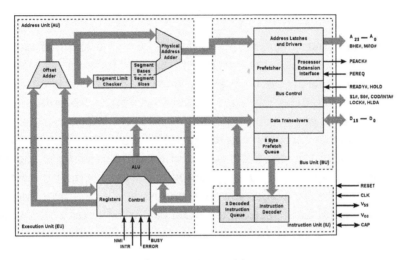

Intel 80286 microarchitecture

Execution units are also essential to microarchitecture. Execution units include arithmetic logic units (ALU), floating point units (FPU), load/store units, branch prediction, and SIMD. These units perform the operations or calculations of the processor. The choice of the number of execution units, their latency and throughput is a central microarchitectural design task. The size, latency, throughput and connectivity of memories within the system are also microarchitectural decisions.

System-level design decisions such as whether or not to include peripherals, such as memory controllers, can be considered part of the microarchitectural design process. This includes decisions on the performance-level and connectivity of these peripherals.

Unlike architectural design, where achieving a specific performance level is the main goal, microarchitectural design pays closer attention to other constraints. Since microarchitecture design decisions directly affect what goes into a system, attention must be paid to issues such as chip area/cost, power consumption, logic complexity, ease of connectivity, manufacturability, ease of debugging, and testability.

Microarchitectural Concepts

Instruction Cycle

In general, all CPUs, single-chip microprocessors or multi-chip implementations run programs by performing the following steps:

1. Read an instruction and decode it

2. Find any associated data that is needed to process the instruction

3. Process the instruction

4. Write the results out

The instruction cycle is repeated continuously until the power is turned off.

Increasing Execution Speed

Complicating this simple-looking series of steps is the fact that the memory hierarchy, which includes caching, main memory and non-volatile storage like hard disks (where the program instructions and data reside), has always been slower than the processor itself. Step (2) often introduces a lengthy (in CPU terms) delay while the data arrives over the computer bus. A considerable amount of research has been put into designs that avoid these delays as much as possible. Over the years, a central goal was to execute more instructions in parallel, thus increasing the effective execution speed of a program. These efforts introduced complicated logic and circuit structures. Initially, these techniques could only be implemented on expensive mainframes or supercomputers due to the amount of circuitry needed for these techniques. As semiconductor manufacturing progressed, more and more of these techniques could be implemented on a single semiconductor chip.

Instruction Set Choice

Instruction sets have shifted over the years, from originally very simple to sometimes very complex (in various respects). In recent years, load-store architectures, VLIW and EPIC types have been in fashion. Architectures that are dealing with data parallelism include SIMD and Vectors. Some labels used to denote classes of CPU architectures are not particularly descriptive, especially so the CISC label; many early designs retroactively denoted "CISC" are in fact significantly simpler than modern RISC processors (in several respects).

However, the choice of instruction set architecture may greatly affect the complexity of implementing high performance devices. The prominent strategy, used to develop the first RISC processors, was to simplify instructions to a minimum of individual semantic complexity combined with high encoding regularity and simplicity. Such uniform instructions were easily fetched, decoded and executed in a pipelined fashion and a simple strategy to reduce the number of logic levels in order to reach high operating frequencies; instruction cache-memories compensated for the higher operating frequency and inherently low code density while large register sets were used to factor out as much of the (slow) memory accesses as possible.

Instruction Pipelining

One of the first, and most powerful, techniques to improve performance is the use of the instruction pipeline. Early processor designs would carry out all of the steps above for one instruction before moving onto the next. Large portions of the circuitry were left idle at any one step; for instance, the instruction decoding circuitry would be idle during execution and so on.

Pipelines improve performance by allowing a number of instructions to work their way through the processor at the same time. In the same basic example, the processor would start to decode (step 1) a new instruction while the last one was waiting for results. This would allow up to four instructions to be "in flight" at one time, making the processor look four times as fast. Although any one instruction takes just as long to complete (there are still four steps) the CPU as a whole "retires" instructions much faster.

RISC makes pipelines smaller and much easier to construct by cleanly separating each stage of the instruction process and making them take the same amount of time — one cycle. The processor as a whole operates in an assembly line fashion, with instructions coming in one side and results out the other. Due to the reduced complexity of the Classic RISC pipeline, the pipelined core and an instruction cache could be placed on the same size die that would otherwise fit the core alone on a CISC design. This was the real reason that RISC was faster. Early designs like the SPARC and MIPS often ran over 10 times as fast as Intel and Motorola CISC solutions at the same clock speed and price.

Pipelines are by no means limited to RISC designs. By 1986 the top-of-the-line VAX implementation (VAX 8800) was a heavily pipelined design, slightly predating the first commercial MIPS and SPARC designs. Most modern CPUs (even embedded CPUs) are now pipelined, and microcoded CPUs with no pipelining are seen only in the most area-constrained embedded processors. Large CISC machines, from the VAX 8800 to the modern Pentium 4 and Athlon, are implemented with both microcode and pipelines. Improvements in pipelining and caching are the two major microarchitectural advances that have enabled processor performance to keep pace with the circuit technology on which they are based.

Cache

It was not long before improvements in chip manufacturing allowed for even more circuitry to be placed on the die, and designers started looking for ways to use it. One of the most common was to add an ever-increasing amount of cache memory on-die. Cache is simply very fast memory, memory that can be accessed in a few cycles as opposed to many needed to "talk" to main memory. The CPU includes a cache controller which automates reading and writing from the cache, if the data is already in the cache it simply "appears", whereas if it is not the processor is "stalled" while the cache controller reads it in.

RISC designs started adding cache in the mid-to-late 1980s, often only 4 KB in total. This number grew over time, and typical CPUs now have at least 512 KB, while more powerful CPUs come with 1 or 2 or even 4, 6, 8 or 12 MB, organized in multiple levels of a memory hierarchy. Generally speaking, more cache means more performance, due to reduced stalling.

Caches and pipelines were a perfect match for each other. Previously, it didn't make much sense to build a pipeline that could run faster than the access latency of off-chip memory. Using on-chip cache memory instead, meant that a pipeline could run at the speed of the cache access latency, a much smaller length of time. This allowed the operating frequencies of processors to increase at a much faster rate than that of off-chip memory.

Branch Prediction

One barrier to achieving higher performance through instruction-level parallelism stems from pipeline stalls and flushes due to branches. Normally, whether a conditional branch will be taken isn't known until late in the pipeline as conditional branches depend on results coming from a register. From the time that the processor's instruction decoder has figured out that it has encountered a conditional branch instruction to the time that the deciding register value can be read out, the pipeline needs to be stalled for several cycles, or if it's not and the branch is taken, the pipeline needs to be flushed. As clock speeds increase the depth of the pipeline increases with it, and some modern processors may have 20 stages or more. On average, every fifth instruction executed is a branch, so without any intervention, that's a high amount of stalling.

Techniques such as branch prediction and speculative execution are used to lessen these branch penalties. Branch prediction is where the hardware makes educated guesses on whether a particular branch will be taken. In reality one side or the other of the branch will be called much more often than the other. Modern designs have rather complex statistical prediction systems, which watch the results of past branches to predict the future with greater accuracy. The guess allows the hardware to prefetch instructions without waiting for the register read. Speculative execution is a further enhancement in which the code along the predicted path is not just prefetched but also executed before it is known whether the branch should be taken or not. This can yield better performance when the guess is good, with the risk of a huge penalty when the guess is bad because instructions need to be undone.

Superscalar

Even with all of the added complexity and gates needed to support the concepts outlined above, improvements in semiconductor manufacturing soon allowed even more logic gates to be used.

In the outline above the processor processes parts of a single instruction at a time. Computer programs could be executed faster if multiple instructions were processed simultaneously. This is what superscalar processors achieve, by replicating functional units such as ALUs. The replication of functional units was only made possible when the die area of a single-issue processor no longer stretched the limits of what could be reliably manufactured. By the late 1980s, superscalar designs started to enter the market place.

In modern designs it is common to find two load units, one store (many instructions have no results to store), two or more integer math units, two or more floating point units, and often a SIMD unit of some sort. The instruction issue logic grows in complexity by reading in a huge list of instructions from memory and handing them off to the different execution units that are idle at that point. The results are then collected and re-ordered at the end.

Out-of-order Execution

The addition of caches reduces the frequency or duration of stalls due to waiting for data to be fetched from the memory hierarchy, but does not get rid of these stalls entirely. In early designs a *cache miss* would force the cache controller to stall the processor and wait. Of course there may be some other instruction in the program whose data *is* available in the cache at that point. Out-of-order execution allows that ready instruction to be processed while an older instruction waits on the cache, then re-orders the results to make it appear that everything happened in the programmed order. This technique is also used to avoid other operand dependency stalls, such as an instruction awaiting a result from a long latency floating-point operation or other multi-cycle operations.

Register Renaming

Register renaming refers to a technique used to avoid unnecessary serialized execution of program instructions because of the reuse of the same registers by those instructions. Suppose we have two groups of instruction that will use the same register. One set of instructions is executed first to leave the register to the other set, but if the other set is assigned to a different similar register, both sets of instructions can be executed in parallel (or) in series.

Multiprocessing and Multithreading

Computer architects have become stymied by the growing mismatch in CPU operating frequencies and DRAM access times. None of the techniques that exploited instruction-level parallelism (ILP) within one program could make up for the long stalls that occurred when data had to be fetched from main memory. Additionally, the large transistor counts and high operating frequencies needed for the more advanced ILP techniques required power dissipation levels that could no longer be cheaply cooled. For these reasons, newer generations of computers have started to exploit higher levels of parallelism that exist outside of a single program or program thread.

This trend is sometimes known as *throughput computing*. This idea originated in the mainframe market where online transaction processing emphasized not just the execution speed of one transaction, but the capacity to deal with massive numbers of transactions. With transaction-based applications such as network routing and web-site serving greatly increasing in the last decade, the computer industry has re-emphasized capacity and throughput issues.

One technique of how this parallelism is achieved is through multiprocessing systems, computer systems with multiple CPUs. Once reserved for high-end mainframes and supercomputers, small-scale (2–8) multiprocessors servers have become commonplace for the small business market. For large corporations, large scale (16–256) multiprocessors are common. Even personal computers with multiple CPUs have appeared since the 1990s.

With further transistor size reductions made available with semiconductor technology advances, multi-core CPUs have appeared where multiple CPUs are implemented on the same silicon chip. Initially used in chips targeting embedded markets, where simpler and smaller CPUs would allow multiple instantiations to fit on one piece of silicon. By 2005, semiconductor technology allowed dual high-end desktop CPUs *CMP* chips to be manufactured in volume. Some designs, such as Sun Microsystems' UltraSPARC T1 have reverted to simpler (scalar, in-order) designs in order to fit more processors on one piece of silicon.

Another technique that has become more popular recently is multithreading. In multithreading, when the processor has to fetch data from slow system memory, instead of stalling for the data to arrive, the processor switches to another program or program thread which is ready to execute. Though this does not speed up a particular program/thread, it increases the overall system throughput by reducing the time the CPU is idle.

Conceptually, multithreading is equivalent to a context switch at the operating system level. The difference is that a multithreaded CPU can do a thread switch in one CPU cycle instead of the hundreds or thousands of CPU cycles a context switch normally requires. This is achieved by replicating the state hardware (such as the register file and program counter) for each active thread.

A further enhancement is simultaneous multithreading. This technique allows superscalar CPUs to execute instructions from different programs/threads simultaneously in the same cycle.

Instruction Set Architecture

An instruction set architecture (ISA) is an abstract model of a computer. It is also referred to as architecture or computer architecture. A realization of an ISA is called an *implementation*. An ISA permits multiple implementations that may vary in performance, physical size, and monetary cost (among other things); because the ISA serves as the interface between software and hardware. Software that has been written for an ISA can run on different implementations of the same ISA. This has enabled binary compatibility between different generations of computers to be easily achieved, and the development of computer families. Both of these developments have helped to lower the cost of computers and to increase their applicability. For these reasons, the ISA is one of the most important abstractions in computing today.

An ISA defines everything a machine language programmer needs to know in order to program a computer. What an ISA defines differs between ISAs; in general, ISAs define the supported data types, what state there is (such as the main memory and registers) and their semantics (such as the memory consistency and addressing modes), the *instruction set* (the set of machine instructions that comprises a computer's machine language), and the input/output model.

Overview

An instruction set architecture is distinguished from a microarchitecture, which is the set of processor design techniques used, in a particular processor, to implement the instruction set. Processors with different microarchitectures can share a common instruction set. For example, the Intel Pentium and the AMD Athlon implement nearly identical versions of the x86 instruction set, but have radically different internal designs.

The concept of an *architecture*, distinct from the design of a specific machine, was developed by Fred Brooks at IBM during the design phase of System/360.

Prior to NPL [System/360], the company's computer designers had been free to honor cost objectives not only by selecting technologies but also by fashioning functional and architectural refinements. The SPREAD compatibility objective, in contrast, postulated a single architecture for a series of five processors spanning a wide range of cost and performance. None of the five engineering design teams could count on being able to bring about adjustments in architectural specifications as a way of easing difficulties in achieving cost and performance objectives.

Some virtual machines that support bytecode as their ISA such as Smalltalk, the Java virtual machine, and Microsoft's Common Language Runtime, implement this by translating the bytecode for commonly used code paths into native machine code. In addition, these virtual machines execute less frequently used code paths by interpretation. Transmeta implemented the x86 instruction set atop VLIW processors in this fashion.

Classification of ISAs

An ISA may be classified in a number of different ways. A common classification is by architectural *complexity*. A complex instruction set computer (CISC) has many specialized instructions, some of which may only be rarely used in practical programs. A reduced instruction set computer (RISC) simplifies the processor by efficiently implementing only the instructions that are frequently used in programs, while the less common operations are implemented as subroutines, having their resulting additional processor execution time offset by infrequent use.

Other types include very long instruction word (VLIW) architectures, and the closely related *long instruction word* (LIW) and *explicitly parallel instruction computing* (EPIC) architectures. These architectures seek to exploit instruction-level parallelism with less hardware than RISC and CISC by making the compiler responsible for instruction issue and scheduling.

Architectures with even less complexity have been studied, such as the minimal instruction set computer (MISC) and one instruction set computer (OISC). These are theoretically important types, but have not been commercialized.

Machine Language

Machine language is built up from discrete *statements* or *instructions*. On the processing architecture, a given instruction may specify:

- particular registers for arithmetic, addressing, or control functions

- particular memory locations or offsets

- particular addressing modes used to interpret the operands

More complex operations are built up by combining these simple instructions, which are executed sequentially, or as otherwise directed by control flow instructions.

Instruction Types

Examples of operations common to many instruction sets include:

Data Handling and Memory Operations

- *Set* a register to a fixed constant value.

- *Copy* data from a memory location to a register, or vice versa (a machine instruction is often called *move*, however the term is misleading). Used to store the contents of a register, result of a computation, or to retrieve stored data to perform a computation on it later. Often called load and store operations.

- *Read* and *write* data from hardware devices.

Arithmetic and Logic Operations

- *Add*, *subtract*, *multiply*, or *divide* the values of two registers, placing the result in a register, possibly setting one or more condition codes in a status register.

- o *increment, decrement* in some ISAs, saving operand fetch in trivial cases.
- Perform bitwise operations, e.g., taking the *conjunction* and *disjunction* of corresponding bits in a pair of registers, taking the *negation* of each bit in a register.
- *Compare* two values in registers.
- *Floating-point instructions* for arithmetic on floating-point numbers.

Control Flow Operations

- *Branch* to another location in the program and execute instructions there.
- *Conditionally branch* to another location if a certain condition holds.
- *Indirectly branch* to another location.
- *Call* another block of code, while saving the location of the next instruction as a point to return to.

Coprocessor Instructions

- Load/store data to and from a coprocessor, or exchanging with CPU registers.
- Perform coprocessor operations.

Complex Instructions

Processors may include "complex" instructions in their instruction set. A single "complex" instruction does something that may take many instructions on other computers. Such instructions are typified by instructions that take multiple steps, control multiple functional units, or otherwise appear on a larger scale than the bulk of simple instructions implemented by the given processor. Some examples of "complex" instructions include:

- transferring multiple registers to or from memory (especially the stack) at once
- moving large blocks of memory (e.g. string copy or DMA transfer)
- complicated integer and floating-point arithmetic (e.g. square root, or transcendental functions such as logarithm, sine, cosine, etc.)
- *SIMD instructions*, a single instruction performing an operation on many homogeneous values in parallel, possibly in dedicated SIMD registers
- performing an atomic test-and-set instruction or other read-modify-write atomic instruction
- instructions that perform ALU operations with an operand from memory rather than a register

Complex instructions are more common in CISC instruction sets than in RISC instruction sets, but RISC instruction sets may include them as well. RISC instruction sets generally do not include ALU operations with memory operands, or instructions to move large blocks of memory, but most RISC instruction sets include SIMD or vector instructions that perform the same arithmetic operation on multiple pieces of data at the same time. SIMD instructions have the ability of manipulating large vectors and matrices in minimal time. SIMD instructions allow easy parallelization of algorithms commonly involved in sound, image, and video processing. Various SIMD implementations have been brought to market under trade names such as MMX, 3DNow!, and AltiVec.

Parts of an Instruction

MIPS32 Add Immediate Instruction

001000	00001	00010	0000000101011110
OP Code	Addr 1	Addr 2	Immediate value

Equivalent mnemonic: **addi** $r1, $r2,

One instruction may have several fields, which identify the logical operation, and may also include source and destination addresses and constant values. This is the MIPS "Add Immediate" instruction, which allows selection of source and destination registers and inclusion of a small constant.

On traditional architectures, an instruction includes an opcode that specifies the operation to perform, such as *add contents of memory to register*—and zero or more operand specifiers, which may specify registers, memory locations, or literal data. The operand specifiers may have addressing modes determining their meaning or may be in fixed fields. In very long instruction word (VLIW) architectures, which include many microcode architectures, multiple simultaneous opcodes and operands are specified in a single instruction.

Some exotic instruction sets do not have an opcode field, such as transport triggered architectures (TTA), only operand(s).

The Forth virtual machine and other "0-operand" instruction sets lack any operand specifier fields, such as some stack machines including NOSC.

Conditional instructions often have a predicate field—a few bits that encode the specific condition to cause the operation to be performed rather than not performed. For example, a conditional branch instruction will be executed, and the branch taken, if the condition is true, so that execution proceeds to a different part of the program, and not executed, and the branch not taken, if the condition is false, so that execution continues sequentially. Some instruction sets also have conditional moves, so that the move will be executed, and the data stored in the target location, if the condition is true, and not executed, and the target location not modified, if the condition is false. Similarly, IBM z/Architecture has a conditional store instruction. A few instruction sets include a predicate field in every instruction; this is called branch predication.

Instruction Length

The size or length of an instruction varies widely, from as little as four bits in some microcontrollers to many hundreds of bits in some VLIW systems. Processors used in personal computers, mainframes, and supercomputers have instruction sizes between 8 and 64 bits. The longest possible instruction on x86 is 15 bytes (120 bits). Within an instruction set, different instructions may have different lengths. In some architectures, notably most reduced instruction set computers (RISC), instructions are a fixed length, typically corresponding with that architecture's word size. In other architectures, instructions have variable length, typically integral multiples of a byte or a halfword. Some, such as the ARM with *Thumb-extension* have *mixed* variable encoding, that is two fixed, usually 32-bit and 16-bit encodings, where instructions can not be mixed freely but must be switched between on a branch (or exception boundary in ARMv8).

A RISC instruction set normally has a fixed instruction width (often 4 bytes = 32 bits), whereas a typical CISC instruction set may have instructions of widely varying length (1 to 15 bytes for x86). Fixed-width instructions are less complicated to handle than variable-width instructions for several reasons (not having to check whether an instruction straddles a cache line or virtual memory page boundary for instance), and are therefore somewhat easier to optimize for speed.

Representation

The instructions constituting a program are rarely specified using their internal, numeric form (machine code); they may be specified by programmers using an assembly language or, more commonly, may be generated from programming languages by compilers.

Design

The design of instruction sets is a complex issue. There were two stages in history for the microprocessor. The first was the CISC (Complex Instruction Set Computer), which had many different instructions. In the 1970s, however, places like IBM did research and found that many instructions in the set could be eliminated. The result was the RISC (Reduced Instruction Set Computer), an architecture that uses a smaller set of instructions. A simpler instruction set may offer the potential for higher speeds, reduced processor size, and reduced power consumption. However, a more complex set may optimize common operations, improve memory and cache efficiency, or simplify programming.

Some instruction set designers reserve one or more opcodes for some kind of system call or software interrupt. For example, MOS Technology 6502 uses 00_H, Zilog Z80 uses the eight codes $C7,CF,D7,DF,E7,EF,F7,FF_H$ while Motorola 68000 use codes in the range $A000..AFFF_H$.

Fast virtual machines are much easier to implement if an instruction set meets the Popek and Goldberg virtualization requirements.

The NOP slide used in immunity-aware programming is much easier to implement if the "unprogrammed" state of the memory is interpreted as a NOP.

On systems with multiple processors, non-blocking synchronization algorithms are much easier to implement if the instruction set includes support for something such as "fetch-and-add", "load-link/store-conditional" (LL/SC), or "atomic compare-and-swap".

Instruction Set Implementation

Any given instruction set can be implemented in a variety of ways. All ways of implementing a particular instruction set provide the same programming model, and all implementations of that instruction set are able to run the same executables. The various ways of implementing an instruction set give different tradeoffs between cost, performance, power consumption, size, etc.

When designing the microarchitecture of a processor, engineers use blocks of "hard-wired" electronic circuitry (often designed separately) such as adders, multiplexers, counters, registers, ALUs, etc. Some kind of register transfer language is then often used to describe the decoding and sequencing of each instruction of an ISA using this physical microarchitecture. There are two basic ways to build a control unit to implement this description (although many designs use middle ways or compromises):

1. Some computer designs "hardwire" the complete instruction set decoding and sequencing (just like the rest of the microarchitecture).

2. Other designs employ microcode routines or tables (or both) to do this—typically as on-chip ROMs or PLAs or both (although separate RAMs and ROMs have been used historically). The Western Digital MCP-1600 is an older example, using a dedicated, separate ROM for microcode.

Some designs use a combination of hardwired design and microcode for the control unit.

Some CPU designs use a writable control store—they compile the instruction set to a writable RAM or flash inside the CPU (such as the Rekursiv processor and the Imsys Cjip), or an FPGA (reconfigurable computing).

An ISA can also be emulated in software by an interpreter. Naturally, due to the interpretation overhead, this is slower than directly running programs on the emulated hardware, unless the hardware running the emulator is an order of magnitude faster. Today, it is common practice for vendors of new ISAs or microarchitectures to make software emulators available to software developers before the hardware implementation is ready.

Often the details of the implementation have a strong influence on the particular instructions selected for the instruction set. For example, many implementations of the instruction pipeline only allow a single memory load or memory store per instruction, leading to a load-store architecture (RISC). For another example, some early ways of implementing the instruction pipeline led to a delay slot.

The demands of high-speed digital signal processing have pushed in the opposite direction—forcing instructions to be implemented in a particular way. For example, to perform digital filters fast enough, the MAC instruction in a typical digital signal processor (DSP) must use a kind of Harvard architecture that can fetch an instruction and two data words simultaneously, and it requires a single-cycle multiply–accumulate multiplier.

Code Density

In early computers, memory was expensive, so minimizing the size of a program to make sure it would fit in the limited memory was often central. Thus the combined size of all the instructions needed to perform a particular task, the *code density*, was an important characteristic of any instruction set. Computers with high code density often have complex instructions for procedure entry, parameterized returns, loops, etc. (therefore retroactively named *Complex Instruction Set Computers*, CISC). However, more typical, or frequent, "CISC" instructions merely combine a basic ALU operation, such as "add", with the access of one or more operands in memory (using addressing modes such as direct, indirect, indexed, etc.). Certain architectures may allow two or three operands (including the result) directly in memory or may be able to perform functions such as automatic pointer increment, etc. Software-implemented instruction sets may have even more complex and powerful instructions.

Reduced instruction-set computers, RISC, were first widely implemented during a period of rapidly growing memory subsystems. They sacrifice code density to simplify implementation circuitry, and try to increase performance via higher clock frequencies and more registers. A single RISC instruction typically performs only a single operation, such as an "add" of registers or a "load" from a memory location into a register. A RISC instruction set normally has a fixed instruction width, whereas a typical CISC instruction set has instructions of widely varying length. However, as RISC computers normally require more and often longer instructions to implement a given task, they inherently make less optimal use of bus bandwidth and cache memories.

Certain embedded RISC ISAs like Thumb and AVR32 typically exhibit very high density owing to a technique called code compression. This technique packs two 16-bit instructions into one 32-bit instruction, which is then unpacked at the decode stage and executed as two instructions.

Minimal instruction set computers (MISC) are a form of stack machine, where there are few separate instructions (16-64), so that multiple instructions can be fit into a single machine word. These type of cores often take little silicon to implement, so they can be easily realized in an FPGA or in a multi-core form. The code density of MISC is similar to the code density of RISC; the increased instruction density is offset by requiring more of the primitive instructions to do a task.

There has been research into executable compression as a mechanism for improving code density. The mathematics of Kolmogorov complexity describes the challenges and limits of this.

Number of Operands

Instruction sets may be categorized by the maximum number of operands *explicitly* specified in instructions.

(In the examples that follow, *a*, *b*, and *c* are (direct or calculated) addresses referring to memory cells, while *reg1* and so on refer to machine registers.)

C = A+B

- 0-operand (*zero-address machines*), so called stack machines: All arithmetic operations take place using the top one or two positions on the stack: *push a, push b, add, pop c*.

    o   *C = A+B* needs *four instructions*. For stack machines, the terms "0-operand" and "zero-address" apply to arithmetic instructions, but not to all instructions, as 1-operand push and pop instructions are used to access memory.

- 1-operand (*one-address machines*), so called accumulator machines, include early computers and many small microcontrollers: most instructions specify a single right operand (that is, constant, a register, or a memory location), with the implicit accumulator as the left operand (and the destination if there is one): *load a, add b, store c.*

  o $C = A+B$ needs *three instructions.*

- 2-operand — many CISC and RISC machines fall under this category:

  o CISC — *move A to C*; then *add B to C.*

    ▪ $C = A+B$ needs *two instructions.* This effectively 'stores' the result without an explicit *store* instruction.

  o CISC — Often machines are limited to one memory operand per instruction: *load a,reg1; add b,reg1; store reg1,c;* This requires a load/store pair for any memory movement regardless of whether the *add* result is an augmentation stored to a different place, as in C = A+B, or the same memory location: A = A+B.

    ▪ $C = A+B$ needs *three instructions.*

  o RISC — Requiring explicit memory loads, the instructions would be: *load a,reg1; load b,reg2; add reg1,reg2; store reg2,c.*

    ▪ $C = A+B$ needs *four instructions.*

- 3-operand, allowing better reuse of data:

  o CISC — It becomes either a single instruction: *add a,b,c*

    ▪ $C = A+B$ needs *one instruction.*

  o CISC — Or, on machines limited to two memory operands per instruction, *move a,reg1; add reg1,b,c;*

    ▪ $C = A+B$ needs *two instructions.*

  o RISC — arithmetic instructions use registers only, so explicit 2-operand load/store instructions are needed: *load a,reg1; load b,reg2; add reg1+reg2->reg3; store reg3,c;*

    ▪ $C = A+B$ needs *four instructions.*

    ▪ Unlike 2-operand or 1-operand, this leaves all three values a, b, and c in registers available for further reuse.

- More operands—some CISC machines permit a variety of addressing modes that allow more than 3 operands (registers or memory accesses), such as the VAX "POLY" polynomial evaluation instruction.

Due to the large number of bits needed to encode the three registers of a 3-operand instruction, RISC architectures that have 16-bit instructions are invariably 2-operand designs, such as the Atmel AVR, TI MSP430, and some versions of ARM Thumb. RISC architectures that have 32-bit instructions are usually 3-operand designs, such as the ARM, AVR32, MIPS, Power ISA, and SPARC architectures.

Each instruction specifies some number of operands (registers, memory locations, or immediate values) *explicitly*. Some instructions give one or both operands implicitly, such as by being stored on top of the stack or in an implicit register. If some of the operands are given implicitly, fewer operands need be specified in the instruction. When a "destination operand" explicitly specifies the destination, an additional operand must be supplied. Consequently, the number of operands encoded in an instruction may differ from the mathematically necessary number of arguments for a logical or arithmetic operation (the arity). Operands are either encoded in the "opcode" representation of the instruction, or else are given as values or addresses following the instruction.

Register Pressure

Register pressure measures the availability of free registers at any point in time during the program execution. Register pressure is high when a large number of the available registers are in use; thus, the higher the register pressure, the more often the register contents must be spilled into memory. Increasing the number of registers in an architecture decreases register pressure but increases the cost.

While embedded instruction sets such as Thumb suffer from extremely high register pressure because they have small register sets, general-purpose RISC ISAs like MIPS and Alpha enjoy low register pressure. CISC ISAs like x86-64 offer low register pressure despite the fact that they have smaller register sets. This due to the many addressing modes and optimizations (such as sub-register addressing, memory operands in ALU instructions, absolute addressing, PC-relative addressing, and register-to-register spills) that CISC ISAs offer.

Technology Trends

- The natural building block for multiprocessors is microprocessor

- Microprocessor performance increases 50% every year

- Transistor count doubles every 18 months

    o Intel Pentium 4 EE 3.4 GHz has 178 M transistors on a 237 mm2 die

    o 130 nm Itanium 2 has 410 M transistors on a 374 mm2 die

    o 90 nm Intel Montecito has 1.7 B transistors on a 596 mm2 die

- Die area is also growing

    o Intel Prescott had 125 M transistors on a 112 mm2 die

- Ever-shrinking process technology

    o Shorter gate length of transistors

- o Can afford to sweep electrons through channel faster

- o Transistors can be clocked at faster rate

- o Transistors also get smaller

- o Can afford to pack more on the die

- o And die size is also increasing

- o What to do with so many transistors?

- Could increase L2 or L3 cache size

  - o Does not help much beyond a certain point

  - o Burns more power

- Could improve microarchitecture

  - o Better branch predictor or novel designs to improve instruction-level parallelism (ILP)

- If cannot improve single-thread performance have to look for thread-level parallelism (TLP)

  - o Multiple cores on the die (chip multiprocessors): IBM POWER4, POWER5, Intel Montecito, Intel Pentium 4, AMD Opteron, Sun UltraSPARC IV

- TLP on chip

  - o Instead of putting multiple cores could put extra resources and logic to run multiple threads simultaneously (simultaneous multi-threading): Alpha 21464 (cancelled), Intel Pentium 4, IBM POWER5, Intel Montecito

- Today's microprocessors are small-scale multiprocessors (dual-core, 2-way SMT)

- Tomorrow's microprocessors will be larger-scale multiprocessors or highly multi-threaded

  - o Sun Niagara is an 8-core (each 4-way threaded) chip: 32 threads on a single chip

Architectural Trends

- Circuits: bit-level parallelism

  - o Started with 4 bits (Intel 4004)

  - o Now 32-bit processor is the norm

  - o 64-bit processors are taking over (AMD Opteron, Intel Itanium, Pentium 4 family); started with Alpha, MIPS, Sun families

- Architecture: instruction-level parallelism (ILP)

  - o Extract independent instruction stream

  - o Key to advanced microprocessor design

- o   Gradually hitting a limit: memory wall

- o   Memory operations are bottleneck

- o   Need memory-level parallelism (MLP)

- o   Also technology limits such as wire delay are pushing for a more distributed control rather than the centralized control in today's processors

- If cannot boost ILP what can be done?

- Thread-level parallelism (TLP)

   - o   Explicit parallel programs already have TLP (inherent)

   - o   Sequential programs that are hard to parallelize or ILP-limited can be speculatively parallelized in hardware

      - ◊   Thread-level speculation (TLS)

- Today's trend: if cannot do anything to boost single-thread performance invest transistors and resources to exploit TLP

Exploiting TLP: NOW

- Simplest solution: take the commodity boxes, connect them over gigabit ethernet and let them talk via messages

   - o   The simplest possible message-passing machine

   - o   Also known as Network of Workstations (NOW)

   - o   Normally PVM (Parallel Virtual Machine) or MPI (Message Passing Interface) is used for programming

   - o   Each processor sees only local memory

   - o   Any remote data access must happen through explicit messages (send/recv calls trapping into kernel)

- Optimizations in the messaging layer are possible (user level messages, active messages)

Supercomputers

- Historically used for scientific computing

- Initially used vector processors

- But uniprocessor performance gap of vector processors and microprocessors is narrowing down

   - o   Microprocessors now have heavily pipelined floating-point units, large on-chip caches, modern techniques to extract ILP

- Microprocessor based supercomputers come in large-scale: 100 to 1000 (called massively parallel processors or MPPs)

- However, vector processor based supercomputers are much smaller scale due to cost disadvantage

  - Cray finally decided to use Alpha μP in T3D

Exploiting TLP: Shared Memory

- Hard to build, but offers better programmability compared to message-passing clusters

- The "conventional" load/store architecture continues to work

- Communication takes place through load/store instructions

- Central to design: a cache coherence protocol

  o Handling data coherency among different caches

- Special care needed for synchronization

Shared Memory MPs

- What is the communication protocol?

  o Could be bus-based

  o Processors share a bus and snoop every transaction on the bus

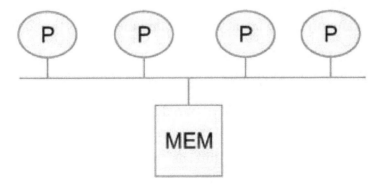

  ◊ The most common design in server and enterprise market

Bus-based MPs

- The memory is "equidistant" from all processors

  o Normally called symmetric multiprocessors (SMPs)

- Fast processors can easily saturate the bus

  o Bus bandwidth becomes a scalability bottleneck

- o In `90s when processors were slow 32P SMPs could be seen
- o Now mostly Sun pushes for large-scale SMPs with advanced bus architecture/technology
- o The bus speed and width have also increased dramatically: Intel Pentium 4 boxes normally come with 400 MHz front-side bus, Xeons have 533 MHz or 800 MHz FSB, PowerPC G5 can clock the bus up to 1.25 GHz

Scaling: DSMs

- Large-scale shared memory MPs are normally built over a scalable switch-based network
- Now each node has its local memory
- Access to remote memory happens through load/store, but may take longer
  - o Non-Uniform Memory Access (NUMA)
  - o Distributed Shared Memory (DSM)
- The underlying coherence protocol is quite different compared to a bus-based SMP
- Need specialized memory controller to handle coherence requests and a router to connect to the network

On-chip TLP

- Current trend:
  - o Tight integration
  - o Minimize communication latency (data communication is the bottleneck)
- Since we have transistors
  - o Put multiple cores on chip (Chip multiprocessing)
  - o They can communicate via either a shared bus or switch-based fabric on-chip (can be custom designed and clocked faster)
  - o Or put support for multiple threads without replicating cores (Simultaneous multi-threading)
  - o Both choices provide a good cost/performance trade-off

Economics

- Ultimately who controls what gets built?
- It is cost vs. performance trade-off
- Given a time budget (to market) and a revenue projection, how much performance can be afforded

- Normal trend is to use commodity microprocessors as building blocks unless there is a very good reason

  o Reuse existing technology as much as possible

- Large-scale scientific computing mostly exploits message-passing machines (easy to build, less costly); even google uses same kind of architecture [use commodity parts]

- Small to medium-scale shared memory multiprocessors are needed in the commercial market (databases)

- Although large-scale DSMs (256 or 512 nodes) are built by SGI, demand is less

References

- Page, Daniel (2009). "11. Compilers". A Practical Introduction to Computer Architecture. Springer. p. 464. ISBN 978-1-84882-255-9

- The evolution of RISC technology at IBM by John Cocke – IBM Journal of R&D, Volume 44, Numbers 1/2, p.48 (2000)

- John L. Hennessy & David A. Patterson (2006). Computer Architecture: A Quantitative Approach (Fourth ed.). Morgan Kaufmann Publishers, Inc. ISBN 0-12-370490-1

- Pugh, Emerson W.; Johnson, Lyle R.; Palmer, John H. (1991). IBM's 360 and Early 370 Systems. MIT Press. ISBN 0-262-16123-0

- Crystal Chen; Greg Novick; Kirk Shimano (December 16, 2006). "RISC Architecture: RISC vs. CISC". cs.stanford.edu. Retrieved February 21, 2015

Computer-Related Pipelines: An Overview

Pipeline in a computing system means a set of data which is connected to one another in such a way that one output is another's input. Some of the examples of computer related pipelines are graphics pipelines, pipelining in software, instruction pipelines and HTTP pipelining. This section is an overview of the subject matter incorporating all the major aspects of pipelining.

Pipeline (Computing)

In computing, a pipeline is a set of data processing elements connected in series, where the output of one element is the input of the next one. The elements of a pipeline are often executed in parallel or in time-sliced fashion; in that case, some amount of buffer storage is often inserted between elements.

Computer-related pipelines include:

- Instruction pipelines, such as the classic RISC pipeline, which are used in central processing units (CPUs) to allow overlapping execution of multiple instructions with the same circuitry. The circuitry is usually divided up into stages and each stage processes one instruction at a time. Examples of stages are instruction decode, arithmetic/logic and register fetch.

- Graphics pipelines, found in most graphics processing units (GPUs), which consist of multiple arithmetic units, or complete CPUs, that implement the various stages of common rendering operations (perspective projection, window clipping, color and light calculation, rendering, etc.).

- Software pipelines, where commands can be written where the output of one operation is automatically fed to the next, following operation. The Unix system call pipe is a classic example of this concept, although other operating systems do support pipes as well.

- HTTP pipelining, where multiple requests are sent without waiting for the result of the first request.

Pipeline Categories

Linear Pipelines

A linear pipeline processor is a series of processing stages and memory access.

Non-linear Pipelines

A non-linear pipelining (also called dynamic pipeline) can be configured to perform various functions at different times. In a dynamic pipeline, there is also feed-forward or feed-back connection. A non-linear pipeline also allows very long instruction words.

Costs and Drawbacks

As the assembly-line example shows, pipelining doesn't decrease the time for processing a single datum; it only increases the throughput of the system when processing a stream of data.

A deeper pipeline increases latency with every additional stage. Latency is the time required for a signal to propagate through the stages of the pipeline from start to finish.

A pipelined system typically requires more resources (circuit elements, processing units, computer memory, etc.) than one that executes one batch at a time, because its stages cannot reuse the resources of a previous stage. Moreover, pipelining may increase the time it takes for an instruction to finish.

A variety of situations can cause a pipeline stall, including jumps (conditional and unconditional branches) and data cache misses. Some processors have a instruction set architecture with certain features designed to reduce the impact of pipeline stalls -- delay slot, conditional instructions such as FCMOV and branch prediction, etc. Some processors spend a lot of energy and transistors in the microarchitecture on features designed to reduce the impact of pipeline stalls -- branch prediction and speculative execution, out-of-order execution, etc. Some optimizing compilers try to reduce the impact of pipeline stalls by replacing some jumps with branch-free code, often at the cost of increasing the binary file size.

Design Considerations

One key aspect of pipeline design is balancing pipeline stages. Using the assembly line example, we could have greater time savings if both the engine and wheels took only 15 minutes. Although the system latency would still be 35 minutes, we would be able to output a new car every 15 minutes. In other words, a pipelined process outputs finished items at a rate determined by its slowest part. (Note that if the time taken to add the engine could not be reduced below 20 minutes, it would not make any difference to the stable output rate if all other components increased their production time to 20 minutes.)

Another design consideration is the provision of adequate buffering between the pipeline stages — especially when the processing times are irregular, or when data items may be created or destroyed along the pipeline.

Graphical Tools

To observe the scheduling of a pipeline (be it static or dynamic), reservation tables are used.

Reservation Table

A reservation table for a linear or a static pipeline can be generated easily because data flow follows a linear stream as static pipeline performs a specific operation. But in case of dynamic pipeline or non-linear pipeline a non-linear pattern is followed so multiple reservation tables can be generated for different functions.

The reservation table mainly displays the time space flow of data through the pipeline for a function. Different functions in a reservation table follow different paths.

The number of columns in a reservation table specifies the evaluation time of a given function.

Implementations

Buffered, Synchronous Pipelines

Conventional microprocessors are synchronous circuits that use buffered, synchronous pipelines. In these pipelines, "pipeline registers" are inserted in-between pipeline stages, and are clocked synchronously. The time between each clock signal is set to be greater than the longest delay between pipeline stages, so that when the registers are clocked, the data that is written to them is the final result of the previous stage.

Buffered, Asynchronous Pipelines

Asynchronous pipelines are used in asynchronous circuits, and have their pipeline registers clocked asynchronously. Generally speaking, they use a request/acknowledge system, wherein each stage can detect when it's "finished". When the stage, S_i, is ready to transmit, it sends a ready signal to stage S_{i+1}. After stage S_{i+1}, receives the incoming data, it returns an acknowledgement signal to S_i.

The AMULET microprocessor is an example of a microprocessor that uses buffered, asynchronous pipelines.

Unbuffered Pipelines

Unbuffered pipelines, called "wave pipelines", do not have registers in-between pipeline stages. Instead, the delays in the pipeline are "balanced" so that, for each stage, the difference between the first stabilized output data and the last is minimized. Thus, data flows in "waves" through the pipeline, and each wave is kept as short (synchronous) as possible.

The maximum rate that data can be fed into a wave pipeline is determined by the maximum difference in delay between the first piece of data coming out of the pipe and the last piece of data, for any given wave. If data is fed in faster than this, it is possible for waves of data to interfere with each other.

Instruction Pipelining

Instruction pipelining is a technique that implements a form of parallelism called instruction-level parallelism within a single processor. It therefore allows faster CPU throughput (the number of instructions that can be executed in a unit of time) than would otherwise be possible at a given clock rate. The basic instruction cycle is broken up into a series called a pipeline. Rather than processing each instruction sequentially (finishing one instruction before starting the next), each instruction is split up into a sequence of dependent steps so different steps can be executed in parallel and instructions can be processed concurrently (starting one instruction before finishing the previous one).

Instr. No.	Pipeline Stage						
1	IF	ID	EX	MEM	WB		
2		IF	ID	EX	MEM	WB	
3			IF	ID	EX	MEM	WB
4				IF	ID	EX	MEM
5					IF	ID	EX
Clock Cycle	1	2	3	4	5	6	7

Basic five-stage pipeline (IF = Instruction Fetch, ID = Instruction Decode, EX = Execute, MEM = Memory access, WB = Register write back). In the fourth clock cycle (the green column), the earliest instruction is in MEM stage, and the latest instruction has not yet entered the pipeline.

The first step is always to fetch the instruction from memory; the final step is usually writing the results of the instruction to processor registers or to memory. Pipelining seeks to let the processor work on as many instructions as there are dependent steps, just as an assembly line builds many vehicles at once, rather than waiting until one vehicle has passed through the line before admitting the next one. Just as the goal of the assembly line is to keep each assembler productive at all times, pipelining seeks to keep every portion of the processor busy with some instruction. Pipelining lets the computer's cycle time be the time of the slowest step, and ideally lets one instruction complete in every cycle.

Pipelining increases instruction throughput by performing multiple operations at the same time, but does not reduce latency, the time needed to complete a single instruction. Indeed, pipelining may increase latency due to additional overhead from breaking the computation into separate steps, and depending on how often the pipeline stalls or needs to be flushed.

The term pipeline is an analogy to the fact that there is fluid in each link of a pipeline, as each part of the processor is occupied with work.

Introduction

Central processing units (CPUs) are driven by a clock. Each clock pulse need not do the same thing; rather, logic in the CPU directs successive pulses to different places to perform a useful sequence. There are many reasons that the entire execution of a machine instruction cannot happen at once; in pipelining, effects that cannot happen at the same time are made into dependent steps of the instruction.

For example, if one clock pulse latches a value into a register or begins a calculation, it will take some time for the value to be stable at the outputs of the register or for the calculation to complete. As another example, reading an instruction out of a memory unit cannot be done at the same time that an instruction writes a result to the same memory unit.

Number of Steps

The number of dependent steps varies with the machine architecture. For example:

- The 1956-1961 IBM Stretch project proposed the terms Fetch, Decode, and Execute that have become common.

- The classic RISC pipeline comprises:

  o   Instruction fetch

  o   Instruction decode and register fetch

  o   Execute

  o   Memory access

  o   Register write back

- The Atmel AVR and the PIC microcontroller each have a two-stage pipeline.

- Many designs include pipelines as long as 7, 10 and even 20 stages (as in the Intel Pentium 4).

- The later "Prescott" and "Cedar Mill" Netburst cores from Intel, used in the latest Pentium 4 models and their Pentium D and Xeon derivatives, have a long 31-stage pipeline.

- The Xelerated X10q Network Processor has a pipeline more than a thousand stages long, although in this case 200 of these stages represent independent CPUs with individually programmed instructions. The remaining stages are used to coordinate accesses to memory and on-chip function units.

As the pipeline is made "deeper" (with a greater number of dependent steps), a given step can be implemented with simpler circuitry, which may let the processor clock run faster. Such pipelines may be called *superpipelines.*

A processor is said to be *fully pipelined* if it can fetch an instruction on every cycle. Thus, if some instructions or conditions require delays that inhibit fetching new instructions, the processor is not fully pipelined.

Hazards

The model of sequential execution assumes that each instruction completes before the next one begins; this assumption is not true on a pipelined processor. A situation where the expected result is problematic is known as a hazard. Imagine the following two register instructions to a hypothetical processor:

```
1: add 1 to R5
```

```
2: copy R5 to R6
```

If the processor has the 5 steps listed in the initial illustration, instruction 1 would be fetched at time t_1 and its execution would be complete at t_5. Instruction 2 would be fetched at t_2 and would be complete at t_6. The first instruction might deposit the incremented number into R5 as its fifth step (register write back) at t_5. But the second instruction might get the number from R5 (to copy to R6) in its second step (instruction decode and register fetch) at time t_3. It seems that the first instruction would not have incremented the value by then. The above code invokes a hazard.

Writing computer programs in a compiled language might not raise these concerns, as the compiler could be designed to generate machine code that avoids hazards.

Workarounds

In some early DSP and RISC processors, the documentation advises programmers to avoid such dependencies in adjacent and nearly adjacent instructions (called delay slots), or declares that the second instruction uses an old value rather than the desired value (in the example above, the processor might counter-intuitively copy the unincremented value), or declares that the value it uses is undefined. The programmer may have unrelated work that the processor can do in the meantime; or, to ensure correct results, the programmer may insert NOPs into the code, partly negating the advantages of pipelining.

Solutions

Pipelined processors commonly use three techniques to work as expected when the programmer assumes that each instruction completes before the next one begins:

- Processors that can compute the presence of a hazard may *stall*, delaying processing of the second instruction (and subsequent instructions) until the values it requires as input are ready. This creates a *bubble* in the pipeline, also partly negating the advantages of pipelining.

- Some processors can not only compute the presence of a hazard but can compensate by having additional data paths that provide needed inputs to a computation step before a subsequent instruction would otherwise compute them, an attribute called operand forwarding.

- Some processors can determine that instructions other than the next sequential one are not dependent on the current ones and can be executed without hazards. Such processors may perform out-of-order execution.

Branches

A branch out of the normal instruction sequence often involves a hazard. Unless the processor can give effect to the branch in a single time cycle, the pipeline will continue fetching instructions sequentially. Such instructions cannot be allowed to take effect because the programmer has diverted control to another part of the program.

A conditional branch is even more problematic. The processor may or may not branch, depending on a calculation that has not yet occurred. Various processors may stall, may attempt branch prediction, and may be able to begin to execute two different program sequences (eager execution), both assuming the branch is and is not taken, discarding all work that pertains to the incorrect guess.

A processor with an implementation of branch prediction that usually makes correct predictions can minimize the performance penalty from branching. However, if branches are predicted poorly, it may create more work for the processor, such as flushing from the pipeline the incorrect code path that has begun execution before resuming execution at the correct location.

Programs written for a pipelined processor deliberately avoid branching to minimize possible loss of speed. For example, the programmer can handle the usual case with sequential execution and branch only on detecting unusual cases. Using programs such as gcov to analyze code coverage lets the programmer measure how often particular branches are actually executed and gain insight with which to optimize the code.

Special Situations

Self-modifying programs

The technique of self-modifying code can be problematic on a pipelined processor. In this technique, one of the effects of a program is to modify its own upcoming instructions. If the processor has an instruction cache, the original instruction may already have been copied into a prefetch input queue and the modification will not take effect.

Uninterruptible instructions

An instruction may be uninterruptible to ensure its atomicity, such as when it swaps two items. A sequential processor permits interrupts between instructions, but a pipelining processor overlaps instructions, so executing an uninterruptible instruction renders portions of ordinary instructions uninterruptible too. The Cyrix coma bug would hang a single-core system using an infinite loop in which an uninterruptible instruction was always in the pipeline.

Design Considerations

Speed

Pipelining keeps all portions of the processor occupied and increases the amount of useful work the processor can do in a given time. Pipelining typically reduces the processor's cycle time and increases the throughput of instructions. The speed advantage is diminished to the extent that execution encounters hazards that require execution to slow below its ideal rate. A non-pipelined processor executes only a single instruction at a time. The start of the next instruction is delayed not based on hazards but unconditionally.

A pipelined processor's need to organize all its work into modular steps may require the duplication of registers that increases the latency of some instructions.

Economy

By making each dependent step simpler, pipelining can enable complex operations more economically than adding complex circuitry, such as for numerical calculations. However, a processor that declines to pursue increased speed with pipelining may be simpler and cheaper to manufacture.

Predictability

Compared to environments where the programmer needs to avoid or work around hazards, use of a non-pipelined processor may make it easier to program and to train programmers. The non-pipelined processor also makes it easier to predict the exact timing of a given sequence of instructions.

Illustrated Example

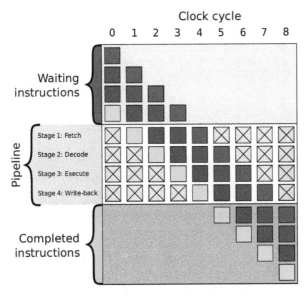

Generic 4-stage pipeline; the colored boxes represent instructions independent of each other

To the right is a generic pipeline with four stages: fetch, decode, execute and write-back. The top gray box is the list of instructions waiting to be executed, the bottom gray box is the list of instructions that have had their execution completed, and the middle white box is the pipeline.

The execution is as follows:

Time	Execution
0	Four instructions are waiting to be executed
1	• The green instruction is fetched from memory
2	• The green instruction is decoded • The purple instruction is fetched from memory
3	• The green instruction is executed (actual operation is performed) • The purple instruction is decoded • The blue instruction is fetched
4	• The green instruction's results are written back to the register file or memory • The purple instruction is executed • The blue instruction is decoded • The red instruction is fetched
5	• The execution of green instruction is completed • The purple instruction is written back • The blue instruction is executed • The red instruction is decoded

6	• The execution of purple instruction is completed
	• The blue instruction is written back
	• The red instruction is executed
7	• The execution of blue instruction is completed
	• The red instruction is written back
8	• The execution of red instruction is completed
9	The execution of all four instructions is completed

Pipeline Bubble

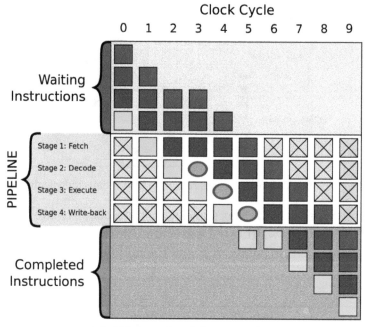

A bubble in cycle 3 delays execution.

A pipelined processor may deal with hazards by stalling and creating a bubble in the pipeline, resulting in one or more cycles in which nothing useful happens.

In the illustration at right, in cycle 3, the processor cannot decode the purple instruction, perhaps because the processor determines that decoding depends on results produced by the execution of the green instruction. The green instruction can proceed to the Execute stage and then to the Write-back stage as scheduled, but the purple instruction is stalled for one cycle at the Fetch stage. The blue instruction, which was due to be fetched during cycle 3, is stalled for one cycle, as is the red instruction after it.

Because of the bubble (the blue ovals in the illustration), the processor's Decode circuitry is idle during cycle 3. Its Execute circuitry is idle during cycle 4 and its Write-back circuitry is idle during cycle 5.

When the bubble moves out of the pipeline (at cycle 6), normal execution resumes. But everything now is one cycle late. It will take 8 cycles (cycle 1 through 8) rather than 7 to completely execute the four instructions shown in colors.

History

Seminal uses of pipelining were in the ILLIAC II project and the IBM Stretch project, though a simple version was used earlier in the Z1 in 1939 and the Z3 in 1941.

Pipelining began in earnest in the late 1970s in supercomputers such as vector processors and array processors. One of the early supercomputers was the Cyber series built by Control Data Corporation. Its main architect, Seymour Cray, later headed Cray Research. Cray developed the XMP line of supercomputers, using pipelining for both multiply and add/subtract functions. Later, Star Technologies added parallelism (several pipelined functions working in parallel), developed by Roger Chen. In 1984, Star Technologies added the pipelined divide circuit developed by James Bradley. By the mid 1980s, supercomputing was used by many different companies around the world.

Today, pipelining and most of the above innovations are implemented by the instruction unit of most microprocessors.

Graphics Pipeline

A computer graphics pipeline, rendering pipeline or simply graphics pipeline, is a conceptual model in computer graphics that describes what steps a graphics system needs to perform to render a 3D scene to a 2D screen. Plainly speaking, once a 3D model has been created, for instance in a video game or any other 3D computer animation, the graphics pipeline is the process of turning that 3D model into what the computer displays. Because the steps required for this operation highly depend on the software and hardware used and the desired display characteristics, there is no universal graphics pipeline suitable for all cases. However, graphics APIs such as Direct3D and OpenGL were created to unify similar steps and to control the graphics pipeline of a given Hardware accelerator. Basically, these APIs abstract the underlying hardware and keep the programmer away from writing some tough code to manipulate the Graphics hardware accelerators (NVIDIA/AMD/Intel etc.).

Three-dimensional real or artificial worlds are a very common part of most modern computer games. The rendering is the process of creating visible images from abstract data.

The model of the graphics pipeline is usually used in real-time rendering. Often, most of the pipeline steps are implemented in hardware, which allows for special optimization. The term "pipeline" is used in a similar sense to the pipeline in processors: the individual steps of the pipeline run parallel but are blocked until the slowest step has been completed.

Concept

The 3D pipeline usually refers to the most common form of computer 3D rendering, 3D polygon rendering, distinct from raytracing, and raycasting. In particular, 3D polygon rendering is similar to raycasting. In raycasting, a ray originates at the point where the camera resides, if that ray hits a surface, then the color and lighting of the point on the surface where the ray hit is calculated. In 3D polygon rendering the reverse happens, the area that is in view of the camera is calculated, and then rays are created from every part of every surface in view of the camera and traced back to the camera.

Structure

A graphics pipeline can be divided into three main parts: Application, Geometry and Rasterization.

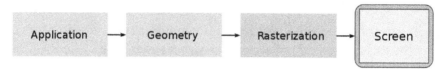

Application

The application step is executed by the software on the main processor (CPU), it cannot be divided into individual steps, which are executed in a pipelined manner. However, it is possible to parallelize it on multi-core processors or multi-processor systems. In the application step, changes are made to the scene as required, for example, by user interaction by means of input devices or during an animation. The new scene with all its primitives, usually triangles, lines and points, is then passed on to the next step in the pipeline.

Examples of tasks that are typically done in the application step are collision detection, animation, morphing, and acceleration techniques using spatial subdivision schemes such as Quadtrees or Octrees. These are also used to reduce the amount of main memory required at a given time. The "world" of a modern computer game is far larger than what could fit into memory at once.

Geometry

The geometry step, which is responsible for the majority of the operations with polygons and their vertices, can be divided into the following five tasks. It depends on the particular implementation of how these tasks are organized as actual parallel pipeline steps.

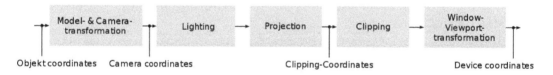

Definitions

A *vertex* (plural: vertices) is a point in the world. Many points are used to join the surfaces. In special cases, point clouds are drawn directly, but this is still the exception.

A *triangle* is the most common geometric primitive of computer graphics. It is defined by its three vertices and a normal vector - the normal vector serves to indicate the front face of the triangle and is a vector that is perpendicular to the surface. The triangle may be provided with a color or with a texture (image "glued" on top of it). Triangles always exist on a single plane, therefore they're preferred over rectangles.

The World Co-ordinate System

The world coordinate system is the coordinate system in which the virtual world is created. This should meet a few conditions for the following mathematics to be easily applicable:

- It must be a rectangular Cartesian coordinate system in which all axes are equally scaled.

How the unit of the coordinate system is defined, is left to the developer. Whether, therefore, the unit vector of the system is to correspond in reality to one meter or an Ångström depends on the application.

- Whether a right-handed or a left-handed coordinate system is to be used may be determined by the graphic library to be used.

  Example: If we are to develop a flight simulator, we can choose the world coordinate system so that the origin is in the middle of the earth and the unit is set to one meter. In addition, in order to make the reference to reality easier, we define that the X axis should intersect the equator on the zero meridian, and the Z axis passes through the poles. In a Right-handed system, the Y-axis runs through the 90°-East meridian (somewhere in the Indian Ocean). Now we have a coordinate system that describes every point on Earth in three-dimensional Cartesian coordinates. In this coordinate system, we are now modeling the principles of our world, mountains, valleys and oceans.

  Note: Aside from computer geometry, geographic coordinates are used for the earth, ie, latitude and longitude, as well as altitudes above sea level. The approximate conversion - if one does not consider the fact that the earth is not an exact sphere - is simple:

  $$\begin{pmatrix} x \\ y \\ z \end{pmatrix} = \begin{pmatrix} (R + hasl) * \cos(lat) * \cos(long) \\ (R + hasl) * \cos(lat) * \sin(long) \\ (R + hasl) * \sin(lat) \end{pmatrix} \text{ with}$$

  R=Radius of the earth [6.378.137m], lat=Latitude, long=Longitude, hasl=height above sea level.

  All of the following examples apply in a right handed system. For a left-handed system the signs may need to be interchanged.

The objects contained within the scene (houses, trees, cars) are often designed in their own object coordinate system (also called model coordinate system or local coordinate system) for reasons of simpler modeling. To assign these objects to coordinates in the world coordinate system or global coordinate system of the entire scene, the object coordinates are transformed by means of translation, rotation or scaling. This is done by multiplying the corresponding transformation matrices. In addition, several differently transformed copies can be formed from one object, for example a forest from a tree; This technique is called instancing.

  In order to place a model of an aircraft in the world, we first determine four matrices. Since we work in three-dimensional space, we need four-dimensional homogeneous matrices for our calculations.

First, we need three rotation matrices, namely one for each of the three aircraft axes (vertical axis, transverse axis, longitudinal axis).

Around the X axis (usually defined as a longitudinal axis in the object coordinate system)

$$R_x = \begin{pmatrix} 1 & 0 & 0 & 0 \\ 0 & \cos(\alpha) & \sin(\alpha) & 0 \\ 0 & -\sin(\alpha) & \cos(\alpha) & 0 \\ 0 & 0 & 0 & 1 \end{pmatrix}$$

Around the Y axis (usually defined as the transverse axis in the object coordinate system)

$$R_y = \begin{pmatrix} \cos(\alpha) & 0 & -\sin(\alpha) & 0 \\ 0 & 1 & 0 & 0 \\ \sin(\alpha) & 0 & \cos(\alpha) & 0 \\ 0 & 0 & 0 & 1 \end{pmatrix}$$

Around the Z axis (usually defined as vertical axis in the object coordinate system)

$$R_z = \begin{pmatrix} \cos(\alpha) & \sin(\alpha) & 0 & 0 \\ -\sin(\alpha) & \cos(\alpha) & 0 & 0 \\ 0 & 0 & 1 & 0 \\ 0 & 0 & 0 & 1 \end{pmatrix}$$

We also use a translation matrix that moves the aircraft to the desired point in our world:

$$T_{x,y,z} = \begin{pmatrix} 1 & 0 & 0 & 0 \\ 0 & 1 & 0 & 0 \\ 0 & 0 & 1 & 0 \\ x & y & z & 1 \end{pmatrix}.$$

Remark: The above matrices are transposed with respect to the ones in the article rotation matrix. An explanation why for this is given below.

Now we could calculate the position of the vertices of the aircraft in world coordinates by multiplying each point successively with these four matrices. Since the multiplication of a matrix with a vector is quite expensive (time consuming), one usually takes another path and first multiplies the four matrices together. The multiplication of two matrices is even more expensive, but must be executed only once for the whole object. The multiplications $((((v*R_x)*R_y)*R_z)*T)$ and $(v*(((R_x*R_y)*R_z)*T))$ are equivalent. Thereafter, the resulting matrix could be applied to the vertices. In practice, however, the multiplication with the vertices is still not applied, but the camera matrices are determined first.

For our example from above, however, the translation has to be determined somewhat differently, since the common meaning of *Up* - apart from at the North Pole - does not coincide with our definition of the positive Z axis and therefore the model must also be rotated around the center of the earth:

$$T_{Kugel} = T_{x,y,z}(0,0,R+hasl) * R_y(\Pi/2-lat) * R_z(long)$$

The first step pushes the origin of the model to the correct height above the earth's surface, then it is rotated by latitude and longitude.

The order in which the matrices are applied is important, because the matrix multiplication is *not* commutative. This also applies to the three rotations, as can be demonstrated by an example: The point (1, 0, 0) lies on the X-axis, if one rotates it first by 90° around the X- and then around The Y axis, it ends up on the Z axis (the rotation around the X axis has no effect on a point that is on the axis). If, on the other hand, one rotates around the Y axis first and then around the X axis, the resulting point is located on the Y axis. The sequence itself is arbitrary as long as it is always the same. The sequence with x, then y, then z (roll, pitch, heading) is often the most intuitive, because the rotation causes the compass direction to coincide with the direction of the "nose".

There are also two conventions to define these matrices, depending on whether you want to work with column vectors or row vectors. Different graphics libraries have different preferences here. OpenGL prefers column vectors, DirectX row vectors. The decision determines from which side the point vectors are to be multiplied by the transformation matrices. For column vectors, the multiplication is performed from the right, ie $v_{out} = M * v_{in}$, where v_{out} and v_{in} are 4x1 colum vectors. The concatenation of the matrices also is done from the right to left, ie, for example $M = T_x * R_x$, when first rotating and then shifting.

In the case of row vectors, this works exactly the other way round. The multiplication now takes place from left as $v_{out} = v_{in} * M$ with 1x4-row vectors and the concatenation is $M = R_x * T_x$ when we also first rotate and then move. The matrices shown above are valid for the second case, while those for column vectors are transposed. The rule $(v * M)^T = M^T * v^T$ applies, which for multiplication with vectors means that you can switch the multiplication order by transposing the matrix.

The interesting thing about this matrix chaining is that a new coordinate system is defined by each such transformation. This can be extended as desired. For example, the propeller of the aircraft may be a separate model, which is then placed by translation to the aircraft nose. This translation only needs to describe the shift from the model coordinate system to the propeller coordinate system. In order to draw the entire aircraft, the transformation matrix for the aircraft is first determined, the points are transformed, and then the propeller model matrix is multiplied to the matrix of the aircraft, and then the propeller points are transformed.

The matrix calculated in this way is also called the *world matrix*. It must be determined for each object in the world before rendering. The application can introduce changes here, for example change the position of the aircraft according to the speed after each frame.

Camera Transform

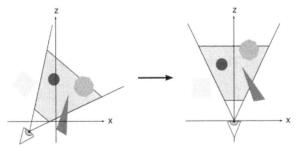

Left: Position and direction of the virtual viewer (camera), as defined by the user. Right: Positioning the objects after the camera transformation. The light gray area is the visible volume.

In addition to the objects, the scene also defines a virtual camera or viewer that indicates the position and direction of view from which the scene is to be rendered. To simplify later projection and clipping, the scene is transformed so that the camera is at the origin, looking along the Z axis. The resulting coordinate system is called the camera coordinate system and the transformation is called *camera transformation* or *View Transformation*.

The view matrix is usually determined from camera position, target point (where the camera looks) and an "up vector" ("up" from the viewer's viewpoint). First three auxiliary vectors are required:

Zaxis = normal(cameraPosition - cameraTarget)

Xaxis = normal(cross(cameraUpVector, zaxis))

Yaxis = cross(zaxis, xaxis)

With normal(v) = normalization of the vector v;

cross(v1, v2) = cross product of v1 and v2.

Finally, the matrix:

$$
\begin{pmatrix}
xaxis.x & yaxis.x & zaxis.x & 0 \\
xaxis.y & yaxis.y & zaxis.y & 0 \\
xaxis.z & yaxis.z & zaxis.z & 0 \\
-dot(xaxis, cameraPosition) & -dot(yaxis, cameraPosition) & -dot(zaxis, cameraPosition) & 1
\end{pmatrix}
$$

with dot(v1, v2) = dot product of v1 and v2.

Projection

The 3D projection step transforms the view volume into a cube with the corner point coordinates (-1, -1, -1) and (1, 1, 1); Occasionally other target volumes are also used. This step is called *projection*, even though it transforms a volume into another volume, since the resulting Z coordinates are not stored in the image, but are only used in Z-buffering in the later rastering step. In a perspectivic illustration, a central projection is used. To limit the number of displayed objects, two additional clipping planes are used; The visual volume is therefore a truncated pyramid (frustum). The parallel or orthogonal projection is used, for example, for technical representations because it has the advantage that all parallels in the object space are also parallel in the image space, and the surfaces and volumes are the same size regardless of the distance from the viewer. Maps use, for example, an orthogonal projection (so-called orthophoto), but oblique images of a landscape cannot be used in this way - although they can technically be rendered, they seem so distorted that we cannot make any use of them. The formula for calculating a perspective mapping matrix is:

$$
\begin{pmatrix}
w & 0 & 0 & 0 \\
0 & h & 0 & 0 \\
0 & 0 & far/(near - far) & -1 \\
0 & 0 & (near * far)/(near - far) & 0
\end{pmatrix}
$$

With h = cot (fieldOfView / 2.0) (aperture angle of the camera); w = h / aspectRatio (aspect ratio of the target image); near = Smallest distance to be visible; far = The longest distance to be visible.

The reasons why the smallest and the greatest distance have to be given here are, on the one hand, that this distance is divided by in order to reach the scaling of the scene (more distant objects are smaller in a perspective image than near objects), and on the other hand to scale the Z values to the range 0..1, for filling the Z-buffer. This buffer often has only a resolution of 16 bits, which is why the near and far values should be chosen carefully. A too large difference between the near and the far value leads to so-called Z-fighting because of the low resolution of the Z-buffer. It can also be seen from the formula that the near value cannot be 0, because this point is the focus point of the projection. There is no picture at this point.

For the sake of completeness, the formula for parallel projection (orthogonal projection):

$$\begin{pmatrix} 2.0/w & 0 & 0 & 0 \\ 0 & 2.0/h & 0 & 0 \\ 0 & 0 & 1.0/(near - far) & -1 \\ 0 & 0 & near/(near - far) & 0 \end{pmatrix}$$

with w = width of the target cube (dimension in units of the world coordinate system); H = w / aspectRatio (aspect ratio of the target image); near = Smallest distance to be visible; far = The longest distance to be visible.

For reasons of efficiency, the camera and projection matrix are usually combined into a transformation matrix so that the camera coordinate system is omitted. The resulting matrix is usually the same for a single image, while the world matrix looks different for each object. In practice, therefore, view and projection are pre-calculated so that only the world matrix has to be adapted during the display. However, more complex transformations such as vertex blending are possible. Freely programmable geometry shaders that modify the geometry can also be executed.

In the actual rendering step, the world matrix * camera matrix * projection matrix is calculated and then finally applied to every single point. Thus, the points of all objects are transferred directly to the screen coordinate system (at least almost, the value range of the axes are still -1..1 for the visible range).

Lighting

Often a scene contains light sources placed at different positions to make the lighting of the objects appear more realistic. In this case, a gain factor for the texture is calculated for each vertex based on the light sources and the material properties associated with the corresponding triangle. In the later rasterization step, the vertex values of a triangle are interpolated over its surface. A general lighting (ambient light) is applied to all surfaces. It is the diffuse and thus direction-independent brightness of the scene. The sun is a directed light source, which can be assumed to be infinitely far away. The illumination effected by the sun on a surface is determined by forming the scalar product of the directional vector from the sun and the normal vector of the surface. If the value is negative, the surface is facing the sun.

Clipping

Only the primitives which are within the visual volume need to actually be rastered (drawn). This visual volume is defined as the inside of a frustum, a shape in the form of a pyramid with a cut off top. Primitives which are completely outside the visual volume are discarded; This is called frustum culling. Further culling methods such as backface culling, which reduce the number of primitives to be considered, can theoretically be executed in any step of the graphics pipeline. Primitives which are only partially inside the cube must be clipped against the cube. The advantage of the previous projection step is that the clipping always takes place against the same cube. Only the - possibly clipped - primitives, which are within the visual volume, are forwarded to the final step.

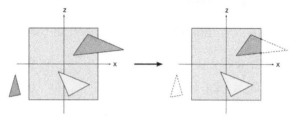

Clipping of primitives against the cube. The blue triangle is discarded while the orange triangle is clipped, creating two new vertices

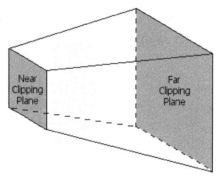

Frustum

Window-Viewport Transformation

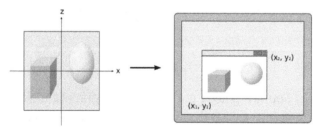

Window-Viewport-Transformation

In order to output the image to any target area (viewport) of the screen, another transformation, the *Window-Viewport transformation*, must be applied. This is a shift, followed by scaling. The resulting coordinates are the device coordinates of the output device. The viewport contains 6 values: height and width of the window in pixels, the upper left corner of the window in window coordinates (usually 0, 0) and the minimum and maximum values for Z (usually 0 and 1).

Formally:
$$\begin{pmatrix} x \\ y \\ z \end{pmatrix} = \begin{pmatrix} vp.X + (1.0 + v.X) * vp.width / 2.0 \\ vp.Y + (1.0 - v.Y) * vp.height / 2.0 \\ vp.minz + v.Z * (vp.maxz - vp.minz) \end{pmatrix}$$

With vp=Viewport; v=Point after projection

On modern hardware, most of the geometry computation steps are performed in the vertex shader. This is, in principle, freely programmable, but generally performs at least the transformation of the points and the illumination calculation. For the DirectX programming interface, the use of a custom vertex shader is necessary from version 10, while older versions still have a standard shader.

Rasterization

In the rastering step, all primitives are rastered, so discrete fragments are created from continuous surfaces.

In this stage of the graphics pipeline, the grid points are also called fragments, for the sake of greater distinctiveness. Each fragment corresponds to one pixel in the frame buffer and this corresponds to one pixel of the screen. These can be colored (and possibly illuminated). Furthermore, it is necessary to determine the visible, closer to the observer fragment, in the case of overlapping polygons. A Z-buffer is usually used for this so-called hidden surface determination. The color of a fragment depends on the illumination, texture, and other material properties of the visible primitive and is often interpolated using the triangle vertice properties. Where available, a fragment shader (also called pixel shader) is run in the rastering step for each fragment of the object. If a fragment is visible, it can now be mixed with already existing color values in the image if transparency or multi-sampling is used. In this step, one or more fragments become a pixel.

To prevent that the user sees the gradual rasterization of the primitives, double buffering takes place. The rasterization is carried out in a special memory area. Once the image has been completely rastered, it is copied to the visible area of the image memory.

Inverse

All matrices used are regular and thus invertible. Since the multiplication of two regular matrices creates another regular matrix, the entire transformation matrix is also invertible. The inverse is required to recalculate world coordinates from screen coordinates - for example, to determine from the mouse pointer position the clicked object. However, since the screen and the mouse have only two dimensions, the third is unknown. Therefore, a ray is projected at the cursor position into the world and then the intersection of this ray with the polygons in the world is determined.

Shader

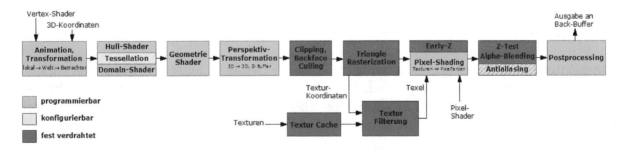

Classic graphics cards are still relatively close to the graphics pipeline. With increasing demands on the GPU, restrictions were gradually removed out to create more flexibility. Modern graphics cards use a freely programmable, shader-controlled pipeline, which allows direct access to individual processing steps. To relieve the main processor, additional processing steps have been moved to the pipeline and the GPU.

The most important shader units are pixel shaders, vertex shaders, and geometry shaders. The Unified Shader has been introduced to take full advantage of all units. This gives you a single large pool of shader units. As required, the pool is divided into different groups of shaders. A strict separation between the shader types is therefore no longer useful.

It is also possible to use a so-called compute-shader to perform any calculations off the display of a graphic on the GPU. The advantage is that they run very parallel, but there are limitations. These universal calculations are also called GPGPU.

HTTP Pipelining

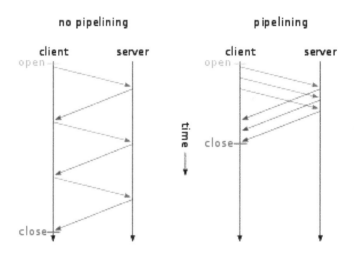

Time diagram of non-pipelined vs. pipelined connection.

HTTP pipelining is a technique in which multiple HTTP requests are sent on a single TCP connection without waiting for the corresponding responses.

The pipelining of requests results in a dramatic improvement in the loading times of HTML pages, especially over high latency connections such as satellite Internet connections. The speedup is less apparent on broadband connections, as the limitation of HTTP 1.1 still applies: the server must send its responses in the same order that the requests were received — so the entire connection remains first-in-first-out and HOL blocking can occur. The asynchronous operation of the upcoming HTTP/2 or SPDY could be a solution for this.

Non-idempotent requests, like those using POST, should not be pipelined. Sequences of GET and HEAD requests can always be pipelined. A sequence of other idempotent requests like PUT and DELETE can be pipelined or not depending on whether requests in the sequence depend on the effect of others.

HTTP pipelining requires both the client and the server to support it. HTTP/1.1 conforming servers are required to support pipelining. This does not mean that servers are required to pipeline responses, but that they are required not to fail if a client chooses to pipeline requests.

Implementation Status

Pipelining was introduced in HTTP/1.1 and was not present in HTTP/1.0.

Implementation in Web Servers

Implementing pipelining in web servers is a relatively simple matter of making sure that network buffers are not discarded between requests. For that reason, most modern web servers handle pipelining without any problem.

Implementation in Web Browsers

Of all the major browsers, only Opera based on Presto layout engine had a fully working implementation that was enabled by default. In all other browsers HTTP pipelining is disabled or not implemented.

- Internet Explorer 8 does not pipeline requests, due to concerns regarding buggy proxies and head-of-line blocking.

- Internet Explorer 11 does not support pipelining.

- Mozilla browsers (such as Mozilla Firefox, SeaMonkey and Camino) support pipelining; however, it is disabled by default. Pipelining is disabled by default to avoid issues with misbehaving servers. When pipelining is enabled, Mozilla browsers use some heuristics, especially to turn pipelining off for older IIS servers. Support for H1 Pipeline was removed from Mozilla Firefox in Version 54.

- Konqueror 2.0 supports pipelining, but it's disabled by default.

- Google Chrome previously supported pipelining, but it has been disabled due to bugs and problems with poorly behaving servers.

Implementation in Web Proxies

Most HTTP proxies do not pipeline outgoing requests.

Some versions of the Squid web proxy will pipeline up to two outgoing requests. This functionality has been disabled by default and needs to be manually enabled for "bandwidth management and access logging reasons." Squid supports multiple requests from clients.

The Polipo proxy pipelines outgoing requests.

Other Implementations

The libwww library made by the World Wide Web Consortium (W3C), supports pipelining since version 5.1 released at 18 February 1997.

Other application development libraries that support HTTP pipelining include:

- Perl modules providing client support for HTTP pipelining are HTTP:Async and the LW-Png library.

- Apache Foundation project HttpComponents provides pipelining support in the HttpCore NIO extensions.

- The Microsoft .NET Framework 3.5 supports HTTP pipelining in the module System.Net. HttpWebRequest.

- Qt class QNetworkRequest, introduced in 4.4.

Some other applications currently exploiting pipelining are:

- IceBreak application server since BUILD389

- phttpget from FreeBSD (a minimalist pipelined HTTP client)

- libcurl has limited support for pipelining using the CURLMOPT_PIPELINING option.

- portsnap (a FreeBSD ports tree distribution system)

- Advanced Packaging Tool (APT) support pipelining.

- Subversion (SVN) has optional support for HTTP pipelining with the serf WebDAV access module (the default module, neon does not have pipelining support).

- Microsoft Message Queuing on Windows Server 2003 utilises pipelining on HTTP by default, and can be configured to use it on HTTPS.

- IBM CICS 3.1 supports HTTP pipelining within its client.

Multipart XHR is implementation of pipelining (without any browser or web server support) done purely in JavaScript in combination with server-side scripting.

Testing tools which support HTTP pipelining include:

- httperf

Pipeline (Software)

In software engineering, a pipeline consists of a chain of processing elements (processes, threads, coroutines, functions, etc.), arranged so that the output of each element is the input of the next; the name is by analogy to a physical pipeline. Usually some amount of buffering is provided between consecutive elements. The information that flows in these pipelines is often a stream of records, bytes or bits, and the elements of a pipeline may be called filters; this is also called the pipes and filters design pattern. Connecting elements into a pipeline is analogous to function composition.

Narrowly speaking, a pipeline is linear and one-directional, though sometimes the term is applied to more general flows. For example, a primarily one-directional pipeline may have some communication in the other direction, known as a *return channel* or *backchannel,* as in the lexer hack, or a pipeline may be fully bi-directional. Flows with one-directional tree and directed acyclic graph topologies behave similarly to (linear) pipelines – the lack of cycles makes them simple – and thus may be loosely referred to as "pipelines".

Implementation

Pipelines are often implemented in a multitasking OS, by launching all elements at the same time as processes, and automatically servicing the data read requests by each process with the data written by the upstream process – this can be called a *multiprocessed pipeline*. In this way, the CPU will be naturally switched among the processes by the scheduler so as to minimize its idle time. In other common models, elements are implemented as lightweight threads or as coroutines to reduce the OS overhead often involved with processes. Depending upon the OS, threads may be scheduled directly by the OS or by a thread manager. Coroutines are always scheduled by a coroutine manager of some form.

Usually, read and write requests are blocking operations, which means that the execution of the source process, upon writing, is suspended until all data could be written to the destination process, and, likewise, the execution of the destination process, upon reading, is suspended until at least some of the requested data could be obtained from the source process. This cannot lead to a deadlock, where both processes would wait indefinitely for each other to respond, since at least one of the two processes will soon thereafter have its request serviced by the operating system, and continue to run.

For performance, most operating systems implementing pipes use pipe buffers, which allow the source process to provide more data than the destination process is currently able or willing to receive. Under most Unices and Unix-like operating systems, a special command is also available which implements a pipe buffer of potentially much larger and configurable size, typically called "buffer". This command can be useful if the destination process is significantly slower than the source process, but it is anyway desired that the source process can complete its task as soon as possible. E.g., if the source process consists of a command which reads an audio track from a CD and the destination process consists of a command which compresses the waveform audio data to a format like MP3. In this case, buffering the entire track in a pipe buffer would allow the CD drive to spin down more quickly, and enable the user to remove the CD from the drive before the encoding process has finished.

Such a buffer command can be implemented using system calls for reading and writing data. Wasteful busy waiting can be avoided by using facilities such as poll or select or multithreading.

Some notable examples of pipeline software systems include:

- RaftLib – C/C++ Apache 2.0 License

VM/CMS and z/OS

CMS Pipelines is a port of the pipeline idea to VM/CMS and z/OS systems. It supports much more complex pipeline structures than Unix shells, with steps taking multiple input streams and producing multiple output streams. (Such functionality is supported by the Unix kernel, but few programs use it as it makes for complicated syntax and blocking modes, although some shells do support it via arbitrary file descriptor assignment).

Traditional application programs on IBM mainframe operating systems have no standard input and output streams to allow redirection or piping. Instead of spawning processes with external programs, CMS Pipelines features a lightweight dispatcher to concurrently execute instances of built-in programs to run the pipeline. More than 200 built-in programs that implement typical UNIX utilities and interface to devices and operating system services. In addition to the built-in programs, CMS Pipelines defines a framework to allow user-written REXX programs with input and output streams that can be used in the pipeline.

Data on IBM mainframes typically resides in a Record-oriented filesystem and connected I/O devices operate in record mode rather than stream mode. As a consequence, data in CMS Pipelines is handled in record mode. For text files, a record holds one line of text. In general, CMS Pipelines does not buffer the data but passes records of data in a lock-step fashion from one program to the next. This ensures a deterministic flow of data through a network of interconnected pipelines.

Object Pipelines

Beside byte stream-based pipelines, there are also object pipelines. In an object pipeline, processing elements output objects instead of text. Windows PowerShell includes an internal object pipeline that transfers .NET objects between functions within the PowerShell runtime. Channels, found in the Limbo programming language, and the IPython ipipe extension are other examples of this metaphor.

Pipelines in GUIs

Graphical environments such as RISC OS and ROX Desktop also make use of pipelines. Rather than providing a save dialog box containing a file manager to let the user specify where a program should write data, RISC OS and ROX provide a save dialog box containing an icon (and a field to specify the name). The destination is specified by dragging and dropping the icon. The user can drop the icon anywhere an already-saved file could be dropped, including onto icons of other programs. If the icon is dropped onto a program's icon, it's loaded and the contents that would otherwise have been saved are passed in on the new program's standard input stream.

For instance, a user browsing the world-wide web might come across a .gz compressed image which they want to edit and re-upload. Using GUI pipelines, they could drag the link to their de-archiving program, drag the icon representing the extracted contents to their image editor, edit it, open the save as dialog, and drag its icon to their uploading software.

Conceptually, this method could be used with a conventional save dialog box, but this would require the user's programs to have an obvious and easily accessible location in the filesystem that can be navigated to. In practice, this is often not the case, so GUI pipelines are rare.

Other Considerations

The name 'pipeline' comes from a rough analogy with physical plumbing in that a pipeline usually allows information to flow in only one direction, like water often flows in a pipe.

Pipes and filters can be viewed as a form of functional programming, using byte streams as data objects; more specifically, they can be seen as a particular form of monad for I/O.

The concept of pipeline is also central to the Cocoon web development framework or to any XProc (the W3C Standards) implementations, where it allows a source stream to be modified before eventual display.

This pattern encourages the use of text streams as the input and output of programs. This reliance on text has to be accounted when creating graphic shells to text programs.

Pipelining and Hazards

Long History

- Starting from long cycle/multi-cycle execution
- Big leap: pipelining
  - Started with single issue
  - Matured into multiple issue
- Next leap: speculative execution
  - Out-of-order issue, in-order completion
- Today's microprocessors feature
  - Speculation at various levels during execution
  - Deep pipelining
  - Sophisticated branch prediction
  - And many more performance boosting hardware

Single-threaded Execution

- Goal of a microprocessor
  - Given a sequential set of instructions it should execute them correctly as fast as possible
  - Correctness is guaranteed as long as the external world sees the execution in-order (i.e. sequential)
  - Within the processor it is okay to re-order the instructions as long as the changes to states are applied in-order
- Performance equation
  - Execution time = average CPI × number of instructions × cycle time

CPI Equation: Analysis

- To reduce the execution time we can try to lower one or more the three terms

- Reducing average CPI (cycles per instruction):
  - The starting point could be CPI=1
  - But complex arithmetic operations e.g. multiplication/division take more than a cycle
  - Memory operations take even longer
  - So normally average CPI is larger than 1
- Reducing number of instructions
  - Better compiler, smart instruction set architecture (ISA)
- Reducing cycle time: faster clock

Life of an Instruction

- Fetch from memory
- Decode/read (figure out the opcode, source and dest registers, read source registers)
- Execute (ALUs, address calculation for memory op)
- Memory access (for load/store)
- Writeback or commit (write result to destination reg)
- During execution the instruction may talk to
  - Register file (for reading source operands and writing results)
  - Cache hierarchy (for instruction fetch and for memory op)

Multi-cycle Execution

- Simplest implementation
  - Assume each of five stages takes a cycle
  - Five cycles to execute an instruction
  - After instruction i finishes you start fetching instruction i+1
  - Without "long latency" instructions CPI is 5
- Alternative implementation
  - You could have a five times slower clock to accommodate all the logic within one cycle
  - Then you can say CPI is 1 excluding mult/div, mem op
  - But overall execution time really doesn't change
- What can you do to lower the CPI?

Pipelining

- Simple observation

  o In the multi-cycle implementation when the ALU is executing, say, an add instruction the decoder is idle

  o Exactly one stage is active at any point in time

  o Wastage of hardware

- Solution: pipelining

  o Process five instructions in parallel

  o Each instruction is in a different stage of processing

  o Each stage is called a pipeline stage

  o Need registers between pipeline stages to hold partially processed instructions (called pipeline latches): why?

More on Pipelining

- What do you gain?

  o Parallelism: called instruction-level parallelism (ILP)

  o Ideal CPI of 1 at the same clock speed as multi-cycle implementation: ideally 5 times reduction in execution time

- What are the problems?

  o Slightly more complex

  o Control and data hazards

  o These hazards put a limit on available ILP

Control Hazard

- Branches pose a problem

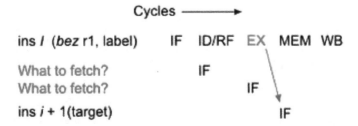

- Two pipeline bubbles: increases average CPI

- Can we reduce it to one bubble?

Branch Delay Slot

- MIPS R3000 has one bubble

    o Called branch delay slot

    o Exploit clock cycle phases

    o On the positive half compute branch condition

    o On the negative half fetch the target

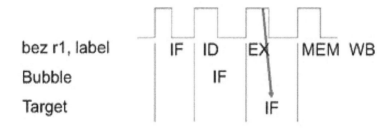

- The PC update hardware (selection between target and next PC) works on the lower edge

- Can we utilize the branch delay slot?

    o Ask the compiler guy

    o The delay slot is always executed (irrespective of the fate of the branch)

    o Boost instructions common to fall through and target paths to the delay slot

    o Not always possible to find

    o You have to be careful also

    o Must boost something that does not alter the outcome of fall-through or target basic blocks

    o If the BD slot is filled with useful instruction then we don't lose anything in CPI; otherwise we pay a branch penalty of one cycle

What else can we do?

- Branch prediction

    o We can put a branch target cache in the fetcher

    o Also called branch target buffer (BTB)

    o Use the lower bits of the instruction PC to index the BTB

    o Use the remaining bits to match the tag

    o In case of a hit the BTB tells you the target of the branch when it executed last time

- o You can hope that this is correct and start fetching from that predicted target provided by the BTB
- o One cycle later you get the real target, compare with the predicted target, and throw away the fetched instruction in case of misprediction; keep going if predicted correctly

Branch Prediction

- BTB will work great for
  - o Loop branches
  - o Subroutine calls
  - o Unconditional branches
- Conditional branch prediction
  - o Rather dynamic in nature
  - o The last target is not very helpful in general (if-then-else)
  - o Need a direction predictor (predicts taken or not taken)
  - o Once that prediction is available we can compute the target
- Return address stack (RAS): push/pop interface

Data Hazards

- Data dependency in instruction stream limits ILP
- True dependency (Read After Write: RAW)

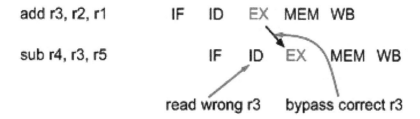

- Need a bypass network to avoid losing cycles
- Without the bypass the fetching of subtraction would have to be delayed by three cycles
- This is an example of RAW hazard

More on RAW

- The most problematic dependencies involve memory ops

- The memory ops may take a large number of cycles to return the value (if missed in cache)

$$lw\ r7,\ 0(r2)$$

$$add\ r4,\ r3,\ r7$$

- This type of dependencies is the primary cause of increase in CPI and lower ILP

Multi-cycle EX Stage

- Thus far we have assumed a single cycle EX
- Consider multiplication and division
- Assume a four-cycle multiplication unit: mult r5, r4, r3   IF ID EX1 EX2 EX3 EX4 MEM WB
- Normally the multiplier is separate
- So the next instruction can start executing when mult moves to EX2 stage and, in fact, can finish before mult
  - More data hazards

WAW Hazard

- Write After Write (WAW)

mult r5, r4, r3	IF	ID	Ex1	Ex2	Ex3	Ex4	MEM	WB
add r5, r6, r12		IF	ID	Ex	MEM	WB		
lw r9, 20 (r10)			IF	ID	Ex	MEM...	(fault)	

- The problem: out-of-order completion
- The final value in r5 will nullify the effect of the add instruction
- The bigger issue: precise exception is violated
- Next load instruction raises an exception (may be due to page fault)
- You handle the exception and start from the load
- But value in r5 does not reflect precise state
- Solution: disallow out-of-order completion

Overall CPI

- CPI = 1.0 + pipeline overhead

- Pipeline overhead comes from
    - Branch penalty (useless delay slots, mispredictions)
    - True data dependencies
    - Multi-cycle instructions (load/store, mult/div)
    - Other data hazards
- So to boost CPI further
    - Need to have better branch prediction
    - Need to hide latency of memory ops, mult/div

Multiple Issue

- Thus far we have assumed that at most one instruction gets advanced to EX stage every cycle
- If we have four ALUs we can issue four independent instructions every cycle
- This is called superscalar execution
- Ideally CPI should go down by a factor equal to issue width (more parallelism)
- Extra hardware needed:
    - Wider fetch to keep the ALUs fed
    - More decode bandwidth, more register file ports; decoded instructions are put in an issue queue
    - Selection of independent instructions for issue
    - In-order completion

Instruction Issue Algorithms

Instruction Selection

- Simplest possible design
    - Issue the instructions sequentially (in-order)
    - Scan the issue queue, stop as soon as you come to an instruction dependent on one already issued
- Cannot issue the last two even though they are independent of the first two: in-order completion is a must for precise exception support

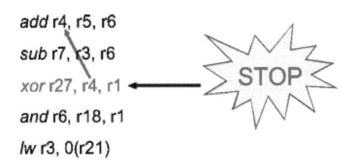

In-order Multi-issue

- Complexity of selection logic

    o Need to check for RAW and WAW

    o Comparisons for RAW: N(N-1) where N is the issue width

    o Comparisons for WAW: N(N-1)/2

    o 18 comparators for 4-issue

- Still need to make sure instructions write back in-order to support precise exception

    o As instructions issue, they are removed from the issue queue and put in a re-order buffer (also called active list in MIPS processors) [Isn't WAW check sufficient?]

    o Instructions write back or retire in-order from re-order buffer (ROB)

Out-of-order Issue

```
lw r4, 0(r6)          Cache miss
addi r5, r4, 0x20
and r10, r5, r19
xor r26, r5, r7
sub r20, r26, r2
andi r27, r8, 0xffff
sll r19, r27, 0x5
beq r20, r19, label
or r12, r15, r16
```

- Issue first cycle, issue second cycle,...

- Taking the parallelism to a new dimension

- Central to all modern microprocessors

- Scan the issue queue completely, select independent instructions and issue as many as possible limited only by the number of functional units

- Need more comparators

- Able to extract more ILP: CPI goes down further

- Possible to overlap the latency of mult/div, load/store with execution of other independent instructions

WAR Hazard

lw r4, 0(r6)   Cache miss

addi r5, r4, 0x20

and r10, r5, r19

xor r26, r5, r7

sub r20, r26, r2

andi r27, r8, 0xffff

sll r19, r27, 0x5

beq r20, r19, label

or r12, r15, r16

- Write After Read (WAR): in-order commit solves it

Modified Bypass

- An executing instruction must broadcast results to the issue queue

  o Waiting instructions compare their source register numbers with the destination register number of the bypassed value

  o Also, now it needs to make sure that it is consuming the right value in program order to avoid WAR

add r19, r2, r3

sub r20, r19, r3

xori r19, r4, 0xf

and r22, r19, r1

- Need to tag every instruction with its last producer

- Can we simplify this?

WAR and WAW

- These are really false dependencies
  - o Arises due to register allocation by the compiler
- Thus far we have assumed that ROB has space to hold the destination values: needs wide ROB entries
- These values are written back to the register file when the instructions retire or commit in-order from ROB
- Also, bypass becomes complicated
- Better way to solve it: rename the destination registers

Register Renaming

- Registers visible to the compiler
  - o Logical or architectural registers
  - o Normally 32 in number for RISC and is fixed by the ISA
- Physical registers inside the processor
  - o Much larger in number
- The destination logical register of every instruction is renamed to a physical register number
- The dependencies are tracked based on physical registers
- MIPS R10000 has 32 logical and 64 physical regs
- Intel Pentium 4 has 8 logical and 128 physical regs

- Assume 64 physical regs and already renamed registers:
  r6=p54, r19=p38, r2=p0, r7=p20, r15=p3, r16=p23

lw r4, 0(r6)	lw p15, 0(p54) [r4 renamed to p15]
addi r5, r4, 0x20	addi p40, p15, 0x20 [r5 renamed to p40]
and r10,r5, r19	and p39, p40, p38 [r10 renamed to p39]
xor r26, r2, r7	xor p62, p0, p20 [r26 renamed to p62]
sub r20, r26, r2	sub p8, p62, p0 [r20 renamed to p8]
andi r27, r8, 0xffff	andi p19, p25, 0xffff [r27 renamed to p19]
sll r19, r27, 0x5	sll p45, p19, 0x5 [r19 renamed to p45]
beq r20, r19, 0x5	beq p8, p45, label
or r12, r15, r16	or p59, p3, p23 [r12 renamed to p59]

mult r5, r4, r3	[r5 gets renamed to, say, p50]
add r5, r6, r12	[r5 gets renamed to, say, p45]

- Now it is safe to issue them in parallel: they are really independent (compiler introduced WAW)

- Register renaming maintains a map table that records logical register to physical register map

- After an instruction is decoded, its logical register numbers are available

- The renamer looks up the map table to find mapping for the logical source regs of this instruction, assigns a free physical register to the destination logical reg, and records the new mapping

- If the renamer runs out of physical registers, the pipeline stalls until at least one register is available

- When do you free a physical register?

  o Suppose a physical register P is mapped to a logical register L which is the destination of instruction I

  o It is safe to free P only when the next producer of L retires (Why not earlier?)

- More physical registers

  o more in-flight instructions

  o possibility of more parallelism

- But cannot make the register file very big

  o Takes time to access

  o Burns power

The pipeline

- Fetch, decode, rename, issue, register file read, ALU, cache, retire

- Fetch, decode, rename are in-order stages, each handles multiple instructions every cycle

- The ROB entry is allocated in rename stage

- Issue, register file, ALU, cache are out-of-order

- Retire is again in-order, but multiple instructions may retire each cycle: need to free the resources and drain the pipeline quickly

What limits ILP now?

- Instruction cache miss (normally not a big issue)

- Branch misprediction

  o Observe that you predict a branch in decode, and the branch executes in ALU

- o There are four pipeline stages before you know outcome

- o Misprediction amounts to loss of at least 4F instructions where F is the fetch width

- • Data cache miss

- o Assuming a issue width of 4, frequency of 3 GHz, memory latency of 120 ns, you need to find 1440 independent instructions to issue so that you can hide the memory latency: this is impossible (resource shortage)

Cycle Time Reduction

- • Execution time = CPI × instruction count × cycle time

- • Talked about CPI reduction or improvement in IPC (instructions retired per cycle)

- • Cycle time reduction is another technique to boost performance

- o Faster clock frequency

- • Pipelining poses a problem

- o Each pipeline stage should be one cycle for balanced progress

- o Smaller cycle time means need to break pipe stages into smaller stages

- • Superpipelining

- o Faster clock frequency necessarily means deep pipes

- o Each pipe stage contains small amount of logic so that it fits in small cycle time

- o May severely degrade CPI if not careful

- o Now branch penalty is even bigger (31 cycles for Intel Prescott): branch mispredictions cause massive loss in performance (93 micro-ops are lost, F=3)

- o Long pipes also put more pressure on resources such as ROB and registers because instruction latency increases (in terms of cycles, not in absolute terms)

- o Instructions occupy ROB entries and registers longer

- o The design becomes increasingly complicated (long wires)

Alternative: VLIW

- • Very Long Instruction Word computers

- o Compiler carries out all dependence analysis

- o Bundles as many independent instructions as allowed by the number of functional units into an instruction packet

- o Hardware is a lot less complex

- o The instructions in the packet issue in parallel

- o Each packet of instructions is pretty long (hence the name)

- o Problem: compiler may not be able to extract as much ILP as a dynamic out-of-order core; many packets may go unutilized

- Big leap from VLIW: EPIC (Explicitly Parallel Instruction Computing) [Itanium family]

Current Research in μP

- Micro-architectural techniques to extract more ILP

  - o Directly helps improve IPC and reduce CPI

  - o Various speculative techniques to hide cache miss latency: prefetching, load value prediction, etc.

- Better branch prediction

  - o Helps deep pipelines

- Faster clocking

  - o Need to cool the chip

  - o Various techniques to reduce power consumption: clock gating, dynamic voltage/frequency scaling (DVFS), power-aware resource usage

  - o Fighting the long wires: scaling micro-architectures against the complexity wall

References

- Glaskowsky, Peter (Aug 18, 2003). "Xelerated's Xtraordinary NPU — World's First 40Gb/s Packet Processor Has 200 CPUs". Microprocessor Report. 18 (8): 12–14. Retrieved 20 March 2017

- C. Michael Pilato; Ben Collins-Sussman; Brian W. Fitzpatrick (2008). Version Control with Subversion. O'Reilly Media. p. 238. ISBN 0-596-51033-0

- Nielsen, Henrik Frystyk; Gettys, Jim; Baird-Smith, Anselm; Prud'hommeaux, Eric; Lie, Håkon Wium; Lilley, Chris (24 June 1997). World Wide Web Consortium. Retrieved 14 January 2010

- "Wayback link of 'Windows Internet Explorer 8 Expert Zone Chat (August 14, 2008)'". Microsoft. August 14, 2008. Retrieved May 10, 2012

- K. Nipp, D. Stoffer; Lineare Algebra; v/d/f Hochschulverlag der ETH Zürich; Zürich 1998, ISBN 3-7281-2649-7

Virtual Memory: An Integrated Study

Virtual memory is a method of managing the memory of a hardware and software system. Virtual memory is very beneficial as it includes freeing application from sharing space, increases security and can use more memory than a physical system. The following chapter will help the readers in developing a better understanding of virtual memory and caches.

Virtual Memory

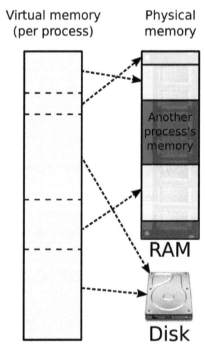

Virtual memory combines active RAM and inactive memory on DASD to form a large range of contiguous addresses.

In computing, virtual memory is a memory management technique that is implemented using both hardware and software. It maps memory addresses used by a program, called *virtual addresses*, into *physical addresses* in computer memory. Main storage as seen by a process or task appears as a contiguous address space or collection of contiguous segments. The operating system manages virtual address spaces and the assignment of real memory to virtual memory. Address translation hardware in the CPU, often referred to as a memory management unit or *MMU*, automatically translates virtual addresses to physical addresses. Software within the operating system may extend these capabilities to provide a virtual address space that can exceed the capacity of real memory and thus reference more memory than is physically present in the computer.

The primary benefits of virtual memory include freeing applications from having to manage a shared memory space, increased security due to memory isolation, and being able to conceptually use more memory than might be physically available, using the technique of paging.

Properties

Virtual memory makes application programming easier by hiding fragmentation of physical memory; by delegating to the kernel the burden of managing the memory hierarchy (eliminating the need for the program to handle overlays explicitly); and, when each process is run in its own dedicated address space, by obviating the need to relocate program code or to access memory with relative addressing.

Memory virtualization can be considered a generalization of the concept of virtual memory.

Usage

Virtual memory is an integral part of a modern computer architecture; implementations usually require hardware support, typically in the form of a memory management unit built into the CPU. While not necessary, emulators and virtual machines can employ hardware support to increase performance of their virtual memory implementations. Consequently, older operating systems, such as those for the mainframes of the 1960s, and those for personal computers of the early to mid-1980s (e.g., DOS), generally have no virtual memory functionality, though notable exceptions for mainframes of the 1960s include:

- The Atlas Supervisor for the Atlas

- THE multiprogramming system for the Electrologica X8 (software based virtual memory without hardware support)

- MCP for the Burroughs B5000

- MTS, TSS/360 and CP/CMS for the IBM System/360 Model 67

- Multics for the GE 645

- The Time Sharing Operating System for the RCA Spectra 70/46

and the operating system for the Apple Lisa is an example of a personal computer operating system of the 1980s that features virtual memory.

During the 1960s and early 70s, computer memory was very expensive. The introduction of virtual memory provided an ability for software systems with large memory demands to run on computers with less real memory. The savings from this provided a strong incentive to switch to virtual memory for all systems. The additional capability of providing virtual address spaces added another level of security and reliability, thus making virtual memory even more attractive to the market place.

Most modern operating systems that support virtual memory also run each process in its own dedicated address space. Each program thus appears to have sole access to the virtual memory.

However, some older operating systems (such as OS/VS1 and OS/VS2 SVS) and even modern ones (such as IBM i) are single address space operating systems that run all processes in a single address space composed of virtualized memory.

Embedded systems and other special-purpose computer systems that require very fast and/or very consistent response times may opt not to use virtual memory due to decreased determinism; virtual memory systems trigger unpredictable traps that may produce unwanted "jitter" during I/O operations. This is because embedded hardware costs are often kept low by implementing all such operations with software (a technique called bit-banging) rather than with dedicated hardware.

History

In the 1940s and 1950s, all larger programs had to contain logic for managing primary and secondary storage, such as overlaying. Virtual memory was therefore introduced not only to extend primary memory, but to make such an extension as easy as possible for programmers to use. To allow for multiprogramming and multitasking, many early systems divided memory between multiple programs without virtual memory, such as early models of the PDP-10 via registers.

The concept of virtual memory was first developed by German physicist Fritz-Rudolf Güntsch at the Technische Universität Berlin in 1956 in his doctoral thesis, *Logical Design of a Digital Computer with Multiple Asynchronous Rotating Drums and Automatic High Speed Memory Operation*; it described a machine with 6 100-word blocks of primary core memory and an address space of 1,000 100-word blocks, with hardware automatically moving blocks between primary memory and secondary drum memory. Paging was first implemented at the University of Manchester as a way to extend the Atlas Computer's working memory by combining its 16 thousand words of primary core memory with an additional 96 thousand words of secondary drum memory. The first Atlas was commissioned in 1962 but working prototypes of paging had been developed by 1959.[p2] In 1961, the Burroughs Corporation independently released the first commercial computer with virtual memory, the B5000, with segmentation rather than paging.

Before virtual memory could be implemented in mainstream operating systems, many problems had to be addressed. Dynamic address translation required expensive and difficult to build specialized hardware; initial implementations slowed down access to memory slightly. There were worries that new system-wide algorithms utilizing secondary storage would be less effective than previously used application-specific algorithms. By 1969, the debate over virtual memory for commercial computers was over; an IBM research team led by David Sayre showed that their virtual memory overlay system consistently worked better than the best manually controlled systems. Throughout the 1970s, the IBM 370 series running their virtual-storage based operating systems provided a means for business users to migrate multiple older systems into fewer, more powerful, mainframes that had improved price/performance. The first minicomputer to introduce virtual memory was the Norwegian NORD-1; during the 1970s, other minicomputers implemented virtual memory, notably VAX models running VMS.

Virtual memory was introduced to the x86 architecture with the protected mode of the Intel 80286 processor, but its segment swapping technique scaled poorly to larger segment sizes. The Intel 80386 introduced paging support underneath the existing segmentation layer, enabling the page fault exception to chain with other exceptions without double fault. However, loading segment descriptors was an expensive operation, causing operating system designers to rely strictly on paging rather than a combination of paging and segmentation.

Paged

Nearly all implementations of virtual memory divide a virtual address space into pages, blocks of contiguous virtual memory addresses. Pages on contemporary systems are usually at least 4 kilobytes in size; systems with large virtual address ranges or amounts of real memory generally use larger page sizes.

Page Tables

Page tables are used to translate the virtual addresses seen by the application into physical addresses used by the hardware to process instructions; such hardware that handles this specific translation is often known as the memory management unit. Each entry in the page table holds a flag indicating whether the corresponding page is in real memory or not. If it is in real memory, the page table entry will contain the real memory address at which the page is stored. When a reference is made to a page by the hardware, if the page table entry for the page indicates that it is not currently in real memory, the hardware raises a page fault exception, invoking the paging supervisor component of the operating system.

Systems can have one page table for the whole system, separate page tables for each application and segment, a tree of page tables for large segments or some combination of these. If there is only one page table, different applications running at the same time use different parts of a single range of virtual addresses. If there are multiple page or segment tables, there are multiple virtual address spaces and concurrent applications with separate page tables redirect to different real addresses.

Paging Supervisor

This part of the operating system creates and manages page tables. If the hardware raises a page fault exception, the paging supervisor accesses secondary storage, returns the page that has the virtual address that resulted in the page fault, updates the page tables to reflect the physical location of the virtual address and tells the translation mechanism to restart the request.

When all physical memory is already in use, the paging supervisor must free a page in primary storage to hold the swapped-in page. The supervisor uses one of a variety of page replacement algorithms such as least recently used to determine which page to free.

Pinned Pages

Operating systems have memory areas that are *pinned* (never swapped to secondary storage). Other terms used are *locked*, *fixed*, or *wired* pages. For example, interrupt mechanisms rely on an array of pointers to their handlers, such as I/O completion and page fault. If the pages containing these pointers or the code that they invoke were pageable, interrupt-handling would become far more complex and time-consuming, particularly in the case of page fault interruptions. Hence, some part of the page table structures is not pageable.

Some pages may be pinned for short periods of time, others may be pinned for long periods of time, and still others may need to be permanently pinned. For example:

- The paging supervisor code and drivers for secondary storage devices on which pages reside must be permanently pinned, as otherwise paging wouldn't even work because the necessary code wouldn't be available.

- Timing-dependent components may be pinned to avoid variable paging delays.

- Data buffers that are accessed directly by peripheral devices that use direct memory access or I/O channels must reside in pinned pages while the I/O operation is in progress because such devices and the buses to which they are attached expect to find data buffers located at physical memory addresses; regardless of whether the bus has a memory management unit for I/O, transfers cannot be stopped if a page fault occurs and then restarted when the page fault has been processed.

In IBM's operating systems for System/370 and successor systems, the term is "fixed", and such pages may be long-term fixed, or may be short-term fixed, or may be unfixed (i.e., pageable). System control structures are often long-term fixed (measured in wall-clock time, i.e., time measured in seconds, rather than time measured in fractions of one second) whereas I/O buffers are usually short-term fixed (usually measured in significantly less than wall-clock time, possibly for tens of milliseconds). Indeed, the OS has a special facility for "fast fixing" these short-term fixed data buffers (fixing which is performed without resorting to a time-consuming Supervisor Call instruction).

Multics used the term "wired". OpenVMS and Windows refer to pages temporarily made nonpageable (as for I/O buffers) as "locked", and simply "nonpageable" for those that are never pageable.

Virtual-real Operation

In OS/VS1 and similar OSes, some parts of systems memory are managed in "virtual-real" mode, called "V=R". In this mode every virtual address corresponds to the same real address. This mode is used for interrupt mechanisms, for the paging supervisor and page tables in older systems, and for application programs using non-standard I/O management. For example, IBM's z/OS has 3 modes (virtual-virtual, virtual-real and virtual-fixed).

Thrashing

When paging and page stealing are used, a problem called "thrashing" can occur, in which the computer spends an unsuitably large amount of time transferring pages to and from a backing store, hence slowing down useful work. A task's working set is the minimum set of pages that should be in memory in order for it to make useful progress. Thrashing occurs when there is insufficient memory available to store the working sets of all active programs. Adding real memory is the simplest response, but improving application design, scheduling, and memory usage can help. Another solution is to reduce the number of active tasks on the system. This reduces demand on real memory by swapping out the entire working set of one or more processes.

Segmented

Some systems, such as the Burroughs B5500, use segmentation instead of paging, dividing virtual address spaces into variable-length segments. A virtual address here consists of a segment number and an offset within the segment. The Intel 80286 supports a similar segmentation scheme as an option, but it is rarely used. Segmentation and paging can be used together by dividing each segment into pages; systems with this memory structure, such as Multics and IBM System/38, are usually paging-predominant, segmentation providing memory protection.

In the Intel 80386 and later IA-32 processors, the segments reside in a 32-bit linear, paged address space. Segments can be moved in and out of that space; pages there can "page" in and out of main memory, providing two levels of virtual memory; few if any operating systems do so, instead using only paging. Early non-hardware-assisted x86 virtualization solutions combined paging and segmentation because x86 paging offers only two protection domains whereas a VMM / guest OS / guest applications stack needs three. The difference between paging and segmentation systems is not only about memory division; segmentation is visible to user processes, as part of memory model semantics. Hence, instead of memory that looks like a single large space, it is structured into multiple spaces.

This difference has important consequences; a segment is not a page with variable length or a simple way to lengthen the address space. Segmentation that can provide a single-level memory model in which there is no differentiation between process memory and file system consists of only a list of segments (files) mapped into the process's potential address space.

This is not the same as the mechanisms provided by calls such as mmap and Win32's MapViewOf-File, because inter-file pointers do not work when mapping files into semi-arbitrary places. In Multics, a file (or a segment from a multi-segment file) is mapped into a segment in the address space, so files are always mapped at a segment boundary. A file's linkage section can contain pointers for which an attempt to load the pointer into a register or make an indirect reference through it causes a trap. The unresolved pointer contains an indication of the name of the segment to which the pointer refers and an offset within the segment; the handler for the trap maps the segment into the address space, puts the segment number into the pointer, changes the tag field in the pointer so that it no longer causes a trap, and returns to the code where the trap occurred, re-executing the instruction that caused the trap. This eliminates the need for a linker completely and works when different processes map the same file into different places in their private address spaces.

Address Space Swapping

Some operating systems provide for swapping entire address spaces, in addition to whatever facilities they have for paging and segmentation. When this occurs, the OS writes those pages and segments currently in real memory to swap files. In a swap-in, the OS reads back the data from the swap files but does not automatically read back pages that had been paged out at the time of the swap out operation.

IBM's MVS, from OS/VS2 Release 2 through z/OS, provides for marking an address space as unswappable; doing so does not pin any pages in the address space. This can be done for the duration of a job by entering the name of an eligible main program in the Program Properties Table with an unswappable flag. In addition, privileged code can temporarily make an address space unswappable With a SYSEVENT Supervisor Call instruction (SVC); certain changes in the address space properties require that the OS swap it out and then swap it back in, using SYSEVENT TRANSWAP.

Memory Address

In computing, memory address is a data concept used at various levels by software and hardware to access the computer's primary storage memory. Memory addresses are fixed-length sequences of digits conventionally displayed and manipulated as unsigned integers. Such numerical semantic bases itself upon features of CPU (such as the instruction pointer and incremental address registers), as well upon use of the memory like an array endorsed by various programming languages.

Types of Memory Addresses

Physical Addresses

A digital computer's memory, more specifically main memory, consists of many memory locations, each having a physical address, a code, which the CPU (or other device) can use to access it. Generally only system software, i.e. the BIOS, operating systems, and some specialized utility programs (e.g., memory testers), address physical memory using machine code operands or processor registers, instructing the CPU to direct a hardware device, called the memory controller, to use the memory bus or system bus, or separate control, address and data busses, to execute the program's commands. The memory controllers' bus consists of a number of parallel lines, each represented by a binary digit (bit). The width of the bus, and thus the number of addressable storage units, and the number of bits in each unit, varies among computers.

Logical Addresses

A computer program uses memory addresses to execute machine code, store and retrieve data. In early computers logical and physical addresses corresponded, but since the introduction of virtual memory most application programs do not have a knowledge of physical addresses. Rather, they address logical addresses, or virtual addresses, using the computer's memory management unit and operating system memory mapping.

Unit of Address Resolution

Most modern computers are *byte-addressable*, with each address identifying a single eight bit byte of storage; data too large to be stored in a single byte may reside in multiple bytes occupying a sequence of consecutive addresses. There exist *word-addressable* computers, where the minimal addressable storage unit is exactly the processor's word. For example, the Data General Nova minicomputer, and the Texas Instruments TMS9900 and National Semiconductor IMP-16 microcomputers used 16 bit words, and there were many 36-bit mainframe computers (e.g., PDP-10) which used 18-bit word addressing, not byte addressing, giving an address space of 2^{18} 36-bit words, approximately 1 megabyte of storage. The efficiency of addressing of memory depends on the bit size of the bus used for addresses – the more bits used, the more addresses are available to the computer. For example, an 8-bit-byte-addressable machine with a 20-bit address bus (e.g. Intel 8086) can address 2^{20} (1,048,576) memory locations, or one MiB of memory, while a 32-bit bus (e.g. Intel 80386) addresses 2^{32} (4,294,967,296) locations, or a 4 GiB address space. In contrast, a 36-bit word-addressable machine with an 18-bit address bus addresses only 2^{18} (262,144) 36-bit locations (9,437,184 bits), equivalent to 1,179,648 8-bit bytes, or 1152 KB, or 1.125 MiB—slightly more than the 8086.

Some older computers (decimal computers), were *decimal digit-addressable*. For example, each address in the IBM 1620's magnetic-core memory identified a single six bit binary-coded decimal digit, consisting of a parity bit, flag bit and four numerical bits. The 1620 used 5-digit decimal addresses, so in theory the highest possible address was 99,999. In practice, the CPU supported 20,000 memory locations, and up to two optional external memory units could be added, each supporting 20,000 addresses, for a total of 60,000 (00000–59999).

Word Size Versus Address Size

A word size is characteristic to a given computer architecture. It denotes the number of digits that a CPU can process at one time. Modern processors, including embedded systems, usually have a word size of 8, 16, 24, 32 or 64 bits; most current general purpose computers use 32 or 64 bits. Many different sizes have been used historically, including 8, 9, 10, 12, 18, 24, 36, 39, 40, 48 and 60 bits.

Very often, when referring to the *word size* of a modern computer, one is also describing the size of address space on that computer. For instance, a computer said to be "32-bit" also usually allows 32-bit memory addresses; a byte-addressable 32-bit computer can address 2^{32} = 4,294,967,296 bytes of memory, or 4 gibibytes (GiB). This allows one memory address to be efficiently stored in one word.

However, this does not always hold true. Computers can have memory addresses larger or smaller than their word size. For instance, many 8-bit processors, such as the MOS Technology 6502, supported 16-bit addresses— if not, they would have been limited to a mere 256 bytes of memory addressing. The 16-bit Intel 8088 and Intel 8086 supported 20-bit addressing via segmentation, allowing them to access 1 MiB rather than 64 KiB of memory. All Intel Pentium processors since the Pentium Pro include Physical Address Extensions (PAE) which support mapping 36-bit physical addresses to 32-bit virtual addresses.

In theory, modern byte-addressable 64-bit computers can address 2^{64} bytes (16 exbibytes), but in practice the amount of memory is limited by the CPU, the memory controller, or the printed circuit board design (e.g. number of physical memory connectors or amount of soldered-on memory).

Contents of Each Memory Location

Each memory location in a stored-program computer holds a binary number or decimal number *of some sort*. Its interpretation, as data of some data type or as an instruction, and use are determined by the instructions which retrieve and manipulate it.

Some early programmers combined instructions and data in words as a way to save memory, when it was expensive: The Manchester Mark 1 had space in its 40-bit words to store little bits of data – its processor ignored a small section in the middle of a word – and that was often exploited as extra data storage. Self-replicating programs such as viruses treat themselves sometimes as data and sometimes as instructions. Self-modifying code is generally deprecated nowadays, as it makes testing and maintenance disproportionally difficult to the saving of a few bytes, and can also give incorrect results because of the compiler or processor's assumptions about the machine's state, but is still sometimes used deliberately, with great care.

Address Space in Application Programming

In modern multitasking environment, an application process usually has in its address space (or spaces) chunks of memory of following types:

- Machine code, including:

  o program's own code (historically known as *code segment* or *text segment*);

  o shared libraries.

- Data, including:

  o initialized data (data segment);

  o uninitialized (but allocated) variables;

  o run-time stack;

  o heap;

  o shared memory and memory mapped files.

Some parts of address space may be not mapped at all.

Addressing Schemes

A computer program can access an address given explicitly – in low-level programming this is usually called an absolute address, or sometimes a specific address, and is known as pointer data type in higher-level languages. But a program can also use relative address which specifies a location in relation to somewhere else (the *base address*). There are many more indirect addressing modes.

Mapping logical addresses to physical and virtual memory also adds several levels of indirection.

Memory Models

Many programmers prefer to address memory such that there is no distinction between code space and data space (cf. above), as well as from physical and virtual memory — in other words, numerically identical pointers refer to exactly the same byte of RAM.

However, many early computers did not support such a *flat memory model* — in particular, Harvard architecture machines force program storage to be completely separate from data storage. Many modern DSPs (such as the Motorola 56000) have three separate storage areas — program storage, coefficient storage, and data storage. Some commonly used instructions fetch from all three areas simultaneously — fewer storage areas (even if there were the same total bytes of storage) would make those instructions run slower.

Memory Models in x86 Architecture

Early x86 computers used the segmented memory model addresses based on a combination of two numbers: a memory segment, and an offset within that segment. Some segments were implicitly treated as *code segments*, dedicated for instructions, *stack segments*, or normal *data segments*. Although the usages were different, the segments did not have different memory protections reflecting this. In the flat memory model all segments (segment registers) are generally set to zero, and only offsets are variable.

Address Space

In computing, an address space defines a range of discrete addresses, each of which may correspond to a network host, peripheral device, disk sector, a memory cell or other logical or physical entity.

For software programs to save and retrieve stored data, each unit of data must have an address where it can be individually located or else the program will be unable to find and manipulate the data. The number of address spaces available will depend on the underlying address structure and these will usually be limited by the computer architecture being used.

Address spaces are created by combining enough uniquely identified qualifiers to make an address unambiguous (within a particular address space). For a person's physical address, the *address space* would be a combination of locations, such as a neighborhood, town, city, or country. Some elements of an address space may be the same— but if any element in the address is different than addresses in said space will reference different entities. An example could be that there are multiple buildings at the same address of "32 Main Street" but in different towns, demonstrating that different towns have different, although similarly arranged, street address spaces.

An address space usually provides (or allows) a partitioning to several regions according to the mathematical structure it has. In the case of total order, as for memory addresses, these are simply chunks. Some nested domains hierarchy appears in the case of directed ordered tree as for the Domain Name System or a directory structure; this is similar to the hierarchical design of postal addresses. In the Internet, for example, the Internet Assigned Numbers Authority (IANA) allocates ranges of IP addresses to various registries in order to enable them to each manage their parts of the global Internet address space.

Examples

Uses of addresses include, but are not limited to the following:

- Memory addresses for main memory, memory-mapped I/O, as well as for virtual memory;
- Device addresses on an expansion bus;
- Sector addressing for disk drives;
- File names on a particular volume;
- Various kinds of network host addresses in computer networks;
- Uniform resource locators in the Internet.

Address Mapping and Translation

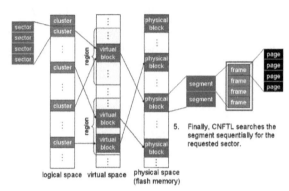

5. Finally, CNFTL searches the segment sequentially for the requested sector.

logical space   virtual space   physical space (flash memory)

Illustration of translation from logical block addressing to physical geometry

Another common feature of address spaces are mappings and translations, often forming numerous layers. This usually means that some higher-level address must be translated to lower-level ones in some way. For example, file system on a logical disk operates linear sector numbers, which have to be translated to *absolute* LBA sector addresses, in simple cases, via addition of the partition's first sector address. Then, for a disk drive connected via Parallel ATA, each of them must be converted to *logical* (means fake) cylinder-head-sector address due to the interface historical shortcomings. It is converted back to LBA by the disk controller and then, finally, to *physical* cylinder, head and sector numbers.

The Domain Name System maps its names to (and from) network-specific addresses (usually IP addresses), which in turn may be mapped to link layer network addresses via Address Resolution Protocol. Also, network address translation may occur on the edge of *different* IP spaces, such as a local area network and the Internet.

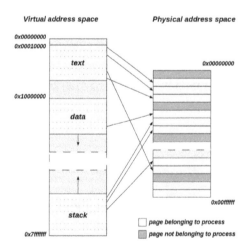

Virtual address space and physical address space relationship

An iconic example of virtual-to-physical address translation is virtual memory, where different pages of virtual address space map either to page file or to main memory physical address space. It is possible that several numerically different virtual addresses all refer to one physical address and hence to the same physical byte of RAM. It is also possible that a single virtual address maps to zero, one, or more than one physical address.

Virtual Address Space

In computing, a virtual address space (VAS) or address space is the set of ranges of virtual addresses that an operating system makes available to a process. The range of virtual addresses usually starts at a low address and can extend to the highest address allowed by the computer's instruction set architecture and supported by the operating system's pointer size implementation, which can be 4 bytes for 32-bit or 8 bytes for 64-bit OS versions. This provides several benefits, one of which is, if each process is given a separate address space, security through process isolation.

Example

When a new application on a 32-bit OS is executed, the process has a 4 GiB VAS: each one of the memory addresses (from 0 to $2^{32}-1$) in that space can have a single byte as a value. Initially, none of them have values ('-' represents no value). Using or setting values in such a VAS would cause a memory exception.

```
            0                                               4GB

VAS         |-----------------------------------------------|
```

Then the application's executable file is mapped into the VAS. Addresses in the process VAS are mapped to bytes in the exe file. The OS manages the mapping:

```
            0                                               4GB

VAS         |---vvvvvvv-------------------------------------|

mapping        |------|

file bytes     app.exe
```

The v's are values from bytes in the mapped file. Then, required DLL files are mapped (this includes custom libraries as well as system ones such as kernel32.dll and user32.dll):

```
            0                                               4GB

VAS         |---vvvvvvv----vvvvvv---vvvv------------------|

mapping        |||||||     ||||||   ||||

file bytes     app.exe     kernel   user
```

The process then starts executing bytes in the exe file. However, the only way the process can use or set '-' values in its VAS is to ask the OS to map them to bytes from a file. A common way to use VAS memory in this way is to map it to the page file. The page file is a single file, but multiple distinct sets of contiguous bytes can be mapped into a VAS:

```
            0                                               4GB

VAS         |---vvvvvvv----vvvvvv---vvvv----vv---v----vvv--|

mapping        |||||||     ||||||   ||||     ||   |    |||

file bytes     app.exe     kernel   user   system_page_file
```

And different parts of the page file can map into the VAS of different processes:

```
            0                                                    4GB
VAS 1       |---vvvv-------vvvvvv---vvvv----vv---v----vvv--|

mapping        | | | |           | | | | | |     | | | |      | |       |        | | |

file bytes     app1 app2   kernel     user     system_page_file

mapping            | | | |   | | | | | |     | | | |              | |      |

VAS 2       |--------vvvv--vvvvvv---vvvv-------vv---v------|
```

On a 32-bit Microsoft Windows installation, by default, only 2 GiB are made available to processes for their own use. The other 2GB are used by the operating system. On later 32-bit editions of Microsoft Windows it is possible to extend the user-mode virtual address space to 3 GiB while only 1 GiB is left for kernel-mode virtual address space by marking the programs as IMAGE_FILE_LARGE_ADDRESS_AWARE and enabling the /3GB switch in the boot.ini file.

On 64-bit Microsoft Windows, in a process running an executable that was linked with /LARGE-ADDRESSAWARE:NO, the operating system artificially limits the process virtual address space to 2 GB. This applies to both 32- and 64-bit executables. Processes running executables that were linked with the /LARGEADDRESSAWARE:YES option, which is the default for 64-bit Visual Studio 2010 and later, have access to more than 2GB of virtual address space: Up to 4 GB for 32-bit executables, up to 8 TB for 64-bit executables in Windows through Windows 8, and up to 128 TB for 64-bit executables in Windows 8.1 and later.

Allocating memory via C's malloc establishes the page file as the backing store for any new virtual address space. However, a process can also explicitly map file bytes.

Linux

For x86 CPUs, Linux 32-bit allows to split the user and kernel address ranges in differents ways: *3G/1G user/kernel* (default) , *1G/3G user/kernel* or *2G/2G user/kernel*.

VA to PA Translation

- The VA generated by the processor is divided into two parts:
  - Page offset and Virtual page number (VPN)
  - Assume a 4 KB page: within a 32-bit VA, lower 12 bits will be page offset (offset within a page) and the remaining 20 bits are VPN (hence 1 M virtual pages total)
  - The page offset remains unchanged in the translation
  - Need to translate VPN to a physical page frame number (PPFN)
  - This translation is held in a page table resident in memory: so first we need to access this page table

- o How to get the address of the page table?

- Accessing the page table

    - o The Page table base register (PTBR) contains the starting physical address of the page table

    - o PTBR is normally accessible in the kernel mode only

    - o Assume each entry in page table is 32 bits (4 bytes)

    - o Thus the required page table address is

$$PTBR + (\text{VPN} << 2)$$

    - o Access memory at this address to get 32 bits of data from the page table entry (PTE)

    - o These 32 bits contain many things: a valid bit, the much needed PPFN (may be 20 bits for a 4 GB physical memory), access permissions (read, write, execute), a dirty/modified bit etc.

Page Fault

- The valid bit within the 32 bits tells you if the translation is valid

- If this bit is reset that means the page is not resident in memory: results in a page fault

- In case of a page fault the kernel needs to bring in the page to memory from disk

- The disk address is normally provided by the page table entry (different interpretation of 31 bits)

- Also kernel needs to allocate a new physical page frame for this virtual page

- If all frames are occupied it invokes a page replacement policy

- Page faults take a long time: order of ms

    - o Need a good page replacement policy

- Once the page fault finishes, the page table entry is updated with the new VPN to PPFN mapping

- Of course, if the valid bit was set, you get the PPFN right away without taking a page fault

- Finally, PPFN is concatenated with the page offset to get the final PA PPFN|Offset

- Processor now can issue a memory request with this PA to get the necessary data

- Really two memory accesses are needed

- Can we improve on this?

Translation Lookaside Buffer

A Translation lookaside buffer (TLB) is a memory cache that is used to reduce the time taken to access a user memory location. It is a part of the chip's memory-management unit (MMU). The TLB stores the recent translations of virtual memory to physical memory and can be called an address-translation cache. A TLB may reside between the CPU and the CPU cache, between CPU cache and the main memory or between the different levels of the multi-level cache. The majority of desktop, laptop, and server processors include one or more TLBs in the memory management hardware, and it is nearly always present in any processor that utilizes paged or segmented virtual memory.

The TLB is sometimes implemented as content-addressable memory (CAM). The CAM search key is the virtual address and the search result is a physical address. If the requested address is present in the TLB, the CAM search yields a match quickly and the retrieved physical address can be used to access memory. This is called a TLB hit. If the requested address is not in the TLB, it is a miss, and the translation proceeds by looking up the page table in a process called a *page walk*. The page walk is time consuming when compared to the processor speed, as it involves reading the contents of multiple memory locations and using them to compute the physical address. After the physical address is determined by the page walk, the virtual address to physical address mapping is entered into the TLB. The PowerPC 604, for example, has a two-way set-associative TLB for data loads and stores. Some processors have different instruction and data address TLBs.

Overview

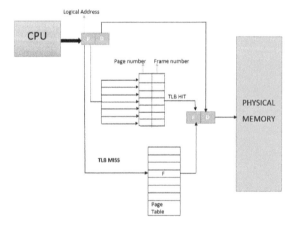

General working of TLB.

A TLB has a fixed number of slots containing page table entries and segment table entries; page table entries map virtual addresses to physical addresses and intermediate table addresses, while segment table entries map virtual addresses to segment addresses, intermediate table addresses and page table addresses. The virtual memory is the memory space as seen from a process; this space is often split into pages of a fixed size (in paged memory), or less commonly into segments of variable sizes (in segmented memory). The page table, generally stored in main memory, keeps track of where the virtual pages are stored in the physical memory. This method uses two memory accesses (one for the page table entry, one for the byte) to access a byte. First, the page table is looked up for the frame number. Second, the frame number with the page offset gives the actual address. Thus any straightforward virtual memory scheme would have the effect of doubling the memory access time. Hence, the TLB is used to reduce the time taken to access the memory locations in the page table method. The TLB is a cache of the page table, representing only a subset of the page table contents.

Referencing the physical memory addresses, a TLB may reside between the CPU and the CPU cache, between the CPU cache and primary storage memory, or between levels of a multi-level cache. The placement determines whether the cache uses physical or virtual addressing. If the cache is virtually addressed, requests are sent directly from the CPU to the cache, and the TLB is accessed only on a cache miss. If the cache is physically addressed, the CPU does a TLB lookup on every memory operation and the resulting physical address is sent to the cache.

In a Harvard architecture or modified Harvard architecture, a separate virtual address space or memory access hardware may exist for instructions and data. This can lead to distinct TLBs for each access type, an Instruction Translation Lookaside Buffer (ITLB) and a Data Translation Lookaside Buffer (DTLB). Various benefits have been demonstrated with separate data and instruction TLBs.

The TLB can be used as a fast lookup hardware cache. The figure shows the working of a TLB. Each entry in the TLB consists of two parts: a tag and a value. If the tag of the incoming virtual address matches the tag in the TLB, the corresponding value is returned. Since the TLB lookup is usually a part of the instruction pipeline, searches are fast and cause essentially no performance penalty. However, to be able to search within the instruction pipeline, the TLB has to be small.

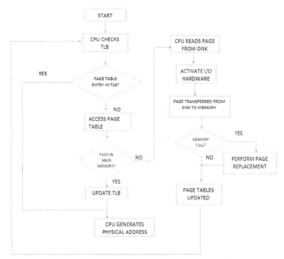

Flowchart shows the working of a Translation Lookaside Buffer. For simplicity,
the page fault routine is not mentioned.

A common optimization for physically addressed caches is to perform the TLB lookup in parallel with the cache access. Upon each virtual memory reference, the hardware checks the TLB to see if the page number is held therein. If yes, it is a TLB hit and the translation is made. The frame number is returned and is used to access the memory. If the page number is not in the TLB, the page table must be checked. Depending on the CPU, this can be done automatically using a hardware or using an interrupt to the operating system. When the frame number is obtained, it can be used to access the memory. In addition, we add the page number and frame number to the TLB, so that they will be found quickly on the next reference. If the TLB is already full, a suitable block must be selected for replacement. There are different replacement methods like Least recently used (LRU), First Come First Out(FIFO) etc.

Performance Implications

The CPU has to access main memory for an instruction cache miss, data cache miss, or TLB miss. The third case (the simplest one) is where the desired information itself actually *is* in a cache, but the information for virtual-to-physical translation is not in a TLB. These are all slow, due to the need to access a slower level of the memory hierarchy, so a well-functioning TLB is important. Indeed, a TLB miss can be more expensive than an instruction or data cache miss, due to the need for not just a load from main memory, but a page walk, requiring several memory accesses.

The flowchart provided explains the working of a TLB. If it is a TLB miss, then the CPU checks the page table for the page table entry. If the 'present bit' is set, then the page is in main memory, and the processor can retrieve the frame number from the page table entry to form the physical address. The processor also updates the TLB to include the new page table entry. Finally, if the present bit is not set, then the desired page is not in the main memory and a page fault is issued. Then a page fault interrupt is called which executes the page fault handling routine.

If the page working set does not fit into the TLB, then TLB thrashing occurs, where frequent TLB misses occur, with each newly cached page displacing one that will soon be used again, degrading performance in exactly the same way as thrashing of the instruction or data cache does. TLB thrashing can occur even if instruction cache or data cache thrashing are not occurring, because these are cached in different size units. Instructions and data are cached in small blocks (cache lines), not entire pages, but address lookup is done at the page level. Thus even if the code and data working sets fit into cache, if the working sets are fragmented across many pages, the virtual address working set may not fit into TLB, causing TLB thrashing. Appropriate sizing of the TLB thus requires considering not only the size of the corresponding instruction and data caches, but also how these are fragmented across multiple pages.

Multiple TLBs

Similar to caches, TLBs may have multiple levels. CPUs can be (and nowadays usually are) built with multiple TLBs, for example a small "L1" TLB (potentially fully associative) that is extremely fast, and a larger "L2" TLB that is somewhat slower. When instruction-TLB (ITLB) and data-TLB (DTLB) are used, a CPU can have three (ITLB1, DTLB1, TLB2) or four TLBs.

For instance, Intel's Nehalem microarchitecture has a four-way set associative L1 DTLB with 64 entries for 4 KiB pages and 32 entries for 2/4 MiB pages, an L1 ITLB with 128 entries for 4 KiB pages using four-way associativity and 14 fully associative entries for 2/4 MiB pages (both parts of the ITLB divided statically between two threads) and a unified 512-entry L2 TLB for 4 KiB pages, both 4-way associative.

Some TLBs may have separate sections for small pages and huge pages.

TLB Miss Handling

Two schemes for handling TLB misses are commonly found in modern architectures:

- With hardware TLB management, the CPU automatically walks the page tables (using the CR3 register on x86 for instance) to see if there is a valid page table entry for the specified virtual address. If an entry exists, it is brought into the TLB and the TLB access is retried: this time the access will hit, and the program can proceed normally. If the CPU finds no valid entry for the virtual address in the page tables, it raises a page fault exception, which the operating system must handle. Handling page faults usually involves bringing the requested data into physical memory, setting up a page table entry to map the faulting virtual address to the correct physical address, and resuming the program. With a hardware-managed TLB, the format of the TLB entries is not visible to software, and can change from CPU to CPU without causing loss of compatibility for the programs.

- With software-managed TLBs, a TLB miss generates a "TLB miss" exception, and operating system code is responsible for walking the page tables and performing the translation in software. The operating system then loads the translation into the TLB and restarts the program from the instruction that caused the TLB miss. As with hardware TLB management, if the OS finds no valid translation in the page tables, a page fault has occurred, and the OS must handle it accordingly. Instruction sets of CPUs that have software-managed TLBs have instructions that allow loading entries into any slot in the TLB. The format of the TLB entry is defined as a part of the instruction set architecture (ISA). The MIPS architecture specifies a software-managed TLB; the SPARC V9 architecture allows an implementation of SPARC V9 to have no MMU, an MMU with a software-managed TLB, or an MMU with a hardware-managed TLB, and the UltraSPARC architecture specifies a software-managed TLB.

The Itanium architecture provides an option of using either software or hardware managed TLBs.

The Alpha architecture's TLB is managed in PALcode, rather than in the operating system. As the PALcode for a processor can be processor-specific and operating-system-specific, this allows different versions of PALcode to implement different page table formats for different operating systems, without requiring that the TLB format, and the instructions to control the TLB, to be specified by the architecture.

Typical TLB

These are typical performance levels of a TLB:

- size: 12–4,096 entries

- hit time: 0.5–1 clock cycle

- miss penalty: 10–100 clock cycles

- miss rate: 0.01–1%

If a TLB hit takes 1 clock cycle, a miss takes 30 clock cycles, and the miss rate is 1%, the effective memory cycle rate is an average of $1 \times 0.99 + (1 + 30) \times 0.01 = 1.30$ (1.30 clock cycles per memory access).

Address Space Switch

On an address space switch, as occurs on a process switch but not on a thread switch, some TLB entries can become invalid, since the virtual-to-physical mapping is different. The simplest strategy to deal with this is to completely flush the TLB. This means that after a switch, the TLB is empty and *any* memory reference will be a miss, and it will be some time before things are running back at full speed. Newer CPUs use more effective strategies marking which process an entry is for. This means that if a second process runs for only a short time and jumps back to a first process, it may still have valid entries, saving the time to reload them.

For example, in the Alpha 21264, each TLB entry is tagged with an "address space number" (ASN), and only TLB entries with an ASN matching the current task are considered valid. Another example in the Intel Pentium Pro, the page global enable (PGE) flag in the register CR4 and the global (G) flag of a page-directory or page-table entry can be used to prevent frequently used pages from being automatically invalidated in the TLBs on a task switch or a load of register CR3.

While selective flushing of the TLB is an option in software managed TLBs, the only option in some hardware TLBs (for example, the TLB in the Intel 80386) is the complete flushing of the TLB on an address space switch. Other hardware TLBs (for example, the TLB in the Intel 80486 and later x86 processors, and the TLB in ARM processors) allow the flushing of individual entries from the TLB indexed by virtual address.

Virtualization and x86 TLB

With the advent of virtualization for server consolidation, a lot of effort has gone into making the x86 architecture easier to virtualize and to ensure better performance of virtual machines on x86 hardware. In a long list of such changes to the x86 architecture, the TLB is the latest.

Normally, entries in the x86 TLBs are not associated with a particular address space; they implicitly refer to the current address space. Hence, every time there is a change in address space, such as a context switch, the entire TLB has to be flushed. Maintaining a tag that associates each TLB entry with an address space in software and comparing this tag during TLB lookup and TLB flush is very expensive, especially since the x86 TLB is designed to operate with very low latency and completely in hardware. In 2008, both Intel (Nehalem) and AMD (SVM) have introduced tags as part of the TLB entry and dedicated hardware that checks the tag during lookup. Even though these are not fully exploited, it is envisioned that in the future, these tags will identify the address space to which every TLB entry belongs. Thus a context switch will not result in the flushing of the TLB – but just changing the tag of the current address space to the tag of the address space of the new task.

- Why can't we cache the most recently used translations?

- Translation Look-aside Buffers (TLB)

- Small set of registers (normally fully associative)

- Each entry has two parts: the tag which is simply VPN and the corresponding PTE

- The tag may also contain a process id

- On a TLB hit you just get the translation in one cycle (may take slightly longer depending on the design)

- On a TLB miss you may need to access memory to load the PTE in TLB (more later)

- Normally there are two TLBs: instruction and data

Cache (Computing)

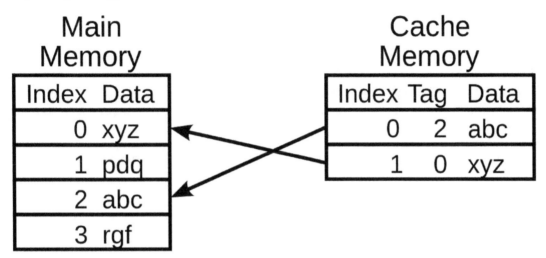

Diagram of a CPU memory cache operation

In computing, a *cache KASH*, is a hardware or software component that stores data so future requests for that data can be served faster; the data stored in a cache might be the result of an earlier computation, or the duplicate of data stored elsewhere. A *cache hit* occurs when the requested data can be found in a cache, while a *cache miss* occurs when it cannot. Cache hits are served by reading data from the cache, which is faster than recomputing a result or reading from a slower data store; thus, the more requests can be served from the cache, the faster the system performs.

To be cost-effective and to enable efficient use of data, caches must be relatively small. Nevertheless, caches have proven themselves in many areas of computing because access patterns in typical computer applications exhibit the locality of reference. Moreover, access patterns exhibit temporal locality if data is requested again that has been recently requested already, while spatial locality refers to requests for data physically stored close to data that has been already requested.

Motivation

There is an inherent trade-off between size and speed (given that a larger resource implies greater physical distances) but also a tradeoff between expensive, premium technologies (such as SRAM) vs cheaper, easily mass-produced commodities (such as DRAM or hard disks).

The buffering provided by a cache benefits both throughput and latency:

Latency

A larger resource incurs a significant latency for access – e.g. it can take hundreds of clock cycles for a modern 4 GHz processor to reach DRAM. This is mitigated by reading in large chunks, in the hope that subsequent reads will be from nearby locations. Prediction or explicit prefetching might also guess where future reads will come from and make requests ahead of time; if done correctly the latency is bypassed altogether.

Throughput and Granularity

The use of a cache also allows for higher throughput from the underlying resource, by assembling multiple fine grain transfers into larger, more efficient requests. In the case of DRAM, this might be served by a wider bus. Imagine a program scanning bytes in a 32bit address space, but being served by a 128bit off chip data bus; individual uncached byte accesses would only allow 1/16th of the total bandwidth to be used, and 80% of the data movement would be addresses. Reading larger chunks reduces the fraction of bandwidth required for transmitting address information.

Operation

Hardware implements cache as a block of memory for temporary storage of data likely to be used again. Central processing units (CPUs) and hard disk drives (HDDs) frequently use a cache, as do web browsers and web servers.

A cache is made up of a pool of entries. Each entry has associated data, which is a copy of the same data in some *backing store*. Each entry also has a tag, which specifies the identity of the data in the backing store of which the entry is a copy.

When the cache client (a CPU, web browser, operating system) needs to access data presumed to exist in the backing store, it first checks the cache. If an entry can be found with a tag matching that of the desired data, the data in the entry is used instead. This situation is known as a cache hit. So, for example, a web browser program might check its local cache on disk to see if it has a local copy of the contents of a web page at a particular URL. In this example, the URL is the tag, and the contents of the web page is the data. The percentage of accesses that result in cache hits is known as the hit rate or hit ratio of the cache.

The alternative situation, when the cache is consulted and found not to contain data with the desired tag, has become known as a cache miss. The previously uncached data fetched from the backing store during miss handling is usually copied into the cache, ready for the next access.

During a cache miss, the CPU usually ejects some other entry in order to make room for the previously uncached data. The heuristic used to select the entry to eject is known as the replacement policy. One popular replacement policy, "least recently used" (LRU), replaces the least recently used entry. More efficient caches compute use frequency against the size of the stored contents, as well as the latencies and throughputs for both the cache and the backing store. This works well for larger amounts of data, longer latencies and slower throughputs, such as experienced with a hard drive and the Internet, but is not efficient for use with a CPU cache.

Writing Policies

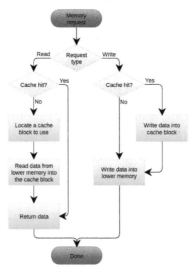

A write-through cache with no-write allocation

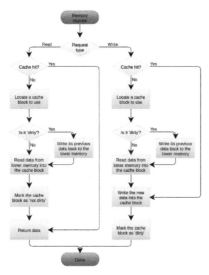

A write-back cache with write allocation

When a system writes data to cache, it must at some point write that data to the backing store as well. The timing of this write is controlled by what is known as the *write policy*.

There are two basic writing approaches:

- *Write-through*: write is done synchronously both to the cache and to the backing store.

- *Write-back* (also called *write-behind*): initially, writing is done only to the cache. The write to the backing store is postponed until the cache blocks containing the data are about to be modified/replaced by new content.

A write-back cache is more complex to implement, since it needs to track which of its locations have been written over, and mark them as *dirty* for later writing to the backing store. The data in these locations are written back to the backing store only when they are evicted from the cache, an effect referred to as a *lazy write*. For this reason, a read miss in a write-back cache (which requires a block to be replaced by another) will often require two memory accesses to service: one to write the replaced data from the cache back to the store, and then one to retrieve the needed data.

Other policies may also trigger data write-back. The client may make many changes to data in the cache, and then explicitly notify the cache to write back the data.

No data is returned on write operations, thus there are two approaches for situations of write-misses:

- *Write allocate* (also called *fetch on write*): data at the missed-write location is loaded to cache, followed by a write-hit operation. In this approach, write misses are similar to read misses.

- *No-write allocate* (also called *write-no-allocate* or *write around*): data at the missed-write location is not loaded to cache, and is written directly to the backing store. In this approach, only the reads are being cached.

Both write-through and write-back policies can use either of these write-miss policies, but usually they are paired in this way:

- A write-back cache uses write allocate, hoping for subsequent writes (or even reads) to the same location, which is now cached.

- A write-through cache uses no-write allocate. Here, subsequent writes have no advantage, since they still need to be written directly to the backing store.

Entities other than the cache may change the data in the backing store, in which case the copy in the cache may become out-of-date or *stale*. Alternatively, when the client updates the data in the cache, copies of those data in other caches will become stale. Communication protocols between the cache managers which keep the data consistent are known as coherency protocols.

Examples of Hardware Caches

CPU Cache

Small memories on or close to the CPU can operate faster than the much larger main memory. Most CPUs since the 1980s have used one or more caches, sometimes in cascaded levels; modern high-end embedded, desktop and server microprocessors may have as many as six types of cache (between levels and functions),. Examples of caches with a specific function are the D-cache and I-cache and the translation lookaside buffer for the MMU.

GPU Cache

Earlier graphics processing units (GPUs) often had limited read-only texture caches, and introduced morton order swizzled textures to improve 2D cache coherency. Cache misses would drastically affect performance, e.g. if mipmapping was not used. Caching was important to leverage 32-bit (and wider) transfers for texture data that was often as little as 4 bits per pixel, indexed in complex patterns by arbitrary UV coordinates and perspective transformations in inverse texture mapping.

As GPUs advanced (especially with GPGPU compute shaders) they have developed progressively larger and increasingly general caches, including instruction caches for shaders, exhibiting increasingly common functionality with CPU caches. For example, GT200 architecture GPUs did not feature an L2 cache, while the Fermi GPU has 768 KB of last-level cache, the Kepler GPU has 1536 KB of last-level cache, and the Maxwell GPU has 2048 KB of last-level cache. These caches have grown to handle synchronisation primitives between threads and atomic operations, and interface with a CPU-style MMU.

DSPs

Digital signal processors have similarly generalised over the years. Earlier designs used scratchpad memory fed by DMA, but modern DSPs such as Qualcomm Hexagon often include a very similar set of caches to a CPU (e.g. Modified Harvard architecture with shared L2, split L1 I-cache and D-cache).

Translation Lookaside Buffer

A memory management unit (MMU) that fetches page table entries from main memory has a specialized cache, used for recording the results of virtual address to physical address translations. This specialized cache is called a translation lookaside buffer (TLB).

Software Caches

Disk Cache

While CPU caches are generally managed entirely by hardware, a variety of software manages other caches. The page cache in main memory, which is an example of disk cache, is managed by the operating system kernel.

While the disk buffer, which is an integrated part of the hard disk drive, is sometimes misleadingly referred to as "disk cache", its main functions are write sequencing and read prefetching. Repeated cache hits are relatively rare, due to the small size of the buffer in comparison to the drive's capacity. However, high-end disk controllers often have their own on-board cache of the hard disk drive's data blocks.

Finally, a fast local hard disk drive can also cache information held on even slower data storage devices, such as remote servers (web cache) or local tape drives or optical jukeboxes; such a scheme is the main concept of hierarchical storage management. Also, fast flash-based solid-state drives (SSDs) can be used as caches for slower rotational-media hard disk drives, working together as hybrid drives or solid-state hybrid drives (SSHDs).

Web Cache

Web browsers and web proxy servers employ web caches to store previous responses from web servers, such as web pages and images. Web caches reduce the amount of information that needs to be transmitted across the network, as information previously stored in the cache can often be re-used. This reduces bandwidth and processing requirements of the web server, and helps to improve responsiveness for users of the web.

Web browsers employ a built-in web cache, but some Internet service providers (ISPs) or organizations also use a caching proxy server, which is a web cache that is shared among all users of that network.

Another form of cache is P2P caching, where the files most sought for by peer-to-peer applications are stored in an ISP cache to accelerate P2P transfers. Similarly, decentralised equivalents exist, which allow communities to perform the same task for P2P traffic, for example, Corelli.

Memoization

A cache can store data that is computed on demand rather than retrieved from a backing store. Memoization is an optimization technique that stores the results of resource-consuming function calls within a lookup table, allowing subsequent calls to reuse the stored results and avoid repeated computation.

Other Caches

The BIND DNS daemon caches a mapping of domain names to IP addresses, as does a resolver library.

Write-through operation is common when operating over unreliable networks (like an Ethernet LAN), because of the enormous complexity of the coherency protocol required between multiple write-back caches when communication is unreliable. For instance, web page caches and client-side network file system caches (like those in NFS or SMB) are typically read-only or write-through specifically to keep the network protocol simple and reliable.

Search engines also frequently make web pages they have indexed available from their cache. For example, Google provides a "Cached" link next to each search result. This can prove useful when web pages from a web server are temporarily or permanently inaccessible.

Another type of caching is storing computed results that will likely be needed again, or memoization. For example, ccache is a program that caches the output of the compilation, in order to speed up later compilation runs.

Database caching can substantially improve the throughput of database applications, for example in the processing of indexes, data dictionaries, and frequently used subsets of data.

A distributed cache uses networked hosts to provide scalability, reliability and performance to the application. The hosts can be co-located or spread over different geographical regions.

Buffer vs. Cache

The semantics of a "buffer" and a "cache" are not necessarily mutually exclusive; even so, there are fundamental differences in intent between the process of caching and the process of buffering.

Fundamentally, caching realizes a performance increase for transfers of data that is being repeatedly transferred. While a caching system may realize a performance increase upon the initial (typically write) transfer of a data item, this performance increase is due to buffering occurring within the caching system.

With read caches, a data item must have been fetched from its residing location at least once in order for subsequent reads of the data item to realize a performance increase by virtue of being able to be fetched from the cache's (faster) intermediate storage rather than the data's residing location. With write caches, a performance increase of writing a data item may be realized upon the first write of the data item by virtue of the data item immediately being stored in the cache's intermediate storage, deferring the transfer of the data item to its residing storage at a later stage or else occurring as a background process. Contrary to strict buffering, a caching process must adhere to a (potentially distributed) cache coherency protocol in order to maintain consistency between the cache's intermediate storage and the location where the data resides. Buffering, on the other hand,

- reduces the number of transfers for otherwise novel data amongst communicating processes, which amortizes overhead involved for several small transfers over fewer, larger transfers,

- provides an intermediary for communicating processes which are incapable of direct transfers amongst each other, or

- ensures a minimum data size or representation required by at least one of the communicating processes involved in a transfer.

With typical caching implementations, a data item that is read or written for the first time is effectively being buffered; and in the case of a write, mostly realizing a performance increase for the application from where the write originated. Additionally, the portion of a caching protocol where individual writes are deferred to a batch of writes is a form of buffering. The portion of a caching protocol where individual reads are deferred to a batch of reads is also a form of buffering, although this form may negatively impact the performance of at least the initial reads (even though it may positively impact the performance of the sum of the individual reads). In practice, caching almost always involves some form of buffering, while strict buffering does not involve caching.

A buffer is a temporary memory location that is traditionally used because CPU instructions cannot directly address data stored in peripheral devices. Thus, addressable memory is used as an intermediate stage. Additionally, such a buffer may be feasible when a large block of data is assembled or disassembled (as required by a storage device), or when data may be delivered in a different order than that in which it is produced. Also, a whole buffer of data is usually transferred sequentially (for example to hard disk), so buffering itself sometimes increases transfer performance or reduces the variation or jitter of the transfer's latency as opposed to caching where the intent is to reduce the latency. These benefits are present even if the buffered data are written to the buffer once and read from the buffer once.

A cache also increases transfer performance. A part of the increase similarly comes from the possibility that multiple small transfers will combine into one large block. But the main performance-gain occurs because there is a good chance that the same data will be read from cache multiple times, or that written data will soon be read. A cache's sole purpose is to reduce accesses to the underlying slower storage. Cache is also usually an abstraction layer that is designed to be invisible from the perspective of neighboring layers.

- Once you have completed the VA to PA translation you have the physical address. What's next?

- You need to access memory with that PA

- Instruction and data caches hold most recently used (temporally close) and nearby (spatially close) data

- Use the PA to access the cache first

- Caches are organized as arrays of cache lines

- Each cache line holds several contiguous bytes (32, 64 or 128 bytes)

Addressing a Cache

- The PA is divided into several parts

- The block offset determines the starting byte address within a cache line

- The index tells you which cache line to access

- In that cache line you compare the tag to determine hit/miss

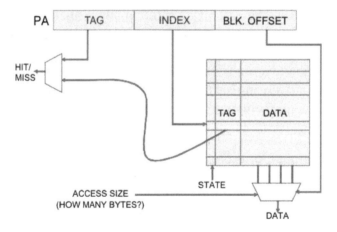

An example

- PA is 32 bits

- Cache line is 64 bytes: block offset is 6 bits

- Number of cache lines is 512: index is 9 bits

- So tag is the remaining bits: 17 bits

- Total size of the cache is 512*64 bytes i.e. 32 KB

- Each cache line contains the 64 byte data, 17-bit tag, one valid/invalid bit, and several state bits (such as shared, dirty etc.)

- Since both the tag and the index are derived from the PA this is called a physically indexed physically tagged cache

Cache Hierarchy and Memory-level Parallelism

Set Associative Cache

- The example assumes one cache line per index
  - Called a direct-mapped cache
  - A different access to a line evicts the resident cache line
  - This is either a capacity or a conflict miss
- Conflict misses can be reduced by providing multiple lines per index
- Access to an index returns a set of cache lines
  - For an n-way set associative cache there are n lines per set
- Carry out multiple tag comparisons in parallel to see if any one in the set hits

2-way Set Associative

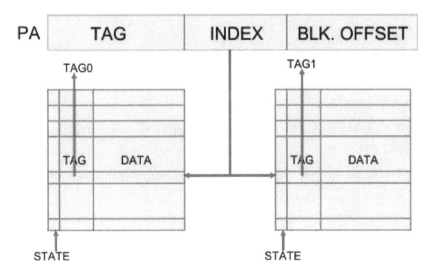

- When you need to evict a line in a particular set you run a replacement policy
  - LRU is a good choice: keeps the most recently used lines (favors temporal locality)
  - Thus you reduce the number of conflict misses
- Two extremes of set size: direct-mapped (1-way) and fully associative (all lines are in a single set)
  - Example: 32 KB cache, 2-way set associative, line size of 64 bytes: number of indices or number of sets=32*1024/(2*64)=256 and hence index is 8 bits wide
  - Example: Same size and line size, but fully associative: number of sets is 1, within the set there are 32*1024/64 or 512 lines; you need 512 tag comparisons for each access

- Ideally want to hold everything in a fast cache

    o   Never want to go to the memory

- But, with increasing size the access time increases

- A large cache will slow down every access

- So, put increasingly bigger and slower caches between the processor and the memory

- Keep the most recently used data in the nearest cache: register file (RF)

- Next level of cache: level 1 or L1 (same speed or slightly slower than RF, but much bigger)

- Then L2: way bigger than L1 and much slower

- Example: Intel Pentium 4 (Netburst)

    o   128 registers accessible in 2 cycles

    o   L1 date cache: 8 KB, 4-way set associative, 64 bytes line size, accessible in 2 cycles for integer loads

    o   L2 cache: 256 KB, 8-way set associative, 128 bytes line size, accessible in 7 cycles

- Example: Intel Itanium 2 (code name Madison)

    o   128 registers accessible in 1 cycle

    o   L1 instruction and data caches: each 16 KB, 4-way set associative, 64 bytes line size, accessible in 1 cycle

    o   Unified L2 cache: 256 KB, 8-way set associative, 128 bytes line size, accessible in 5 cycles

    o   Unified L3 cache: 6 MB, 24-way set associative, 128 bytes line size, accessible in 14 cycles

Cache Hierarchy

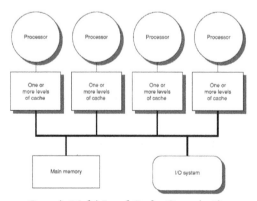

Generic Multi-Level Cache Organization

Cache hierarchy or Multi-level caches refers to a memory model designed generally to hold data which is more likely to be requested by processors. The purpose of such memory models is to provide a faster execution of memory related instructions, and faster overall performance of the system.

This model was for CPU cores to run at faster clocks, needing to hide the memory latency of the main memory access. Today Multi-level caches are the optimum solution to provide such a fast access to data residing in main memory. The access time to memory that acts as a bottleneck for the CPU core performance can be relaxed by using a hierarchical cache structure in order to reduce the latency and hence speed up the CPU clock.

Background

In the history of computer and electronic chip developments, there was a time that CPUs were getting faster and faster while memory access speeds had not much of such improvements. At the time, this gap and difference between CPUs and memories became a trigger point of need for enhancements in memory access time. With getting CPUs faster, systems were capable of running and executing more instructions in a given time rather than before, but the time limitation in data access from memory prevented programmers to benefit this capability. This issue was the motivation behind thoughts for achieving memory models with higher access rate in order to company with processors for a better and faster performance. Therefore, the needs for such memory models resulted to the concept of Cache memory. This concept was first proposed by Maurice Wilkes a British computer scientist in University of Cambridge in 1965, but at the time he called such memories as "slave memory". Roughly between 1970-1990 there were lots of papers and articles proposed by many people like Anant Agarwal, Alan Jay Smith, Mark D. Hill, Thomas R. Puzak, etc., regarding enhancement and analysis for a better cache memory designs. First cache memory models were implemented at that time, but as researchers were investigating and proposing better designs, the need for faster memory models still could have been sensed. Because although those cache models improved data access latency, they could not have enough storage capacity to cover much data compared to main memory and there was lots of data to be accessed in the old fashioned way with high latency. Therefore, approximately from 1990 and so on, gradually ideas like adding another cache level (second-level) to such memory models as a backup for the first level cache came into thoughts and proposals. Many people like Jean-Loup Baer, Wen-Hann Wang, Andrew W. Wilson, etc. have conducted researches on this model. When several simulations and implementations demonstrated the advantages of such two-level cache models in having a faster data access from memory, concept of multi-level caches formed as a new and generally better model of cache memories compared to its previous single form. From year 2000 until now multi-level cache models received a widespread attention and it is implemented wildly in many systems as we can find three level-caches in Intel Core i7 products.

Multi-level Cache

Access to the main memory for each instruction execution may result in the very slow processing with the clock speed dependent on the time taken to find the data in main memory and fetch it. In order to hide this memory latency from the processor, data caching is used. Whenever the data is required by the processor, it is fetched from the memory and stored in the small structure called Cache. For any further references to that data, the cache is searched first before going to main memory. This structure resides closer to the processor in terms of time taken to search and fetch data with respect to Main Memory. The advantages of using cache can be proven by calculating the Average Access Time (AAT) for the memory hierarchy without cache and with the cache.

Average Access Time (AAT)

Cache, being small in the size, may result in frequent misses and we might eventually have to go to main memory to fetch data. And hence, the AAT depends on the miss rate of all the structures that it searches through for the data.

$$AAT = hit\ time + ((miss\ rate) \times (miss\ penalty))$$

AAT for main memory is given by Hit time $_{main\ memory}$. AAT for caches can be given by

Hit time$_{cache}$ + (Miss rate$_{cache}$ + Miss Penalty$_{time\ taken\ to\ go\ to\ main\ memory\ after\ missing\ cache}$).

Hit time for caches is very less as compared to main memory and hence the resulting AAT after using cache in the memory hierarchy is improved significantly.

Trade-offs

While using the cache to improve the memory latency, it may not always result in the required improvement for the time taken to fetch data due to the way caches are organized and traversed. E.g. The same size direct mapped caches usually have more miss rate than the fully associative caches. This may also depend on upon the benchmark that we are testing the processor upon and the pattern of instructions. But always using the fully associative cache may result in more power consumption as it has to search the whole cache every time. Due to this, the trade-off between the power consumption and the size of the cache becomes critical in the cache design.

Evolution

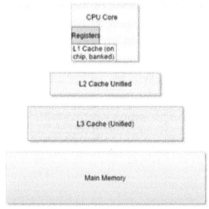

Cache hierarchy for up-to L3 level of cache and main memory with on chip L1.

In the case of a miss in the cache, the purpose of using such a structure will be rendered useless and we will ultimately have to go to main memory to fetch the required data. The idea of using multiple levels of cache comes into picture here. This means that if we miss the cache closest to the processor, we will search for the data in the next closest level of cache and will keep on doing that until we run out of levels of caches and will finally search the main memory. The general trend is to keep L1 cache small and at a distance of 1–2 CPU clock cycles from the processor with the lower levels of caches increasing in the size to store more data than L1 and hence have lower miss rate. This, in turn, results into a better AAT. The number of levels of cache can be designed by architects as per the requirement after checking for the trade-offs between cost, AATs, and size.

Performance Gains

With the technology scaling which made memory systems feasible and smaller to accommodate on a single chip, most of the modern day processors go for up to 3 or 4 levels of caches. The reduction in the AAT can be understood by this example where we check AAT for different configurations up to 3-level caches.

Example: Main memory = 50ns, L1 = 1ns (10% miss rate), L2 = 5ns (1% miss rate), L3 = 10 ns (0.2% miss rate) ·

1. AAT (No cache) = 50ns

2. AAT (L1 cache+ Main Memory) = 1ns + (0.1 × 50ns) = 6ns

3. AAT (L1 cache + L2 cache + Main Memory) = 1ns + (0.1 × (5 + 0.01(50ns)) = 1.505ns

4. AAT (L1 cache + L2 cache + L3 cache + Main Memory) = 1ns + (0.1 × (5 + 0.01(10 + 0.002 × 50ns))) = 1.5001ns

Disadvantages

- Increase in the cost of memories and hence the overall system.

- Cached data is stored only until power supply is provided.

- Increase in area consumed by memory system on chip.

- In case of a large programs with poor temporal locality, even the multi-level caches cannot help improve the performance and eventually, main memory needs to be reached to fetch the data.

Properties

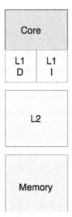

Cache organization with L1 cache as Separate and L2 cache as Unified

Banked Versus Unified

In a banked cache, the cache is divided into instruction cache and data cache. In contrast, a unified cache contains both the instructions and data combined in the same cache. During a process, the upper-level cache is accessed to get the instructions to the processor in each cycle. The cache will also be accessed to get data. Requiring both actions to be implemented at the same time requires multiple ports in the cache and as well as takes more access time. Having multiple ports requires additional hardware and wiring leading to huge structure. Therefore, the L1 cache is organized as a banked cache which results in fewer ports, less hardware and low access time.

The lower level caches L2 and L3 are accessed only when there is a miss in the L1 cache implies the frequency of access to the lower level caches is less compared to the L1 cache. Therefore, the unified organization is implemented in the lower level caches as having a single port will suffice.

Inclusion Policies

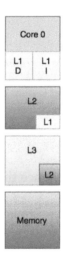

Inclusive cache organization

Whether a block present in the upper cache layer can be present in the lower cache level is governed by the inclusion policies below:

- Inclusive

- Exclusive

- Non-Inclusive Non-Exclusive (NINE)

In the Inclusive policy, all the blocks present in the upper-level cache has to be present in the lower level cache as well. Each upper-level cache component is a subset of the lower level cache component. In this case, since there is a duplication of blocks there is some wastage of memory. However checking is better in the case of inclusive because if the lower level cache doesn't have the block then we can be sure that the upper-level cache can no way have that block.

In the exclusive policy, all the cache hierarchy components are completely exclusive which implies that any element in the upper-level cache will not be present in any of the lower cache component.

This enables complete usage of the cache memory as no same block is present in the other cache component. However, there is a high memory access latency.

The above policies require a set on rules to be followed in order to implement them. If none of these are forced, the resulting inclusion policy is called Non-Inclusive Non-Exclusive (NINE). This means that the upper level cache may or may not be present in the lower level cache.

Write Policies

There are two policies which define the way in which a modified cache block will be updated in the main memory:

- Write Through
- Write Back

In the case of Write Through policy whenever the value of the cache block changes, it is further modified in the lower-level memory hierarchy as well. This policy ensures that the data is stored safely as it is written throughout the hierarchy.

However, in the case of the Write Back policy, the changed cache block will be updated in the lower-level hierarchy only when the cache block is evicted. Writing back every cache block which is evicted is not efficient. Therefore, we use the concept of a Dirty bit attached to each cache block. The dirty bit is made high whenever the cache block is modified and during eviction, only the blocks with dirty bit high will be written to the lower-level hierarchy and then the dirty bit is cleared. In this policy, there is data losing risk as the only valid copy is stored in the cache and therefore need some correction techniques to be implemented.

In case of a write where the byte is not present in the cache block the write policies below determine whether the byte has to be brought to the cache or not:

- Write Allocate
- Write No-Allocate

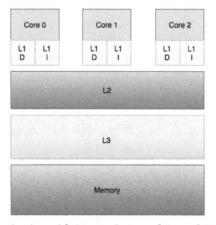

Cache organization with L1 as private and L2 and L3 as shared

Write Allocate policy states that in case of a write miss, the block is fetched from the main memory and placed in the cache before writing. In the Write No-Allocate policy, if the block is missed in the cache it will just write in the lower level memory hierarchy without fetching the block into the cache.

The common combinations of the policies are Write Back Write Allocate and Write Through Write No-Allocate.

Shared Versus Private

A private cache is private to that particular core and cannot be accessed by the other cores. Since each core has its own private cache there might be duplicate blocks in the cache which leads to reduced capacity utilization. However, this organization leads to a lower latency.

A shared cache is where it is shared among multiple cores and therefore can be directly accessed by any of the cores. Since it is shared, each block in the cache is unique and therefore has more hit rate as there will be no duplicate blocks. However, the cache hit latency is larger as multiple cores try to access the same cache.

In the multi-core processors, the organization of the cache to be shared or private impacts the performance of the processor. In practice, the upper-level cache L1 (or sometimes L2) is implemented as private and lower level caches are implemented as shared.

Recent Implementation Models

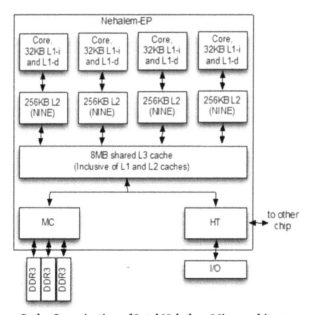

Cache Organization of Intel Nehalem Microarchitecture

Intel Broadwell Microarchitechture (2014)

- L1 Cache (Instruction and Data) – 64kB per core

- L2 Cache – 256kB per core

- L3 Cache – 2MB to 6MB shared

- L4 Cache – 128MB of eDRAM (Iris Pro Models only)

Intel Kaby Lake Microarchitechture (2016)

- L1 Cache (Instruction and Data) – 64kB per core

- L2 Cache – 256kB per core

- L3 Cache – 8192kB shared

IBM Power 7

- L1 Cache (Instruction and Data) – Each 64-banked, each bank has 2rd+1wr ports 32kB, 8-way associative, 128B block, Write through

- L2 Cache – 256kB, 8-way, 128B block, Write back, Inclusive of L1, 2ns access latency

- L3 Cache – 8 regions of 4MB (total 32MB), local region 6ns, remote 30ns, each region 8-way associative, DRAM data array, SRAM tag array

States of a Cache Line

- The life of a cache line starts off in invalid state (I)

- An access to that line takes a cache miss and fetches the line from main memory

- If it was a read miss the line is filled in shared state (S) [we will discuss it later; for now just assume that this is equivalent to a valid state]

- In case of a store miss the line is filled in modified state (M); instruction cache lines do not normally enter the M state (no store to Icache)

- The eviction of a line in M state must write the line back to the memory (this is called a writeback cache); otherwise the effect of the store would be lost

Inclusion policy

- A cache hierarchy implements inclusion if the contents of level n cache (exclude the register file) is a subset of the contents of level n+1 cache

  o Eviction of a line from L2 must ask L1 caches (both instruction and data) to invalidate that line if present

  o A store miss fills the L2 cache line in M state, but the store really happens in L1 data cache; so L2 cache does not have the most up-to-date copy of the line

  o Eviction of an L1 line in M state writes back the line to L2

  o Eviction of an L2 line in M state first asks the L1 data cache to send the most up-to-date copy (if any), then it writes the line back to the next higher level (L3 or main memory)

  o Inclusion simplifies the on-chip coherence protocol (more later)

The First Instruction

- Accessing the first instruction
  - Take the starting PC
  - Access iTLB with the VPN extracted from PC: iTLB miss
  - Invoke iTLB miss handler
  - Calculate PTE address
  - If PTEs are cached in L1 data and L2 caches, look them up with PTE address: you will miss there also
  - Access page table in main memory: PTE is invalid: page fault
  - Invoke page fault handler
  - Allocate page frame, read page from disk, update PTE, load PTE in iTLB, restart fetch
- Now you have the physical address
  - Access Icache: miss
  - Send refill request to higher levels: you miss everywhere
  - Send request to memory controller (north bridge)
  - Access main memory
  - Read cache line
  - Refill all levels of cache as the cache line returns to the processor
  - Extract the appropriate instruction from the cache line with the block offset
- This is the longest possible latency in an instruction/data access

TLB Access

- For every cache access (instruction or data) you need to access the TLB first
- Puts the TLB in the critical path
- Want to start indexing into cache and read the tags while TLB lookup takes place
  - Virtually indexed physically tagged cache
  - Extract index from the VA, start reading tag while looking up TLB
  - Once the PA is available do tag comparison
  - Overlaps TLB reading and tag reading
  - Memory Op Latency

- L1 hit: ~1 ns

- L2 hit: ~5 ns

- L3 hit: ~10-15 ns

- Main memory: ~70 ns DRAM access time + bus transfer etc. = ~110-120 ns

- If a load misses in all caches it will eventually come to the head of the ROB and block instruction retirement (in-order retirement is a must)

- Gradually, the pipeline backs up, processor runs out of resources such as ROB entries and physical registers

- Ultimately, the fetcher stalls: severely limits ILP

MLP

- Need memory-level parallelism (MLP)

  o Simply speaking, need to mutually overlap several memory operations

- Step 1: Non-blocking cache

  o Allow multiple outstanding cache misses

  o Mutually overlap multiple cache misses

  o Supported by all microprocessors today (Alpha 21364 supported 16 outstanding cache misses)

- Step 2: Out-of-order load issue

  o Issue loads out of program order (address is not known at the time of issue)

  o How do you know the load didn't issue before a store to the same address? Issuing stores must check for this memory-order violation

Out-of-order Loads

```
sw   0(r7), r6

… /* other instructions */

lw   r2, 80(r20)
```

- Assume that the load issues before the store because r20 gets ready before r6 or r7

- The load accesses the store buffer (used for holding already executed store values before they are committed to the cache at retirement)

- If it misses in the store buffer it looks up the caches and, say, gets the value somewhere

- After several cycles the store issues and it turns out that 0(r7)==80(r20) or they overlap; now what?

Load/Store Ordering

- Out-of-order load issue relies on speculative memory disambiguation

  o Assumes that there will be no conflicting store

  o If the speculation is correct, you have issued the load much earlier and you have allowed the dependents to also execute much earlier

  o If there is a conflicting store, you have to squash the load and all the dependents that have consumed the load value and re-execute them systematically

  o Turns out that the speculation is correct most of the time

  o To further minimize the load squash, microprocessors use simple memory dependence predictors (predicts if a load is going to conflict with a pending store based on that load's or load/store pairs' past behavior)

MLP and Memory Wall

- Today microprocessors try to hide cache misses by initiating early prefetches:

  o Hardware prefetchers try to predict next several load addresses and initiate cache line prefetch if they are not already in the cache

  o All processors today also support prefetch instructions; so you can specify in your program when to prefetch what: this gives much better control compared to a hardware prefetcher

- Researchers are working on load value prediction

- Even after doing all these, memory latency remains the biggest bottleneck

- Today microprocessors are trying to overcome one single wall: the memory wall

References

- D. Abramson, J. Jackson, S. Muthrasanallur, G. Neiger, G. Regnier, R. Sankaran, I. Schoin-as, R. Uhlig, B. Vembu, and J. Wiegert. Intel Virtualization Technology for Directed I/O. Intel Technology Journal, 10(03):179–192

- Burroughs (1964). Burroughs B5500 Information Processing System Reference Manual (PDF). Burroughs Corporation. 1021326. Retrieved November 28, 2013

- Bensoussan, André; Clingen, CharlesT.; Daley, Robert C. (May 1972). "The Multics Vir-tual Memory: Concepts and Design". Communications of the ACM. 15 (5): 308–318. doi:10.1145/355602.361306

- R. J. Creasy, "The origin of the VM/370 time-sharing system", IBM Journal of Research & Development, Vol. 25, No. 5 (September 1981), p. 486

- Cragon, Harvey G. (1996). Memory Systems and Pipelined Processors. Jones and Bartlett Publishers. p. 113. ISBN 0-86720-474-5

- "Control swapping (DONTSWAP, OKSWAP, TRANSWAP)". IBM Knowledge Center. z/OS MVS Programming: Authorized Assembler Services Reference SET-WTO SA23-1375-00. 1990–2014. Retrieved October 9, 2016

- Chen, J. Bradley; Borg, Anita; Jouppi, Norman P. (1992). "A Simulation Based Study of TLB Performance". SIGARCH Computer Architecture News (20): 114–123. doi:10.1145/146628.139708

- Quintero, Dino, et.al. (May 1, 2013). IBM Power Systems Performance Guide: Implement-ing and Optimizing. IBM Corporation. p. 138. ISBN 0738437662. Retrieved July 18, 2017

- "IPv4 Address Space Registry". Internet Assigned Numbers Authority (IANA). March 11, 2009. Retrieved September 1, 2011

- Paul, S; Z Fei (1 February 2001). "Distributed caching with centralized control". Computer Communications. 24 (2): 256–268. doi:10.1016/S0140-3664(00)00322-4

- Sharma, Dp (2009). Foundation of Operating Systems. Excel Books India. p. 62. ISBN 978- 81-7446-626-6. Retrieved July 18, 2017

- Frank Uyeda (2009). "Lecture 7: Memory Management" (PDF). CSE 120: Principles of Operating Systems. UC San Diego. Retrieved 2013-12-04

- David A. Patterson; John L. Hennessy (2009). Computer Organization And Design. Hard-ware/Software interface. 4th edition. Burlington, MA 01803, USA: Morgan Kaufmann Publishers. p. 503. ISBN 978-0-12-374493-7

- Jessen, E. (1996). "Die Entwicklung des virtuellen Speichers". Informatik-Spektrum (in German). Springer Berlin / Heidelberg. 19 (4): 216–219. ISSN 0170-6012. doi:10.1007/s002870050034

A Brief Introduction to Synchronization

Synchronization can be of two types, synchronization of processes and of data. The two concepts of synchronization are linked. Synchronization is important for both multi-processor systems and simple processor systems. This chapter provides a plethora of interdisciplinary topics for better comprehension of synchronization.

Synchronization (Computer Science)

In computer science, synchronization refers to one of two distinct but related concepts: synchronization of processes, and synchronization of data. *Process synchronization* refers to the idea that multiple processes are to join up or handshake at a certain point, in order to reach an agreement or commit to a certain sequence of action. *Data synchronization* refers to the idea of keeping multiple copies of a dataset in coherence with one another, or to maintain data integrity. Process synchronization primitives are commonly used to implement data synchronization.

The Need for Synchronization

The need for synchronization does not arise merely in multi-processor systems but for any kind of concurrent processes; even in single processor systems. Mentioned below are some of the main needs for synchronization:

Forks and Joins: When a job arrives at a fork point, it is split into N sub-jobs which are then serviced by n tasks. After being serviced, each sub-job waits until all other sub-jobs are done processing. Then, they are joined again and leave the system. Thus, in parallel programming, we require synchronization as all the parallel processes wait for several other processes to occur.

Producer-Consumer: In a producer-consumer relationship, the consumer process is dependent on the producer process till the necessary data has been produced.

Exclusive use resources: When multiple processes are dependent on a resource and they need to access it at the same time the operating system needs to ensure that only one processor accesses it at a given point in time. This reduces concurrency.

Thread or Process Synchronization

Thread synchronization is defined as a mechanism which ensures that two or more concurrent processes or threads do not simultaneously execute some particular program segment known as critical section. Processes' access to critical section is controlled by using synchronization techniques. When one thread starts executing the critical section (serialized segment of the program) the other thread should wait until the first thread finishes. If proper synchronization techniques are not applied, it may cause a race condition where the values of variables may be unpredictable and vary depending on the timings of context switches of the processes or threads.

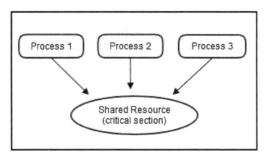

Three processes accessing a shared resource (critical section) simultaneously.

For example, suppose that there are three processes, namely 1, 2, and 3. All three of them are concurrently executing, and they need to share a common resource (critical section) as shown in Figure above. Synchronization should be used here to avoid any conflicts for accessing this shared resource. Hence, when Process 1 and 2 both try to access that resource, it should be assigned to only one process at a time. If it is assigned to Process 1, the other process (Process 2) needs to wait until Process 1 frees that resource (as shown in Figure below).

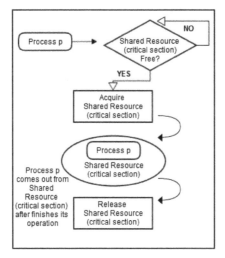

A process accessing a shared resource if available, based on some synchronization technique.

Another synchronization requirement which needs to be considered is the order in which particular processes or threads should be executed. For example, we cannot board a plane until we buy a ticket. Similarly, we cannot check e-mails without validating our credentials (i.e., user name and password). In the same way, an ATM will not provide any service until we provide it with a correct PIN.

Other than mutual exclusion, synchronization also deals with the following:

- deadlock, which occurs when many processes are waiting for a shared resource (critical section) which is being held by some other process. In this case, the processes just keep waiting and execute no further;

- starvation, which occurs when a process is waiting to enter the critical section, but other processes monopolize the critical section, and the first process is forced to wait indefinitely;

- priority inversion, which occurs when a high-priority process is in the critical section, and it is interrupted by a medium-priority process. This violation of priority rules can happen under certain circumstances and may lead to serious consequences in real-time systems;

- busy waiting, which occurs when a process frequently polls to determine if it has access to a critical section. This frequent polling robs processing time from other processes.

Minimizing Synchronization

One of the challenges for exascale algorithm design is to minimize or reduce synchronization. Synchronization takes more time than computation, especially in distributed computing. Reducing synchronization drew attention from computer scientists for decades. Whereas it becomes an increasingly significant problem recently as the gap between the improvement of computing and latency increases. Experiments have shown that (global) communications due to synchronization on a distributed computers takes a dominated share in a sparse iterative solver. This problem is receiving increasing attention after the emergence of a new benchmark metric,the High Performance Conjugate Gradient(HPCG), for ranking the top 500 supercomputers.

Classic Problems of Synchronization

The following are some classic problems of synchronization:

- The Producer–Consumer Problem (also called The Bounded Buffer Problem);

- The Readers–Writers Problem;

- The Dining Philosophers Problem.

These problems are used to test nearly every newly proposed synchronization scheme or primitive.

Hardware Synchronization

Many systems provide hardware support for critical section code.

A single processor or uniprocessor system could disable interrupts by executing currently running code without preemption, which is very inefficient on multiprocessor systems. "The key ability we require to implement synchronization in a multiprocessor is a set of hardware primitives with the ability to atomically read and modify a memory location. Without such a capability, the cost of building basic synchronization primitives will be too high and will increase as the processor count increases. There are a number of alternative formulations of the basic hardware primitives, all of which provide the ability to atomically read and modify a location, together with some way to tell if the read and write were performed atomically. These hardware primitives are the basic building blocks that are used to build a wide variety of user-level synchronization operations, including things such as locks and barriers. In general, architects do not expect users to employ the basic hardware primitives, but instead expect that the primitives will be used by system programmers to build a synchronization library, a process that is often complex and tricky." Many modern hardware provides special atomic hardware instructions by either test-and-set the memory word or compare-and-swap contents of two memory words.

Synchronization Strategies in Programming Languages

In Java, to prevent thread interference and memory consistency errors, blocks of code are wrapped into synchronized *(lock_object)* sections. This forces any thread to acquire the said lock object before it can execute the block. The lock is automatically released when thread leaves the block or enter the waiting state within the block. Any variable updates, made by the thread in synchronized block, become visible to other threads whenever those other threads similarly acquires the lock.

In addition to mutual exclusion and memory consistency, Java *synchronized* blocks enable signaling, sending events from those threads, which have acquired the lock and execute the code block to those which are waiting for the lock within the block. This means that Java synchronized sections combine functionality of mutexes and events. Such primitive is known as synchronization monitor.

Any object is fine to be used as a lock/monitor in Java. The declaring object is implicitly implied as lock object when the whole method is marked with *synchronized*.

The .NET framework has synchronization primitives. "Synchronization is designed to be cooperative, demanding that every thread or process follow the synchronization mechanism before accessing protected resources (critical section) for consistent results." In .NET, locking, signaling, lightweight synchronization types, spinwait and interlocked operations are some of mechanisms related to synchronization.

Implementation of Synchronization

Spinlock

Another effective way of implementing synchronization is by using spinlocks. Before accessing any shared resource or piece of code, every processor checks a flag. If the flag is reset, then the processor sets the flag and continues executing the thread. But, if the flag is set (locked), the threads would keep spinning in a loop and keep checking if the flag is set or not. But, spinlocks are effective only if the flag is reset for lower cycles otherwise it can lead to performance issues as it wastes many processor cycles waiting.

Barriers

Barriers are simple to implement and provide good responsiveness. They are based on the concept of implementing wait cycles to provide synchronization.Consider three threads running simultaneously, starting from barrier 1. After time t, thread1 reaches barrier 2 but it still has to wait for thread 2 and 3 to reach barrier2 as it does not have the correct data. Once, all the threads reach barrier 2 they all start again. After time t, thread 1 reaches barrier3 but it will have to wait for threads 2 and 3 and the correct data again.

Thus, in barrier synchronization of multiple threads there will always be a few threads that will end up waiting for other threads as in the above example thread 1 keeps waiting for thread 2 and 3. This results in severe degradation of the process performance.

The barrier synchronization wait function for i^{th} thread can be represented as:

(Wbarrier)i = f ((Tbarrier)i, (Rthread)i)

Where Wbarrier is the wait time for a thread, Tbarrier is the number of threads has arrived, and Rthread is the arrival rate of threads.

Experiments show that 34% of the total execution time is spent in waiting for other slower threads.

Semaphores

Semaphores are signalling mechanisms which can allow one or more threads/processors to access a section. A Semaphore has a flag which has a certain fixed value associated with it and each time a thread wishes to access the section, it decrements the flag. Similarly, when the thread leaves the section, the flag is incremented. If the flag is zero, the thread cannot access the section and gets blocked if it chooses to wait.

Some semaphores would allow only one thread or process in the code section. Such Semaphores are called binary semaphore and are very similar to Mutex. Here, if the value of semaphore is 1, the thread is allowed to access and if the value is 0, the access is denied.

Mathematical Foundations

Synchronization was originally a process-based concept whereby a lock could be obtained on an object. Its primary usage was in databases. There are two types of (file) lock; read-only and read–write. Read-only locks may be obtained by many processes or threads. Readers–writer locks are exclusive, as they may only be used by a single process/thread at a time.

Although locks were derived for file databases, data is also shared in memory between processes and threads. Sometimes more than one object (or file) is locked at a time. If they are not locked simultaneously they can overlap, causing a deadlock exception.

Java and Ada only have exclusive locks because they are thread based and rely on the compare-and-swap processor instruction.

An abstract mathematical foundation for synchronization primitives is given by the history monoid. There are also many higher-level theoretical devices, such as process calculi and Petri nets, which can be built on top of the history monoid.

Synchronization Examples

Following are some synchronization examples with respect to different platforms.

Synchronization in Windows

Windows provides:

- interrupt masks, which protect access to global resources (critical section) on uniprocessor systems;

- spinlocks, which prevent, in multiprocessor systems, spinlocking-thread from being pre-empted;

- dispatchers, which act like mutexes, semaphores, events, and timers.

Synchronization in Linux

Linux provides:

- semaphores

- spinlock

- barriers

- mutex

- readers–writer locks, for the longer section of codes which are accessed very frequently but don't change very often

- Read-copy-update (RCU)

Enabling and disabling of kernel preemption replaced spinlocks on uniprocessor systems. Prior to kernel version 2.6, Linux disabled interrupt to implement short critical sections. Since version 2.6 and later, Linux is fully preemptive.

Synchronization in Solaris

Solaris provides:

- semaphores;

- condition variables;

- adaptive mutexes, binary semaphores that are implemented differently depending upon the conditions;

- readers–writer locks:

- turnstiles, queue of threads which are waiting on acquired lock.

Pthreads Synchronization

Pthreads is a platform-independent API that provides:

- mutexes;

- condition variables;

- readers–writer locks;

- spinlocks;

- barriers.

Data Synchronization

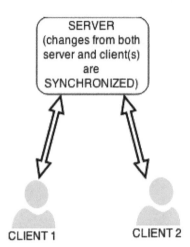

Changes from both server and client(s) are synchronized.

A distinctly different (but related) concept is that of data synchronization. This refers to the need to keep multiple copies of a set of data coherent with one another or to maintain data integrity, Figure above. For example, database replication is used to keep multiple copies of data synchronized with database servers that store data in different locations.

Examples include:

- File synchronization, such as syncing a hand-held MP3 player to a desktop computer;

- Cluster file systems, which are file systems that maintain data or indexes in a coherent fashion across a whole computing cluster;

- Cache coherency, maintaining multiple copies of data in sync across multiple caches;

- RAID, where data is written in a redundant fashion across multiple disks, so that the loss of any one disk does not lead to a loss of data;

- Database replication, where copies of data on a database are kept in sync, despite possible large geographical separation;

- Journaling, a technique used by many modern file systems to make sure that file metadata are updated on a disk in a coherent, consistent manner.

Challenges in Data Synchronization

Some of the challenges which user may face in data synchronization:

- data formats complexity;

- real-timeliness;

- data security;

- data quality;

- performance.

Data Formats Complexity

When we start doing something, the data we have usually is in a very simple format. It varies with time as the organization grows and evolves and results not only in building a simple interface between the two applications (source and target), but also in a need to transform the data while passing them to the target application. ETL (extraction transformation loading) tools can be very helpful at this stage for managing data format complexities.

Real-timeliness

This is an era of real-time systems. Customers want to see the current status of their order in e-shop, the current status of a parcel delivery—a real time parcel tracking—, the current balance on their account, etc. This shows the need of a real-time system, which is being updated as well to enable smooth manufacturing process in real-time, e.g., ordering material when enterprise is running out stock, synchronizing customer orders with manufacturing process, etc. From real life, there exist so many examples where real-time processing gives successful and competitive advantage.

Data Security

There are no fixed rules and policies to enforce data security. It may vary depending on the system which you are using. Even though the security is maintained correctly in the source system which captures the data, the security and information access privileges must be enforced on the target systems as well to prevent any potential misuse of the information. This is a serious issue and particularly when it comes for handling secret, confidential and personal information. So because of the sensitivity and confidentiality, data transfer and all in-between information must be encrypted.

Data Quality

Data quality is another serious constraint. For better management and to maintain good quality of data, the common practice is to store the data at one location and share with different people and different systems and/or applications from different locations. It helps in preventing inconsistencies in the data.

Performance

There are five different phases involved in the data synchronization process:

- data extraction from the source (or master, or main) system;

- data transfer;

- data transformation;

- data load to the target system.

Each of these steps is very critical. In case of large amounts of data, the synchronization process needs to be carefully planned and executed to avoid any negative impact on performance.

Fork–join Model

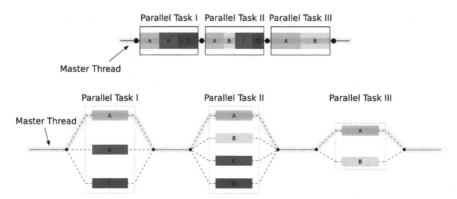

An illustration of the fork–join paradigm, in which three regions of the program permit parallel execution of the variously colored blocks. Sequential execution is displayed on the top, while its equivalent fork–join execution is on the bottom.

In parallel computing, the fork–join model is a way of setting up and executing parallel programs, such that execution branches off in parallel at designated points in the program, to "join" (merge) at a subsequent point and resume sequential execution. Parallel sections may fork recursively until a certain task granularity is reached. Fork–join can be considered a parallel design pattern. It was formulated as early as 1963.

By nesting fork–join computations recursively, one obtains a parallel version of the divide and conquer paradigm, expressed by the following generic pseudocode:

```
solve(problem):
    if problem is small enough:
        solve problem directly (sequential algorithm)
    else:
        for part in subdivide(problem)
            fork subtask to solve part
        join all subtasks spawned in previous loop
        combine results from subtasks
```

Examples

The simple parallel merge sort of CLRS is a fork–join algorithm.

```
mergesort(A, lo, hi):
    if lo < hi:                     // at least one element of input
        mid = ⌊lo+ (hi - lo) / 2⌋
            fork mergesort(A, lo, mid)  // process (potentially) in parallel with
main task
```

```
    mergesort(A, mid, hi)        // main task handles second recursion

    join

    merge(A, lo, mid, hi)
```

The first recursive call is "forked off", meaning that its execution may run in parallel (in a separate thread) with the following part of the function, up to the join that causes all threads to synchronize. While the join may look like a barrier, it is different because the threads will continue to work after a barrier, while after a join only one thread continues.

The second recursive call is not a fork in the pseudocode above; this is intentional, as forking tasks may come at an expense. If both recursive calls were set up as subtasks, the main task would not have any additional work to perform before being blocked at the join.

Implementations

Implementations of the fork–join model will typically fork *tasks, fibers* or *lightweight threads*, not operating-system-level "heavyweight" threads or processes, and use a thread pool to execute these tasks: the fork primitive allows the programmer to specify *potential* parallelism, which the implementation then maps onto actual parallel execution. The reason for this design is that creating new threads tends to result in too much overhead.

The lightweight threads used in fork–join programming will typically have their own scheduler (typically a work stealing one) that maps them onto the underlying thread pool. This scheduler can be much simpler than a fully featured, preemptive operating system scheduler: general-purpose thread schedulers must deal with blocking for locks, but in the fork–join paradigm, threads only block at the join point.

Fork–join is the main model of parallel execution in the OpenMP framework, although OpenMP implementations may or may not support nesting of parallel sections. It is also supported by the Java concurrency framework, the Task Parallel Library for .NET, and Intel's Threading Building Blocks (TBB). The Cilk programming language has language-level support for fork and join, in the form of the spawn and sync keywords, or cilk_spawn and cilk_sync in Cilk Plus.

Producer–consumer Problem

In computing, the producer–consumer problem (also known as the bounded-buffer problem) is a classic example of a multi-process synchronization problem. The problem describes two processes, the producer and the consumer, who share a common, fixed-size buffer used as a queue. The producer's job is to generate data, put it into the buffer, and start again. At the same time, the consumer is consuming the data (i.e., removing it from the buffer), one piece at a time. The problem is to make sure that the producer won't try to add data into the buffer if it's full and that the consumer won't try to remove data from an empty buffer.

The solution for the producer is to either go to sleep or discard data if the buffer is full. The next time the consumer removes an item from the buffer, it notifies the producer, who starts to fill the buffer again. In the same way, the consumer can go to sleep if it finds the buffer to be empty. The next time the producer puts data into the buffer, it wakes up the sleeping consumer. The solution can be reached by means of inter-process communication, typically using semaphores. An inadequate solution could result in a deadlock where both processes are waiting to be awakened. The problem can also be generalized to have multiple producers and consumers.

Inadequate Implementation

To solve the problem, a less experienced programmer might come up with a solution shown below. In the solution two library routines are used, sleep and wakeup. When sleep is called, the caller is blocked until another process wakes it up by using the wakeup routine. The global variable itemCount holds the number of items in the buffer.

```
int itemCount = 0;


procedure producer() {
    while (true) {
        item = produceItem();


        if (itemCount == BUFFER_SIZE) {
            sleep();
        }


        putItemIntoBuffer(item);
        itemCount = itemCount + 1;


        if (itemCount == 1) {
            wakeup(consumer);
        }
    }
}


procedure consumer() {
    while (true) {


        if (itemCount == 0) {
```

```
            sleep();

        }


        item = removeItemFromBuffer();

        itemCount = itemCount - 1;


        if (itemCount == BUFFER_SIZE - 1) {

            wakeup(producer);

        }


        consumeItem(item);

    }

}
```

The problem with this solution is that it contains a race condition that can lead to a deadlock. Consider the following scenario:

1. The consumer has just read the variable itemCount, noticed it's zero and is just about to move inside the if block.

2. Just before calling sleep, the consumer is interrupted and the producer is resumed.

3. The producer creates an item, puts it into the buffer, and increases itemCount.

4. Because the buffer was empty prior to the last addition, the producer tries to wake up the consumer.

5. Unfortunately the consumer wasn't yet sleeping, and the wakeup call is lost. When the consumer resumes, it goes to sleep and will never be awakened again. This is because the consumer is only awakened by the producer when itemCount is equal to 1.

6. The producer will loop until the buffer is full, after which it will also go to sleep.

Since both processes will sleep forever, we have run into a deadlock. This solution therefore is unsatisfactory.

An alternative analysis is that if the programming language does not define the semantics of concurrent accesses to shared variables (in this case itemCount) without use of synchronization, then the solution is unsatisfactory for that reason, without needing to explicitly demonstrate a race condition.

Using Semaphores

Semaphores solve the problem of lost wakeup calls. In the solution below we use two semaphores, fillCount and emptyCount, to solve the problem. fillCount is the number of items already in the buffer and available to be read, while emptyCount is the number of available spaces in the buffer where items could be written. fillCount is incremented and emptyCount decremented when a new item is put into the buffer. If the producer tries to decrement emptyCount when its value is zero, the producer is put to sleep. The next time an item is consumed, emptyCount is incremented and the producer wakes up. The consumer works analogously.

```
semaphore fillCount = 0; // items produced

semaphore emptyCount = BUFFER_SIZE; // remaining space


procedure producer() {

    while (true) {

        item = produceItem();

        down(emptyCount);

        putItemIntoBuffer(item);

        up(fillCount);

    }

}


procedure consumer() {

    while (true) {

        down(fillCount);

        item = removeItemFromBuffer();

        up(emptyCount);

        consumeItem(item);

    }

}
```

The solution above works fine when there is only one producer and consumer. With multiple producers sharing the same memory space for the item buffer, or multiple consumers sharing the same memory space, this solution contains a serious race condition that could result in two or more processes reading or writing into the same slot at the same time. To understand how this is possible, imagine how the procedure put ItemIntoBuffer() can be implemented. It could contain two actions, one determining the next available slot and the other writing into it. If the procedure can be executed concurrently by multiple producers, then the following scenario is possible:

1. Two producers decrement emptyCount

2. One of the producers determines the next empty slot in the buffer

3. Second producer determines the next empty slot and gets the same result as the first producer

4. Both producers write into the same slot

To overcome this problem, we need a way to make sure that only one producer is executing putItemIntoBuffer() at a time. In other words, we need a way to execute a critical section with mutual exclusion. The solution for multiple producers and consumers is shown below.

```
mutex buffer_mutex; // similar to "semaphore buffer_mutex = 1", but different
semaphore fillCount = 0;


semaphore emptyCount = BUFFER_SIZE;


procedure producer() {
    while (true) {
        item = produceItem();
        down(emptyCount);
            down(buffer_mutex);
                putItemIntoBuffer(item);
            up(buffer_mutex);
        up(fillCount);
    }
}


procedure consumer() {
    while (true) {
        down(fillCount);
            down(buffer_mutex);
                item = removeItemFromBuffer();
            up(buffer_mutex);
        up(emptyCount);
        consumeItem(item);
    }
}
```

Notice that the order in which different semaphores are incremented or decremented is essential: changing the order might result in a deadlock. It is important to note here that though mutex seems to work as a semaphore with value of 1 (binary semaphore), but there is difference in the fact that mutex has ownership concept. Ownership means that mutex can only be "incremented" back (set to 1) by the same process that "decremented" it (set to 0), and all others tasks wait until mutex is available for decrement (effectively meaning that resource is available), which ensures mutual exclusivity and avoids deadlock. Thus using mutexes improperly can stall many processes when exclusive access is not required, but mutex is used instead of semaphore.

Using Monitors

The following pseudo code shows a solution to the producer–consumer problem using monitors. Since mutual exclusion is implicit with monitors, no extra effort is necessary to protect the critical section. In other words, the solution shown below works with any number of producers and consumers without any modifications. It is also noteworthy that using monitors makes race conditions much less likely than when using semaphores.

```
monitor ProducerConsumer {

    int itemCount;

    condition full;

    condition empty;


    procedure add(item) {

        while (itemCount == BUFFER_SIZE) {

            wait(full);

        }


        putItemIntoBuffer(item);

        itemCount = itemCount + 1;


        if (itemCount == 1) {

            notify(empty);

        }

    }

    procedure remove() {

        while (itemCount == 0) {
```

```
            wait(empty);

        }


        item = removeItemFromBuffer();

        itemCount = itemCount - 1;


        if (itemCount == BUFFER_SIZE - 1) {

            notify(full);

        }



        return item;

    }

}


procedure producer() {

    while (true) {

        item = produceItem();

        ProducerConsumer.add(item);

    }

}


procedure consumer() {

    while (true) {

        item = ProducerConsumer.remove();

        consumeItem(item);

    }

}
```

Note the use of while statements in the above code, both when testing if the buffer is full or empty. With multiple consumers, there is a race condition where one consumer gets notified that an item has been put into the buffer but another consumer is already waiting on the monitor so removes it from the buffer instead. If the while was instead an if, too many items might be put into the buffer or a remove might be attempted on an empty buffer.

Without Semaphores or Monitors

The producer–consumer problem, particularly in the case of a single producer and single consumer, strongly relates to implementing a FIFO or a channel. The producer–consumer pattern can provide highly efficient data communication without relying on semaphores, mutexes, or monitors *for data transfer*. Use of those primitives can give performance issues as they are expensive to implement. Channels and FIFOs are popular just because they avoid the need for end-to-end atomic synchronization. A basic example coded in C is shown below. Note that:

- Atomic read-modify-write access to shared variables is avoided, as each of the two Count variables is updated only by a single thread. Also, these variables stay incremented all the time; the relation remains correct when their values wrap around on an integer overflow.

- This example does not put threads to sleep, which may be acceptable depending on the system context. The sched_yield() is there just to behave nicely and could be removed. Thread libraries typically require semaphores or condition variables to control the sleep/wakeup of threads. In a multi-processor environment, thread sleep/wakeup would occur much less frequently than passing of data tokens, so avoiding atomic operations on data passing is beneficial.

- This example does not work for multiple producers and/or consumers because there is a race condition when checking the state. For example, if only one token is in the storage buffer and two consumers find the buffer non-empty, then both will consume the same token and possibly increase the count of consumed tokens over produced counter.

- This example, as written, requires that UINT_MAX + 1 is evenly divisible by BUFFER_SIZE; if it is not evenly divisible, [Count % BUFFER_SIZE] produces the wrong buffer index after Count wraps past UINT_MAX back to zero. An alternate solution without this restriction would employ two additional Idx variables to track the current buffer index for the head (producer) and tail (consumer). These Idx variables would be used in place of [Count % BUFFER_SIZE], and each of them would have to be incremented at the same time as the respective Count variable is incremented, as follows: Idx = (Idx + 1) % BUFFER_SIZE.

```
volatile unsigned int produceCount = 0, consumeCount = 0;

TokenType buffer[BUFFER_SIZE];


void producer(void) {

    while (1) {

        while (produceCount - consumeCount == BUFFER_SIZE)
```

```
            sched_yield(); /* `buffer` is full */
        /* You must update the field in the buffer _before_ incrementing your
         * pointer.
         */
        buffer[produceCount % BUFFER_SIZE] = produceToken();
        ++produceCount;
    }
}

void consumer(void) {
    while (1) {
        while (produceCount - consumeCount == 0)
            sched_yield(); /* `buffer` is empty */

        consumeToken(&buffer[consumeCount % BUFFER_SIZE]);
        ++consumeCount;
    }
}
```

Waiting Algorithms

Complication with Stores

- In OOO execution instructions issue out of program order
  - A store may issue out of program order
  - But it cannot write its value to cache until it retires i.e. comes to the head of ROB; Why? (assume 1p)
  - So its value is kept in a store buffer (this is normally part of the store queue entry occupied by the store)
  - If it hits in the cache (i.e. a write hit), nothing happens
  - If it misses in the cache, either a ReadX or an Upgrade request is issued on the bus depending on the state of the requested cache line
  - Until the store retires subsequent loads from the same processor to the same address can steal the value from store buffer (why not the old value?)

What about others?

- Take the following example (assume invalidation-based protocol)

  o   P0 writes x, P1 reads x

  o   P0 issues store, assume that it hits in cache, but it commits much later (any simple reason?)

  o   P1 issues BusRd (Can it hit in P1's cache?)

  o   Snoop logic in P0's cache controller finds that it is responsible for sourcing the cache line (M state)

  o   What value of x does the launched cache line contain? New value or the old value?

  o   After this BusRd what is the state of P0's line?

  o   After this BusRd can the loads from P0 still continue to use the value written by the store?

  o   What happens when P0 ultimately commits the store?

- Take the following example (assume invalidation-based protocol)

  o   P0 writes x, P1 reads x

  o   P0 issues store, assume that it hits in cache, but it commits much later (any simple reason?)

  o   P1 issues BusRd (Can it hit in P1's cache?)

  o   Snoop logic in P0's cache controller finds that it is responsible for sourcing the cache line (M state)

  o   What value of x does the launched cache line contain? New value or the old value? OLD VALUE

  o   After this BusRd what is the state of P0's line? S

  o   After this BusRd can the matching loads from P0 still continue to use the value written by the store? YES

  o   What happens when P0 ultimately commits the store? UPGRADE MISS

More Example

- In the previous example same situation may arise even if P0 misses in the cache; the timing of P1's read decides whether the race happens or not

- Another example

  o   P0 writes x, P1 writes x

- o   Suppose the race does happen i.e. P1 launches BusRdX before P0's store commits (Can P1 launch upgrade?)

- o   Surely the launched cache line will have old value of x as before

- o   Is it safe for the matching loads from P0 to use the new value of x from store buffer?

- o   What happens when P0's store ultimately commits?

- In the previous example same situation may arise even if P0 misses in the cache; the timing of P1's read decides whether the race happens or not

- Another example

- o   P0 writes x, P1 writes x

- o   Suppose the race does happen i.e. P1 launches BusRdX before P0's store commits (Can P1 launch upgrade?)

- o   Surely the launched cache line will have old value of x as before

- o   Is it safe for the matching loads from P0 to use the new value of x from store buffer? YES

- o   What happens when P0 's store ultimately commits? READ-EXCLUSIVE MISS

Yet Another Example

- Another example

- o   P0 reads x, P0 writes x, P1 writes x

- o   Suppose the race does happen i.e. P1 launches BusRdX before P0's store commits

- o   Surely the launched cache line will have old value of x as before

- o   What value does P0's load commit?

Synchronization Types

- Mutual exclusion

- o   Synchronize entry into critical sections

- o   Normally done with locks

- Point-to-point synchronization

- o   Tell a set of processors (normally set cardinality is one) that they can proceed

- o   Normally done with flags

- Global synchronization

- o Bring every processor to sync
- o Wait at a point until everyone is there
- o Normally done with barriers

Synchronization

- Normally a two-part process: acquire and release; acquire can be broken into two parts: intent and wait
  - o Intent: express intent to synchronize (i.e. contend for the lock, arrive at a barrier)
  - o Wait: wait for your turn to synchronization (i.e. wait until you get the lock)
  - o Release: proceed past synchronization and enable other contenders to synchronize
  - o Waiting algorithms do not depend on the type of synchronization

Waiting Algorithms

- Busy wait (common in multiprocessors)
  - o Waiting processes repeatedly poll a location (implemented as a load in a loop)
  - o Releasing process sets the location appropriately
  - o May cause network or bus transactions
- Block
  - o Waiting processes are de-scheduled
  - o Frees up processor cycles for doing something else
- Busy waiting is better if
  - o De-scheduling and re-scheduling take longer than busy waiting
  - o No other active process
  - o Does not work for single processor
- Hybrid policies: busy wait for some time and then block

Implementation

- Popular trend
  - o Architects offer some simple atomic primitives
  - o Library writers use these primitives to implement synchronization algorithms

- o   Normally hardware primitives for acquire and possibly release are provided

- o   Hard to offer hardware solutions for waiting

- o   Also hardwired waiting may not offer that much of flexibility

Hardwired Locks

- Not popular today

  - o   Less flexible

  - o   Cannot support large number of locks

- Possible designs

  - o   Dedicated lock line in bus so that the lock holder keeps it asserted and waiters snoop the lock line in hardware

  - o   Set of lock registers shared among processors and lock holder gets a lock register (Cray Xmp)

Software Locks

- Bakery algorithm

```
Shared: choosing[P] = FALSE, ticket[P] = 0;

Acquire: choosing[i] = TRUE; ticket[i] = max(ticket,…,ticket[P-1]) + 1;
choosing[i] = FALSE;

  for j = 0 to P-1

  while (choosing[j]);

  while (ticket[j] && ((ticket[j], j) < (ticket[i], i)));

  endfor

Release: ticket[i] = 0;
```

- Does it work for multiprocessors?

  - o   Assume sequential consistency

  - o   Performance issues related to coherence?

- Too much overhead: need faster and simpler lock algorithms

  - o   Need some hardware support

Hardware Support

- Start with a simple software lock

```
Shared: lock = 0;

Acquire: while (lock); lock = 1;

Release or Unlock: lock = 0;
```

- Assembly translation

```
Lock: lw register, lock_addr  /* register is any processor register */
      bnez register, Lock
      addi register, register, 0x1
      sw register, lock_addr


Unlock: xor register, register, register
        sw register, lock_addr
```

- Does it work?

    o   What went wrong?

    o   We wanted the read-modify-write sequence to be atomic

Atomic Exchange

- We can fix this if we have an atomic exchange instruction

```
          addi register, r0, 0x1            /* r0 is hardwired to 0 */
Lock:     xchg register, lock_addr    /* An atomic load and store */
          bnez register, Lock
```

Unlock remains unchanged

- Various processors support this type of instruction

    o   Intel x86 has xchg, Sun UltraSPARC has ldstub (load-store-unsigned byte), UltraS-PARC also has swap

    o   Normally easy to implement for bus-based systems: whoever wins the bus for xchg can lock the bus

    o   Difficult to support in distributed memory systems

Test and Set

- Less general compared to exchange

```
Lock:   ts register, lock_addr
        bnez register, Lock
```

Unlock remains unchanged

- Loads current lock value in a register and sets location always with 1

    o   Exchange allows to swap any value

- A similar type of instruction is fetch & op

    o   Fetch memory location in a register and apply op on the memory location

    o   Op can be a set of supported operations e.g. add, increment, decrement, store etc.

    o   In Test & set op=set

Fetch and Op

- Possible to implement a lock with fetch & clear then add (used to be supported in BBN Butterfly 1)

```
        addi reg1, r0, 0x1

 Lock:  fetch & clr then add reg1, reg2, lock_addr          /* fetch in
 reg2, clear, add reg1 */

        bnez reg2, Lock
```

- Butterfly 1 also supports fetch & clear then xor

- Sequent Symmetry supports fetch & store

- More sophisticated: compare & swap

    o   Takes three operands: reg1, reg2, memory address

    o   Compares the value in reg1 with address and if they are equal swaps the contents of reg2 and address

    o   Not in line with RISC philosophy (same goes for fetch & add)

Compare and Swap

```
        addi reg1, r0, 0x0          /* reg1 has 0x0 */

        addi reg2, r0, 0x1          /* reg2 has 0x1 */

Lock: compare & swap reg1, reg2, lock_addr

        bnez reg2, Lock
```

Traffic of Test and Set

- In some machines (e.g., SGI Origin 2000) uncached fetch & op is supported

    o   every such instruction will generate a transaction (may be good or bad depending on the support in memory controller; will discuss later)

- Let us assume that the lock location is cacheable and is kept coherent

- Every invocation of test & set must generate a bus transaction; Why? What is the transaction? What are the possible states of the cache line holding lock_addr?

- Therefore all lock contenders repeatedly generate bus transactions even if someone is still in the critical section and is holding the lock

- Can we improve this?

  - Test & set with backoff

Backoff Test and Set

- Instead of retrying immediately wait for a while

  - How long to wait?

  - Waiting for too long may lead to long latency and lost opportunity

  - Constant and variable backoff

  - Special kind of variable backoff: exponential backoff (after the i th attempt the delay is k*ci where k and c are constants)

  - Test & set with exponential backoff works pretty well

```
        delay = k
Lock:   ts register, lock_addr
            bez register, Enter_CS
            pause (delay)                /* Can be simulated as a timed loop */
            delay = delay*c
            j Lock
```

Test and Test and Set

- Reduce traffic further

  - Before trying test & set make sure that the lock is free

```
Lock: ts register, lock_addr
            bez register, Enter_CS
Test:   lw register, lock_addr
            bnez register, Test
            j Lock
```

- How good is it?

o In a cacheable lock environment the Test loop will execute from cache until it receives an invalidation (due to store in unlock); at this point the load may return a zero value after fetching the cache line

o If the location is zero then only everyone will try test & set

TTS Traffic Analysis

- Recall that unlock is always a simple store

- In the worst case everyone will try to enter the CS at the same time

  o First time P transactions for ts and one succeeds; every other processor suffers a miss on the load in Test loop; then loops from cache

  o The lock-holder when unlocking generates an upgrade (why?) and invalidates all others

  o All other processors suffer read miss and get value zero now; so they break Test loop and try ts and the process continues until everyone has visited the CS

  o $(P+(P-1)+1+(P-1))+((P-1)+(P-2)+1+(P-2))+... = (3P-1) + (3P-4) + (3P-7) + ... \sim 1.5P^2$ asymptotically

  o For distributed shared memory the situation is worse because each invalidation becomes a separate message (more later)

Goals of a Lock Algorithm

- Low latency: if no contender the lock should be acquired fast

- Low traffic: worst case lock acquire traffic should be low; otherwise it may affect unrelated transactions

- Scalability: Traffic and latency should scale slowly with the number of processors

- Low storage cost: Maintaining lock states should not impose unrealistic memory overhead

- Fairness: Ideally processors should enter CS according to the order of lock request (TS or TTS does not guarantee this)

Ticket Lock

- Similar to Bakery algorithm but simpler

- A nice application of fetch & inc

- Basic idea is to come and hold a unique ticket and wait until your turn comes

  o Bakery algorithm failed to offer this uniqueness thereby increasing complexity

```
Shared:   ticket = 0, release_count = 0;
```

```
Lock:       fetch & inc reg1, ticket_addr

Wait:       lw reg2, release_count_addr              /* while (release_count
!= ticket); */

            sub reg3, reg2, reg1

            bnez reg3, Wait


Unlock:  addi reg2, reg2, 0x1  /* release_count++ */
        sw reg2, release_count_addr
```

- Initial fetch & inc generates O(P) traffic on bus-based machines (may be worse in DSM depending on implementation of fetch & inc)

- But the waiting algorithm still suffers from 0.5P2 messages asymptotically

  - Researchers have proposed proportional backoff i.e. in the wait loop put a delay proportional to the difference between ticket value and last read release_count

- Latency and storage-wise better than Bakery

- Traffic-wise better than TTS and Bakery (I leave it to you to analyze the traffic of Bakery)

- Guaranteed fairness: the ticket value induces a FIFO queue

Array-based Lock

- Solves the $O(P^2)$ traffic problem

- The idea is to have a bit vector (essentially a character array if boolean type is not supported)

- Each processor comes and takes the next free index into the array via fetch & inc

- Then each processor loops on its index location until it becomes set

- On unlock a processor is responsible to set the next index location if someone is waiting

- Initial fetch & inc still needs O(P) traffic, but the wait loop now needs O(1) traffic

- Disadvantage: storage overhead is O(P)

- Performance concerns

  - Avoid false sharing: allocate each array location on a different cache line

  - Assume a cache line size of 128 bytes and a character array: allocate an array of size 128P bytes and use every 128th position in the array

- o For distributed shared memory the location a processor loops on may not be in its local memory: on acquire it must take a remote miss; allocate P pages and let each processor loop on one bit in a page? Too much wastage; better solution: MCS lock (Mellor-Crummey & Scott)

- Correctness concerns

  - o Make sure to handle corner cases such as determining if someone is waiting on the next location (this must be an atomic operation) while unlocking

  - o Remember to reset your index location to zero while unlocking

RISC Processors

- All these atomic instructions deviate from the RISC line

  - o Instruction needs a load as well as a store

- Also, it would be great if we can offer a few simple instructions with which we can build most of the atomic primitives

  - o Note that it is impossible to build atomic fetch & inc with xchg instruction

- MIPS, Alpha and IBM processors support a pair of instructions: LL and SC

  - o Load linked and store conditional

LL/SC

- Load linked behaves just like a normal load with some extra tricks

  - o Puts the loaded value in destination register as usual

  - o Sets a load_linked bit residing in cache controller to 1

  - o Puts the address in a special lock_address register residing in the cache controller

- Store conditional is a special store

  - o sc reg, addr stores value in reg to addr only if load_linked bit is set; also it copies the value in load_linked bit to reg and resets load_linked bit

- Any intervening "operation" (e.g., bus transaction or cache replacement) to the cache line containing the address in lock_address register clears the load_linked bit so that subsequent sc fails

Locks with LL/SC

- Test & set

```
Lock:   LL r1, lock_addr            /* Normal read miss/BusRead */
            addi r2, r0, 0x1
```

```
        SC r2, lock_addr              /* Possibly upgrade miss */

        beqz r2, Lock                 /* Check if SC succeeded */

        bnez r1, Lock                 /* Check if someone is in CS */
```

- LL/SC is best-suited for test & test & set locks

```
Lock:   LL r1, lock_addr

        bnez r1, Lock

        addi r1, r0, 0x1

        SC r1, lock_addr

        beqz r1, Lock
```

Fetch and Op with LL/SC

- Fetch & inc

```
Try:    LL r1, addr

        addi r1, r1, 0x1

        SC r1, addr

        beqz r1, Try
```

- Compare & swap: Compare with r1, swap r2 and memory location (here we keep on trying until comparison passes)

```
Try:    LL r3, addr

        sub r4, r3, r1

        bnez r4, Try

        add r4, r2, r0

        SC r4, addr

        beqz r4, Try

        add r2, r3, r0
```

Store Conditional and OOO

- Execution of SC in an OOO pipeline

  o Rather subtle

  o For now assume that SC issues only when it comes to the head of ROB i.e. non-speculative execution of SC

  o It first checks the load_linked bit; if reset doesn't even access cache (saves cache bandwidth and unnecessary bus transactions) and returns zero in register

- o   If load_linked bit is set, it accesses cache and issues bus transaction if needed (Bus-ReadX if cache line in I state and BusUpgr if in S state)

- o   Checks load_linked bit again before writing to cache (note that cache line goes to M state in any case)

- o   Can wake up dependents only when SC graduates (a case where a store initiates a dependence chain)

Speculative SC?

- What happens if SC is issued speculatively?

   - o   Actual store happens only when it graduates and issuing a store early only starts the write permission process

   - o   Suppose two processors are contending for a lock

   - o   Both do LL and succeed because nobody is in CS

   - o   Both issue SC speculatively and due to some reason the graduation of SC in both of them gets delayed

   - o   So although initially both may get the line one after another in M state in their caches, the load_linked bit will get reset in both by the time SC tries to graduate

   - o   They go back and start over with LL and may issue SC again speculatively leading to a livelock (probability of this type of livelock increases with more processors)

   - o   Speculative issue of SC with hardwired backoff may help

   - o   Better to turn off speculation for SC

- What about the branch following SC?

   - o   Can we speculate past that branch?

   - o   Assume that the branch predictor tells you that the branch is not taken i.e. fall through: we speculatively venture into the critical section

   - o   We speculatively execute the critical section

   - o   This may be good and bad

   - o   If the branch prediction was correct we did great

   - o   If the predictor went wrong, we might have interfered with the execution of the processor that is actually in CS: may cause unnecessary invalidations and extra traffic

   - o   Any correctness issues?

Point-to-point Synch

- Normally done in software with flags

```
P0: A = 1; flag = 1;

P1: while (!flag); print A;
```

- Some old machines supported full/empty bits in memory

  o Each memory location is augmented with a full/empty bit

  o Producer writes the location only if bit is reset

  o Consumer reads location if bit is set and resets it

  o Lot less flexible: one producer-one consumer sharing only (one producer-many con-
     sumers is very popular); all accesses to a memory location become synchronized (un-
     less compiler flags some accesses as special)

- Possible optimization for shared memory

  o Allocate flag and data structures (if small) guarded by flag in same cache line e.g., flag
     and A in above example

Barrier (Computer Science)

In parallel computing, a barrier is a type of synchronization method. A barrier for a group of
threads or processes in the source code means any thread/process must stop at this point and
cannot proceed until all other threads/processes reach this barrier.

Many collective routines and directive-based parallel languages impose implicit barriers. For example, a parallel *do* loop in Fortran with OpenMP will not be allowed to continue on any thread
until the last iteration is completed. This is in case the program relies on the result of the loop immediately after its completion. In message passing, any global communication (such as reduction
or scatter) may imply a barrier.

Implementation

The basic barrier has mainly two variables, one of which records the pass/stop state of the barrier,
the other of which keeps the total number of threads that have entered in the barrier. The barrier
state was initialized to be "stop" by the first threads coming into the barrier. Whenever a thread
enters, based on the number of threads already in the barrier, only if it is the last one, the thread
set the barrier state to be "pass" so that all the threads can get out of the barrier. On the other hand,
when the incoming thread is not the last one, it is trapped in the barrier and keeps testing if the
barrier state is changed from "stop" to "pass" and it gets out only when the barrier state changes to
be "pass". The pseudocode below demonstrate this.

```
int barrierCounter = 0

int barrierFlag = 0
```

```
function barrier()
{
    Lock()

    if (barrierCounter == 0)
        barrierFlag = 0                              // reset flag is first

    barrierCounter = barrierCounter + 1
    myCount = barrierCounter                         // myCount local

    UnLock()

    if (myCount == numProcessors)                    // last thread
        barrierCounter = 0                           // reset
        barrierFlag = 1                              // release
    else
        wait for barrierFlag == 1
}
```

The potential problems are as follows:

1. When sequential barriers using the same pass/block state variable are implemented, a deadlock could happen in the first barrier whenever a thread reaches the second and there are still some threads have not got out of the first barrier.

2. Due to all the threads repeatedly accessing the global variable for pass/stop, the communication traffic is rather high, which decreases the scalability.

The following Sense-Reversal Centralized Barrier is designed to resolve the first problem. And the second problem can be resolved by regrouping the threads and using multi-level barrier, e.g. Combining Tree Barrier. Also hardware implementations may have the advantage of higher scalability.

Sense-Reversal Centralized Barrier

A Sense-Reversal Centralized Barrier solves the potential deadlock problem arising when sequential barriers are used. Instead of using the same value to represent pass/stop, sequential barriers use opposite values for pass/stop state. For example, if barrier 1 uses 0 to stop the threads, barrier 2 will use 1 to stop threads and barrier 3 will use 0 to stop threads again and so on. The pseudo code below demonstrates this.

```
int barrierCounter
int barrierFlag


function barrier()
{
    sense = !sense                          //toggle private sense


    Lock()


    barrierCounter = barrierCounter + 1
    myCount = barrierCounter                //myCount local


    UnLock()


    if (myCount == numProcessors)           //last thread
        barrierCounter = 0                  //reset
        barrierFlag = sense                 //release
    else
        wait for barrierFlag != sense



}
```

Combining Tree Barrier

A Combining Tree Barrier is a hierarchical way of implementing barrier to resolve the scalibility by avoiding the case that all threads spinning on a same location.

In k-Tree Barrier, all threads are equally divided into subgroups of k threads and a first-round synchronizations are done within these subgroups. Once all subgroups have done their synchronizations, the first thread in each subgroup enters the second level for further synchronization. In the second level, like in the first level, the threads form new subgroups of k threads and synchronize within groups, sending out one thread in each subgroup to next level and so on. Eventually, in the final level there is only one subgroup to be synchronized. After the final-level synchronization, the releasing signal is transmitted to upper levels and all threads get past the barrier.

Hardware Barrier Implementation

The hardware barrier uses hardware to implement the above basic barrier model.

The simplest hardware implementation uses dedicated wires to transmit signal to implement barrier. This dedicated wire performs OR/AND operation to act as the pass/block flags and thread counter. For small systems, such a model works and communication speed is not a major concern. In large multiprocessor systems this hardware design can make barrier implementation have high latency. The network connection among processors is one implementation to lower the latency, which is analogous to Combining Tree Barrier.

Memory Barrier

A memory barrier, also known as a membar, memory fence or fence instruction, is a type of barrier instruction that causes a central processing unit (CPU) or compiler to enforce an ordering constraint on memory operations issued before and after the barrier instruction. This typically means that operations issued prior to the barrier are guaranteed to be performed before operations issued after the barrier.

Memory barriers are necessary because most modern CPUs employ performance optimizations that can result in out-of-order execution. This reordering of memory operations (loads and stores) normally goes unnoticed within a single thread of execution, but can cause unpredictable behaviour in concurrent programs and device drivers unless carefully controlled. The exact nature of an ordering constraint is hardware dependent and defined by the architecture's memory ordering model. Some architectures provide multiple barriers for enforcing different ordering constraints.

Memory barriers are typically used when implementing low-level machine code that operates on memory shared by multiple devices. Such code includes synchronization primitives and lock-free data structures on multiprocessor systems, and device drivers that communicate with computer hardware.

An Illustrative Example

When a program runs on a single-CPU machine, the hardware performs the necessary bookkeeping to ensure that the program executes as if all memory operations were performed in the order specified by the programmer (program order), so memory barriers are not necessary. However, when the memory is shared with multiple devices, such as other CPUs in a multiprocessor system, or memory mapped peripherals, out-of-order access may affect program behavior. For example, a second CPU may see memory changes made by the first CPU in a sequence which differs from program order.

The following two-processor program gives an example of how such out-of-order execution can affect program behavior:

Initially, memory locations x and f both hold the value 0. The program running on processor #1 loops while the value of f is zero, then it prints the value of x. The program running on processor #2 stores the value 42 into x and then stores the value 1 into f. Pseudo-code for the two program fragments is shown below. The steps of the program correspond to individual processor instructions.

Processor #1:

```
while (f == 0);
```

```
 // Memory fence required here

 print x;

Processor #2:

 x = 42;

 // Memory fence required here

 f = 1;
```

One might expect the print statement to always print the number "42"; however, if processor #2's store operations are executed out-of-order, it is possible for f to be updated *before* x, and the print statement might therefore print "0". Similarly, processor #1's load operations may be executed out-of-order and it is possible for x to be read *before* f is checked, and again the print statement might therefore print an unexpected value. For most programs neither of these situations are acceptable. A memory barrier can be inserted before processor #2's assignment to f to ensure that the new value of x is visible to other processors at or prior to the change in the value of f. Another can be inserted before processor #1's access to x to ensure the value of x is not read prior to seeing the change in the value of f.

Low-level Architecture-specific Primitives

Memory barriers are low-level primitives and part of an architecture's memory model, which, like instruction sets, vary considerably between architectures, so it is not appropriate to generalize about memory barrier behavior. The conventional wisdom is that using memory barriers correctly requires careful study of the architecture manuals for the hardware being programmed. That said, the following paragraph offers a glimpse of some memory barriers which exist in contemporary products.

Some architectures, including the ubiquitous x86/x64, provide several memory barrier instructions including an instruction sometimes called "full fence". A full fence ensures that all load and store operations prior to the fence will have been committed prior to any loads and stores issued following the fence. Other architectures, such as the Itanium, provide separate "acquire" and "release" memory barriers which address the visibility of read-after-write operations from the point of view of a reader (sink) or writer (source) respectively. Some architectures provide separate memory barriers to control ordering between different combinations of system memory and I/O memory. When more than one memory barrier instruction is available it is important to consider that the cost of different instructions may vary considerably.

Multithreaded Programming and Memory Visibility

Multithreaded programs usually use synchronization primitives provided by a high-level programming environment, such as Java and .NET Framework, or an application programming interface (API) such as POSIX Threads or Windows API. Synchronization Primitives such as mutexes and semaphores are provided to synchronize access to resources from parallel threads of execution. These primitives are usually implemented with the memory barriers required to provide the expected memory visibility semantics. In such environments explicit use of memory barriers is not generally necessary.

Each API or programming environment in principle has its own high-level memory model that defines its memory visibility semantics. Although programmers do not usually need to use memory barriers in such high level environments, it is important to understand their memory visibility semantics, to the extent possible. Such understanding is not necessarily easy to achieve because memory visibility semantics are not always consistently specified or documented.

Just as programming language semantics are defined at a different level of abstraction than machine language opcodes, a programming environment's memory model is defined at a different level of abstraction than that of a hardware memory model. It is important to understand this distinction and realize that there is not always a simple mapping between low-level hardware memory barrier semantics and the high-level memory visibility semantics of a particular programming environment. As a result, a particular platform's implementation of (say) POSIX Threads may employ stronger barriers than required by the specification. Programs which take advantage of memory visibility as implemented rather than as specified may not be portable.

Out-of-order Execution Versus Compiler Reordering Optimizations

Memory barrier instructions address reordering effects only at the hardware level. Compilers may also reorder instructions as part of the program optimization process. Although the effects on parallel program behavior can be similar in both cases, in general it is necessary to take separate measures to inhibit compiler reordering optimizations for data that may be shared by multiple threads of execution. Note that such measures are usually necessary only for data which is not protected by synchronization primitives such as those discussed in the prior section.

In C and C++, the volatile keyword was intended to allow C and C++ programs to directly access memory-mapped I/O. Memory-mapped I/O generally requires that the reads and writes specified in source code happen in the exact order specified with no omissions. Omissions or reorderings of reads and writes by the compiler would break the communication between the program and the device accessed by memory-mapped I/O. A C or C++ compiler may not omit reads from and writes to volatile memory locations, nor may it reorder read/writes relative to other such actions for the same volatile location (variable). The keyword volatile *does not guarantee a memory barrier* to enforce cache-consistency. Therefore, the use of "volatile" alone is not sufficient to use a variable for inter-thread communication on all systems and processors.

The C and C++ standards prior to C11 and C++11 do not address multiple threads (or multiple processors), and as such, the usefulness of volatile depends on the compiler and hardware. Although volatile guarantees that the volatile reads and volatile writes will happen in the exact order specified in the source code, the compiler may generate code (or the CPU may re-order execution) such that a volatile read or write is reordered with regard to non-volatile reads or writes, thus limiting its usefulness as an inter-thread flag or mutex. Preventing such is compiler specific, but some compilers, like gcc, will not reorder operations around in-line assembly code with volatile and "memory" tags, like in: asm volatile ("" : : : "memory"). Moreover, it is not guaranteed that volatile reads and writes will be seen in the same order by other processors or cores due to caching, cache coherence protocol and relaxed memory ordering, meaning volatile variables alone may not even work as inter-thread flags or mutexes.

Some languages and compilers may provide sufficient facilities to implement functions which address both the compiler reordering and machine reordering issues. In Java version 1.5 (also known as version 5), the volatile keyword is now guaranteed to prevent certain hardware *and* compiler re-orderings, as part of the new Java Memory Model. C++11 standardizes special atomic types and operations with semantics similar to those of volatile in the Java Memory Model.

Barrier

- High-level classification of barriers

  o   Hardware and software barriers

- Will focus on two types of software barriers

  o   .Centralized barrier: every processor polls a single count

  o   Distributed tree barrier: shows much better scalability

- Performance goals of a barrier implementation

  o   Low latency: after all processors have arrived at the barrier, they should be able to leave quickly

  o   Low traffic: minimize bus transaction and contention

  o   Scalability: latency and traffic should scale slowly with the number of processors

  o   Low storage: barrier state should not be big

  o   Fairness: Preserve some strict order of barrier exit (could be FIFO according to arrival order); a particular processor should not always be the last one to exit

Centralized Barrier

```
struct bar_type {

    int counter;

    struct lock_type lock;

    int flag = 0;

} bar_name;


BARINIT (bar_name) {

    LOCKINIT(bar_name.lock);

    bar_name.counter = 0;
```

```
    }


    BARRIER (bar_name, P) {

        int my_count;

        LOCK (bar_name.lock);

        if (!bar_name.counter) {

            bar_name.flag = 0; /* first one */

        }

        my_count = ++bar_name.counter;

        UNLOCK (bar_name.lock);

        if (my_count == P) {

            bar_name.counter = 0;

            bar_name.flag = 1; /* last one */

        }

        else {

            while (!bar_name.flag);

        }

    }
```

Sense Reversal

- The last implementation fails to work for two consecutive barrier invocations

  o Need to prevent a process from entering a barrier instance until all have left the previous instance

  o Reverse the sense of a barrier i.e. every other barrier will have the same sense: basically attach parity or sense to a barrier

```
    BARRIER (bar_name, P) {

        local sense = !local_sense; /* this is private per processor */

        LOCK (bar_name.lock);

        bar_name.counter++;

        if (bar_name.counter == P) {

            UNLOCK (bar_name.lock);
```

```
        bar_name.counter = 0;

        bar_name.flag = local_sense;

    }

    else {

        UNLOCK (bar_name.lock);

        while (bar_name.flag != local_sense);

    }

}
```

Centralized Barrier

- How fast is it?

  o Assume that the program is perfectly balanced and hence all processors arrive at the barrier at the same time

  o Latency is proportional to P due to the critical section (assume that the lock algorithm exhibits at most O(P) latency)

  o The amount of traffic of acquire section (the CS) depends on the lock algorithm; after everyone has settled in the waiting loop the last processor will generate a BusRdX during release (flag write) and others will subsequently generate BusRd before releasing: O(P)

  o Scalability turns out to be low partly due to the critical section and partly due to O(P) traffic of release

  o No fairness in terms of who exits first

Tree Barrier

- Does not need a lock, only uses flags

  o Arrange the processors logically in a binary tree (higher degree also possible)

  o Two siblings tell each other of arrival via simple flags (i.e. one waits on a flag while the other sets it on arrival)

  o One of them moves up the tree to participate in the next level of the barrier

  o Introduces concurrency in the barrier algorithm since independent subtrees can proceed in parallel

  o Takes log(P) steps to complete the acquire

  o A fixed processor starts a downward pass of release waking up other processors that in turn set other flags o   Shows much better scalability compared to centralized barriers in DSM multiprocessors; the advantage in small bus-based systems is not much, since all transactions are any way serialized on the bus; in fact the additional log (P) delay may hurt performance in bus-based SMPs

```
TreeBarrier (pid, P) {

    unsigned int i, mask;

    for (i = 0, mask = 1; (mask & pid) != 0; ++i, mask <<= 1) {

        while (!flag[pid][i]);

        flag[pid][i] = 0;

    }

    if (pid < (P - 1)) {

        flag[pid + mask][i] = 1;

        while (!flag[pid][MAX- 1]);

        flag[pid][MAX - 1] = 0;

    }

    for (mask >>= 1; mask > 0; mask >>= 1) {

flag[pid - mask][MAX-1] = 1;

    }

}
```

- Convince yourself that this works

- Take 8 processors and arrange them on leaves of a tree of depth 3

- You will find that only odd nodes move up at every level during acquire (implemented in the first for loop)

- The even nodes just set the flags (the first statement in the if condition): they bail out of the first loop with mask=1

- The release is initiated by the last processor in the last for loop; only odd nodes execute this loop (7 wakes up 3, 5, 6; 5 wakes up 4; 3 wakes up 1, 2; 1 wakes up 0)

- Each processor will need at most log (P) + 1 flags

- Avoid false sharing: allocate each processor's flags on a separate chunk of cache lines

- With some memory wastage (possibly worth it) allocate each processor's flags on a separate page and map that page locally in that processor's physical memory

    o   Avoid remote misses in DSM multiprocessor

    o　Does not matter in bus-based SMPs

Hardware Support

- Read broadcast

  o　Possible to reduce the number of bus transactions from P-1 to 1 in the best case

  o　A processor seeing a read miss to flag location (possibly from a fellow processor) backs off and does not put its read miss on the bus

  o　Every processor picks up the read reply from the bus and the release completes with one bus transaction

  o　Needs special hardware/compiler support to recognize these flag addresses and resort to read broadcast

Hardware Barrier

- Useful if frequency of barriers is high

  o　Need a couple of wired-AND bus lines: one for odd barriers and one for even barriers

  o　A processor arrives at the barrier and asserts its input line and waits for the wired-AND line output to go HIGH

  o　Not very flexible: assumes that all processors will always participate in all barriers

  o　Bigger problem: what if multiple processes belonging to the same parallel program are assigned to each processor?

  o　No SMP supports it today

  o　However, possible to provide flexible hardware barrier support in the memory controller of DSM multiprocessors: memory controller can recognize accesses to special barrier counter or barrier flag, combine them in memory and reply to processors only when the barrier is complete (no retry due to failed lock)

Speculative Synch

- Speculative synchronization

  o　Basic idea is to introduce speculation in the execution of critical sections

  o　Assume that no other processor will have conflicting data accesses in the critical section and hence don't even try to acquire the lock

  o　Just venture into the critical section and start executing

  o　Note the difference between this and speculative execution of critical section due to speculation on the branch following SC: there you still contend for the lock generating network transactions

- Martinez and Torrellas. In ASPLOS 2002.

- Rajwar and Goodman. In ASPLOS 2002.

- We will discuss Martinez and Torrellas

Why is it good?

- In many cases compiler/user inserts synchronization conservatively

  o Hard to know exact access pattern

  o The addresses accessed may depend on input

- Take a simple example of a hash table

  o When the hash table is updated by two processes you really do not know which bins they will insert into

  o So you conservatively make the hash table access a critical section

  o For certain input values it may happen that the processes could actually update the hash table concurrently

How does it work?

- Speculative locks

  o Every processor comes to the critical section and tries to acquire the lock

  o One of them succeeds and the rest fail

  o The successful processor becomes the safe thread

  o The failed ones don't retry but venture into the critical section speculatively as if they have the lock; at this point a speculative thread also takes a checkpoint of its register state in case a rollback is needed

  o The safe thread executes the critical section as usual

  o The speculative threads are allowed to consume values produced by the safe thread but not by the sp. threads

  o All stores from a speculative thread are kept inside its cache hierarchy in a special "speculative modified" state; these lines cannot be sent to memory until it is known to be safe; if such a line is replaced from cache either it can be kept in a small buffer or the thread can be stalled

- Speculative locks (continued)

  o If a speculative thread receives a request for a cache line that is in speculative M state, that means there is a data race inside the critical section and by design the receiver thread is rolled back to the beginning of critical section

- o   Why can't the requester thread be rolled back?

- o   In summary, the safe thread is never squashed and the speculative threads are not squashed if there is no cross-thread data race

- o   If a speculative thread finishes executing the critical section without getting squashed, it still must wait for the safe thread to finish the critical section before committing the speculative state (i.e. changing speculative M lines to M); why?

- Speculative locks (continued)

  - o   Upon finishing the critical section, a speculative thread can continue executing beyond the CS, but still remaining in speculative mode

  - o   When the safe thread finishes the CS all speculative threads that have already completed CS, can commit in some non-deterministic order and revert to normal execution

  - o   The speculative threads that are still inside the critical section remain speculative; a dedicated hardware unit elects one of them the lock owner and that becomes the safe non-speculative thread; the process continues

  - o   Clearly, under favorable conditions speculative synchronization can reduce lock contention enormously

Why is it correct?

- In a non-speculative setting there is no order in which the threads execute the CS

  - o   Even if there is an order that must be enforced by the program itself

- In speculative synchronization some threads are considered safe (depends on time of arrival) and there is exactly one safe thread at a time in a CS

- The speculative threads behave as if they complete the CS in some order after the safe thread(s)

- A read from a thread (spec. or safe) after a write from another speculative thread to the same cache line triggers a squash

  - o   It may not be correct to consume the speculative value

  - o   Same applies to write after write

Performance Concerns

- Maintaining a safe thread guarantees forward progress

  - o   Otherwise if all were speculative, cross-thread races may repeatedly squash all of them

- False sharing?

  - o   What if two bins of a hash table belong to the same cache line?

  - o   Two threads are really not accessing the same address, but the speculative thread will still suffer from a squash

- Possible to maintain per-word speculative state

Speculative Flags and Barriers

- Speculative flags are easy to support

  - Just continue past an unset flag in speculative mode

  - The thread that sets the flag is always safe

  - The thread(s) that read the flag will speculate

- Speculative barriers come for free

  - Barriers use locks and flags

  - However, since the critical section in a barrier accesses a counter, multiple threads venturing into the CS are guaranteed to have conflicts

  - So just speculate on the flag and let the critical section be executed conventionally

Speculative Flags and Branch Prediction

```
P0: A=1; flag=1;

P1: while (!flag); print A;

Assembly of P1's code

Loop:    lw register, flag_addr

             beqz register, Loop

         ...
```

- What if I pass a hint via the compiler (say, a single bit in each branch instruction) to the branch predictor asking it to always predict not taken for this branch?

  - Isn't it achieving the same effect as speculative flag, but with a much simpler technique? No.

References

- Silberschatz, Abraham; Gagne, Greg; Galvin, Peter Baer (July 11, 2008). "Chapter 6: Process Synchronization". Operating System Concepts (Eighth ed.). John Wiley & Sons. ISBN 978-0-470-12872-5

- "Synchronization Primitives in .NET framework". MSDN, The Microsoft Developer Net-work. Microsoft. Retrieved 23 November 2014

- Hennessy, John L.; Patterson, David A. (September 30, 2011). "Chapter 5: Thread-Level Parallelism". Computer Architecture: A Quantitative Approach (Fifth ed.). Morgan Kauf-mann. ISBN 978-0-123-83872-8

- M. M., Rahman (2012). "Process synchronization in multiprocessor and multi-core pro-cessor". Informatics, Electronics & Vision (ICIEV), 2012 International Conference. doi:10.1109/ICIEV.2012.6317471

- Nyman, Linus; Laakso, Mikael. "Notes on the History of Fork and Join". IEEE Annals of the History of Computing. IEEE Computer Society. 38 (3): 84–87. doi:10.1109/MAHC.2016.34. Retrieved 9 September 2016

- Solihin, Yan (2015-01-01). Fundamentals of Parallel Multicore Architecture (1st ed.). Chap-man & Hall/CRC. ISBN 1482211181

- Boehm, Hans (June 2005). Threads cannot be implemented as a library. Proceedings of the 2005 ACM SIGPLAN conference on Programming language design and implementa-tion. Association for Computing Machinery. doi:10.1145/1065010.1065042

- Cormen, Thomas H.; Leiserson, Charles E.; Rivest, Ronald L.; Stein, Clifford (2009) [1990]. Introduction to Algorithms (3rd ed.). MIT Press and McGraw-Hill. ISBN 0-262-03384-4

Directory-Based Cache Coherence

A directory is a system used for cataloging files on the computer. They can also be known as folders or drawers. Some of the topics discussed in this chapter are virtual networks, replacement of S blocks and Sequent NUMA-Q. The aspects elucidated in this chapter are of vital importance, and provide a better understanding of computer architecture.

Directory (Computing)

```
C:\Temp> dir
 Volume in drive C is C
 Volume Serial Number is 74F5-B93C

 Directory of C:\Temp

2009-08-25  11:59    <DIR>          .
2009-08-25  11:59    <DIR>          ..
2007-03-01  11:37         2,321,600 AdobeUpdater12345.exe
2009-04-03  10:01            27,988 dd_depcheckdotnetfx30.txt
2009-04-03  10:01               764 dd_dotnetfx3error.txt
2009-04-03  10:01            32,572 dd_dotnetfx3install.txt
2009-06-09  13:46            35,145 GenProfile.log
2009-08-05  12:11               155 KB969856.log
2009-04-20  08:37               402 MSI29e0b.LOG
2009-04-09  16:34            38,895 offcln11.log
2009-04-03  16:02    <DIR>          OfficePatches
2009-07-14  14:30    <DIR>          OHotfix
2009-08-25  10:52            16,384 Perflib_Perfdata_c30.dat
2009-04-03  10:01             1,744 uxeventlog.txt
2009-08-25  11:42        50,245,632 WFV2F.tmp
2009-04-20  10:07             1,397 {AC76BA86-7AD7-1033-7B44-A81200000003}.ini
2009-04-20  10:13               617 {AC76BA86-7AD7-1033-7B44-A81300000003}.ini
              13 File(s)     52,723,295 bytes
               4 Dir(s)  83,570,208,768 bytes free
```

Screenshot of a Windows / MS-DOS command prompt window showing a directory listing.

In computing, a directory is a file system cataloging structure which contains references to other computer files, and possibly other directories. On many computers, directories are known as folders, or drawers to provide some relevancy to a workbench or the traditional office file cabinet.

Files are organized by storing related files in the same directory. In a hierarchical filesystem (that is, one in which files and directories are organized in a manner that resembles a tree), a directory contained inside another directory is called a subdirectory. The terms parent and child are often used to describe the relationship between a subdirectory and the directory in which it is cataloged, the latter being the parent. The top-most directory in such a filesystem, which does not have a parent of its own, is called the root directory.

Overview

Historically, and even on some modern embedded systems, the file systems either had no support for directories at all or only had a "flat" directory structure, meaning subdirectories were not supported; there were only a group of top-level directories each containing files. In modern systems, a directory can contain a mix of files and subdirectories.

A reference to a location in a directory system is called a path.

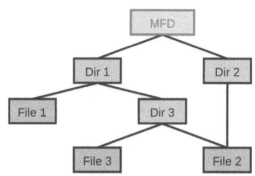

Diagram of a hierarchal directory tree. The root directory is here called 'MFD', for Master File Directory.

In many operating systems, programs have an associated working directory in which they execute. Typically, file names accessed by the program are assumed to reside within this directory if the file names are not specified with an explicit directory name.

Some operating systems restrict a user's access to only their home directory or project directory, thus isolating their activities from all other users. In early versions of Unix the root directory was the home directory of the root user, but modern Unix usually uses another directory such as /root for this purpose.

In keeping with Unix philosophy, Unix systems treat directories as a type of file.

Folder Metaphor

Sample folder icon (from KDE).

The name *folder*, presenting an analogy to the file folder used in offices, and used in a hierarchical file system design for the Electronic Recording Machine, Accounting (ERMA) Mark 1 published in 1958 as well as by Xerox Star, is used in almost all modern operating systems' desktop environments. Folders are often depicted with icons which visually resemble physical file folders.

There is a difference between a *directory*, which is a file system concept, and the graphical user interface metaphor that is used to represent it (a *folder*). For example, Microsoft Windows uses the concept of special folders to help present the contents of the computer to the user in a fairly consistent way that frees the user from having to deal with absolute directory paths, which can vary between versions of Windows, and between individual installations. Many operating systems also have the concept of "smart folders" that reflect the results of a file system search or other operation. These folders do not represent a directory in the file hierarchy. Many email clients allow the creation of folders to organize email. These folders have no corresponding representation in the filesystem structure.

If one is referring to a *container of documents*, the term *folder* is more appropriate. The term *directory* refers to the way a structured list of document files and folders is stored on the computer. The distinction can be due to the way a directory is accessed; on Unix systems, /usr/bin/ is usually referred to as a directory when viewed in a command line console, but if accessed through a graphical file manager, users may sometimes call it a folder.

Lookup Cache

Operating systems that support hierarchical filesystems (practically all modern ones) implement a form of caching to RAM of recent path lookups. In the Unix world, this is usually called Directory Name Lookup Cache (DNLC), although it is called dcache on Linux.

For local filesystems, DNLC entries normally expire only under pressure from other more recent entries. For network file systems a coherence mechanism is necessary to ensure that entries have not been invalidated by other clients.

Basics of Directory

- Theoretically speaking each directory entry should have a dirty bit and a bitvector of length P.

  - On a read from processor k, if dirty bit is off read cache line from memory, send it to k, set bit[k] in vector; if dirty bit is on read owner id from vector (different interpretation of bitvector), send read intervention to owner, owner replies line directly to k (how?), sends a copy to home, home updates memory, directory controller sets bit[k] and bit[owner] in vector.

  - On a write from processor k, if dirty bit is off send invalidations to all sharers marked in vector, wait for acknowledgments, read cache line from memory, send it to k, zero out vector and write k in vector, set dirty bit; if dirty bit on same as read, but now intervention is of readX type and memory does not write the line back, dirty bit is set and vector=k.

Directory Organization

- Centralized vs. distributed

  - Centralized directory helps to resolve many races, but becomes a bandwidth bottleneck

  - One solution is to provide a banked directory structure: with each memory bank associate its directory bank

  - But since memory is distributed, this essentially leads to distributed directory structure i.e. each node is responsible for holding the directory entries corresponding to the memory lines it is holding

  - Why did we decide to have a distributed memory organization instead of dance hall?

Is directory useful?

- One drawback of directory

- o   Before looking up the directory you cannot decide what to do (even if you start reading memory speculatively)

- o   So directory introduces one level of indirection in every request that misses in processor's cache hierarchy

- o   Therefore, broadcast is definitely preferable over directory if the system can offer enough memory controller and router bandwidth to handle broadcast messages (network link bandwidth is normally not the bottleneck since most messages do not carry data; observe that you would never broadcast a reply); AMD Opteron adopted this scheme, but target is small scale

- Directory is preferable

  - o   If number of sharers is small because in this case a broadcast would waste enormous amount of memory controller bandwidth

Sharing Pattern

- Problem is with the writes

  - o   Frequently written cache lines exhibit a small number of sharers; so small number of invalidations

  - o   Widely shared data are written infrequently; so large number of invalidations, but rare

  - o   Synchronization variables are notorious: heavily contended locks are widely shared and written in quick succession generating a burst of invalidations; require special solutions such as queue locks or tree barriers

  - o   What about interventions? These are very problematic because in these cases you cannot send the interventions before looking up the directory and any speculative memory lookup would be useless

  - o   For scientific applications interventions are small due to mostly one producer-many consumer pattern; for database workloads these take the lion's share due to migratory pattern and tend to increase with bigger cache

- Optimizing interventions related to migratory sharing has been a major focus of high-end scalable servers

  - o   AlphaServer GS320 employs few optimizations to quickly resolve races related to migratory hand-off (more later)

  - o   Some academic research looked at destination or owner prediction to speculatively send interventions even before consulting the directory (Martin and Hill 2003, Acacio et al 2002)

- In general, directory provides far better utilization of bandwidth for scalable MPs compared to broadcast

Directory Organization

- How to find source of directory information

  - Centralized: just access the directory (bandwidth limited)

  - Distributed: flat scheme distributes directory with memory and every cache line has a home node where its memory and directory reside

  - Hierarchical scheme organizes the processors as the leaves of a logical tree (need not be binary) and an internal node stores the directory entries for the memory lines local to its children; a directory entry essentially tells you which of its children subtrees are caching the line and if some subtree which is not its children is also caching; finding the directory entry of a cache line involves a traversal of the tree until the entry is found (inclusion is maintained between level k and k+1 directory node where the root is at the highest level i.e. in the worst case may have to go to the root to find dir.)

- Format of a directory entry

  - Varies a lot: no specific rule

  - Memory-based scheme: directory entry is co-located in the home node with the memory line; various organizations can be used; the most popular one is a simple bit vector (with a 128 bytes line, storage overhead for 64 nodes is 6.35%, for 256 nodes 25%, for 1024 nodes 100%); clearly does not scale with P (more later)

  - Cache-based scheme: Organize the directory as a distributed linked-list where the sharer nodes form a chain; the cache tag is extended to hold a node number; the home node only knows the id of the first sharer; on a read miss the requester adds itself to the head (involves home and first sharer); on a write miss traverse list and invalidate (essentially serialized chain of messages); advantage: distributes contention and does not make the home node a hot-spot, storage overhead is fixed; but very complex (IEEE SCI standard)

- Lot of research has been done to reduce directory storage overhead

  - The trade-off is between preciseness of information and performance

  - Normal trick is to have a superset of information e.g., group every two sharers into a cluster and have a bit per cluster: may lead to one useless invalidation per cluster

  - Memory-based bitvector scheme is very popular: invalidations can be overlapped or multicast

  - Cache-based schemes incur serialized message chain for invalidation

  - Hierarchical schemes are not used much due to high latency and volume of messages (up and down tree); also root may become a bandwidth bottleneck

Directory Overhead

- Quadratic in number of processors for bitvector

- o   Assume P processors, each with M amount of local memory (i.e. total shared memory size is M^*P)

- o   Let the coherence granularity (cache block size) be B

- o   Number of cache blocks per node = M/B = number of directory entries per node

- o   Size of one directory entry = P + O(1)

- o   Total size of directory memory across all processors = $(M/B)(P+O(1))^*P = O(P^2)$

Path of a Read Miss

- Assume that the line is not shared by anyone

  - o   Load issues from load queue (for data) or fetcher accesses icache; looks up TLB and gets PA

  - o   Misses in L1, L2, L3,... caches

  - o   Launches address and request type on system bus

  - o   The request gets queued in memory controller and registered in OTT or TTT (Outstanding Transaction Table or Transactions in Transit Table)

  - o   Memory controller eventually schedules the request

  - o   Decodes home node from upper few bits of address

  - o   Local home: access directory and data memory (how?)

  - o   Remote home: request gets queued in network interface

- From NI onward

  - o   Eventually the request gets forwarded to the router and through the network to the home

  - o   At the home the request gets queued in NI and waits for being scheduled by the home memory controller

  - o   After it is scheduled home memory controller looks up directory and data memory

  - o   Reply returns through the same path

- Total time (by log model and memory latency m)

  - o   Local home: max(k_ho, m)

  - o   Remote home: $k_r o + g_{h+a} + N\ell\, g_{h+a} + max(k_h o,\ m) + g_{h+a+d} + N\ell + g_{h+a+d} + k_r o$

Correctness Issues

- Serialization to a location

  - o   Schedule order at home

- o   Use NACKs (extra traffic and livelock) or smarter techniques (back-off, NACK-free)

- Flow control deadlock

  - o   Avoid buffer dependence cycles

  - o   Avoid network queue dependence cycles

  - o   Virtual networks multiplexed on physical networks

  - o   Coherence protocol dictates the virtual network usage

Tree Structure

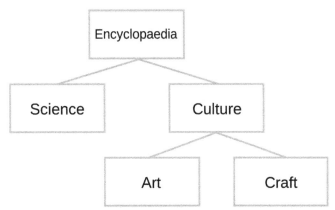

A tree structure showing the possible hierarchical organization of an encyclopedia.

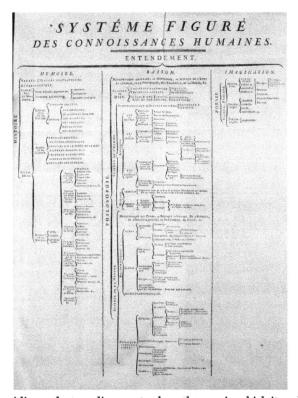

The original Encyclopédie used a tree diagram to show the way in which its subjects were ordered.

A tree structure or tree diagram is a way of representing the hierarchical nature of a structure in a graphical form. It is named a "tree structure" because the classic representation resembles a tree, even though the chart is generally upside down compared to an actual tree, with the "root" at the top and the "leaves" at the bottom. A tree structure is conceptual, and appears in several forms.

Terminology and Properties

The tree elements are called "nodes". The lines connecting elements are called "branches". Nodes without children are called leaf nodes, "end-nodes", or "leaves".

Every finite tree structure has a member that has no superior. This member is called the "root" or root node. The root is the starting node. But the converse is not true: infinite tree structures may or may not have a root node.

The names of relationships between nodes model the kinship terminology of family relations. The gender-neutral names "parent" and "child" have largely displaced the older "father" and "son" terminology, although the term "uncle" is still used for other nodes at the same level as the parent.

- A node's "parent" is a node one step higher in the hierarchy (i.e. closer to the root node) and lying on the same branch.

- "Sibling" ("brother" or "sister") nodes share the same parent node.

- A node's "uncles" are siblings of that node's parent.

- A node that is connected to all lower-level nodes is called an "ancestor". The connected lower-level nodes are "descendants" of the ancestor node.

In the example, "encyclopedia" is the parent of "science" and "culture", its children. "Art" and "craft" are siblings, and children of "culture", which is their parent and thus one of their ancestors. Also, "encyclopedia", as the root of the tree, is the ancestor of "science", "culture", "art" and "craft". Finally, "science", "art" and "craft", as leaves, are ancestors of no other node.

Tree structures can depict all kinds of taxonomic knowledge, such as family trees, the biological evolutionary tree, the evolutionary tree of a language family, the grammatical structure of a language (a key example being S → NP VP, meaning a sentence is a noun phrase and a verb phrase, with each in turn having other components which have other components), the way web pages are logically ordered in a web site, mathematical trees of integer sets, et cetera.

The Oxford English Dictionary records use of both the terms "tree structure" and "tree-diagram" from 1965 in Noam Chomsky's *Aspects of the Theory of Syntax*.

In a tree structure there is one and only one path from any point to any other point.

Examples of Tree Structures

- Internet:

- usenet hierarchy

- Document Object Model's logical structure, Yahoo! subject index, DMOZ

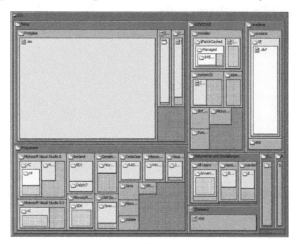

A tree map used to represent a directory structure as a nested set.

- Operating system: directory structure

- Information management: Dewey Decimal System, PSH, this hierarchical bulleted list

- Management: hierarchical organizational structures

- Computer Science:

  - binary search tree

  - Red-Black Tree

  - AVL tree

  - R-tree

- Biology: evolutionary tree

- Business: pyramid selling scheme

- Project management: work breakdown structure

- Linguistics:

  - (Syntax) Phrase structure trees

  - (Historical Linguistics) Tree model of language change

- Sports: business chess, playoffs brackets

- Mathematics: Von Neumann universe

- Group theory: descendant trees

Representing Trees

There are many ways of visually representing tree structures. Almost always, these boil down to variations, or combinations, of a few basic styles:

Classical Node-link Diagrams

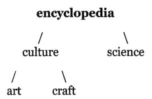

Classical node-link diagrams, that connect nodes together with line segments.

Nested Sets

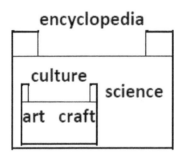

Nested sets that use enclosure/containment to show parenthood, examples include TreeMaps and fractal maps.

Layered "Icicle" Diagrams

encyclopedia	
culture	science
art	craft	

Layered "icicle" diagrams that use alignment/adjacency.

Outlines and Tree Views

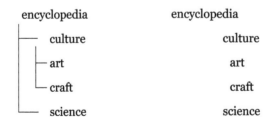

Lists or diagrams that use indentation, sometimes called "outlines" or "tree views".

Nested Parentheses

((art,craft)culture,science)encyclopedia

or

Encyclopedia(Culture(Art,Craft),Science)

A correspondence to nested parentheses was first noticed by Sir Arthur Cayley.

Radial Trees

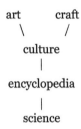

art   craft

\\   /

culture

|

encyclopedia

|

science

Unix Filesystem

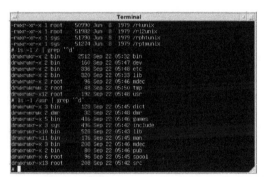

Version 7 Unix filesystem layout: subdirectories of "/" and "/usr"

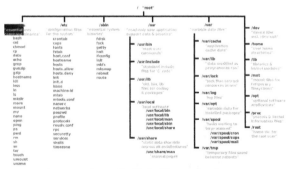

An overview of a Unix filesystem layout

In Unix and operating systems inspired by it, the file system is considered a central component of the operating system. It was also one of the first parts of the system to be designed and implemented by Ken Thompson in the first experimental version of Unix, dated 1969.

As in other operating systems, the filesystem provides information storage and retrieval, and one of several forms of interprocess communication, in that the many small programs that traditionally form a Unix system can store information in files so that other programs can read them, although pipes complemented it in this role starting with the Third Edition. Also, the filesystem provides access to other resources through so-called *device files* that are entry points to terminals, printers, and mice.

The rest of this article uses *Unix* as a generic name to refer to both the original Unix operating system and its many workalikes.

Principles

The filesystem appears as one rooted tree of directories. Instead of addressing separate volumes such as disk partitions, removable media, and network shares as separate trees (as done in DOS and Windows: each *drive* has a drive letter that denotes the root of its file system tree), such volumes can be *mounted* on a directory, causing the volume's file system tree to appear as that directory in the larger tree. The root of the entire tree is denoted /.

In the original Bell Labs Unix, a two-disk setup was customary, where the first disk contained startup programs, while the second contained users' files and programs. This second disk was mounted at the empty directory named usr on the first disk, causing the two disks to appear as one filesystem, with the second's disks contents viewable at /usr.

Unix directories do not *contain* files. Instead, they contain the names of files paired with references to so-called inodes, which in turn contain both the file and its metadata (owner, permissions, time of last access, etc., but no name). Multiple names in the file system may refer to the same file, a feature termed a *hard link*. The mathematical traits of hard links make the file system a limited type of directed acyclic graph, although the *directories* still form a tree, as they typically may not be hard-linked. (As originally envisioned in 1969, the Unix file system would in fact be used as a general graph with hard links to directories providing navigation, instead of path names.)

File Types

The original Unix file system supported three types of files: ordinary files, directories, and "special files", also termed device files. The Berkeley Software Distribution (BSD) and System V each added a file type to be used for interprocess communication: BSD added sockets, while System V added FIFO files.

BSD also added symbolic links (often termed "symlinks") to the range of file types, which are files that refer to other files, and complement hard links. Symlinks were modeled after a similar feature in Multics, and differ from hard links in that they may span filesystems and that their existence is independent of the target object. Other Unix systems may support added types of files.

Conventional Directory Layout

Certain conventions exist for locating some kinds of files, such as programs, system configuration files, and users' home directories. These were first documented in the hier(7) man page since Version 7 Unix; subsequent versions, derivatives and clones typically have a similar man page.

The details of the directory layout have varied over time. Although the file system layout is not part of the Single UNIX Specification, several attempts exist to standardize (parts of) it, such as the System V Application Binary Interface, the Intel Binary Compatibility Standard, the Common Operating System Environment, and Linux Foundation's Filesystem Hierarchy Standard (FHS).

Here is a generalized overview of common locations of files on a Unix operating system:

Directory or file	Description
/	The slash / character alone denotes the root of the filesystem tree.
/bin	Stands for *binaries* and contains certain fundamental utilities, such as ls or cp, that are needed to mount /usr, when that is a separate filesystem, or to run in one-user (administrative) mode when /usr cannot be mounted. In System V.4, this is a symlink to /usr/bin.
/boot	Contains all the files needed for successful booting process. In Research Unix, this was one file rather than a directory.
/dev	Stands for *devices*. Contains file representations of peripheral devices and pseudo-devices.
/etc	Contains system-wide configuration files and system databases; the name stands for *et cetera*. Originally also contained "dangerous maintenance utilities" such as init, but these have typically been moved to /sbin or elsewhere.
/home	Contains user home directories on Linux and some other systems. In the original version of Unix, home directories were in /usr instead. Some systems use or have used different locations still: OS X has home directories in /Users, older versions of BSD put them in /u, FreeBSD has /usr/home.
/lib	Originally *essential libraries*: C libraries, but not Fortran ones. On modern systems, it contains the shared libraries needed by programs in /bin, and possibly loadable kernel module or device drivers. Linux distributions may have variants /lib32 and /lib64 for multi-architecture support.
/media	Default mount point for removable devices, such as USB sticks, media players, etc.
/mnt	Stands for *mount*. Empty directory commonly used by system administrators as a temporary mount point.
/opt	Contains locally installed software. Originated in System V, which has a package manager that installs software to this directory (one subdirectory per package).
/proc	procfs virtual filesystem showing information about processes as files.
/root	The home directory for the superuser *root* - that is, the system administrator. This account's home directory is usually on the initial filesystem, and hence not in /home (which may be a mount point for another filesystem) in case specific maintenance needs to be performed, during which other filesystems are not available. Such a case could occur, for example, if a hard disk drive suffers physical failures and cannot be properly mounted.
/sbin	Stands for "system (or superuser) binaries" and contains fundamental utilities, such as init, usually needed to start, maintain and recover the system.
/srv	Server data (data for services provided by system).
/sys	In some Linux distributions, contains a sysfs virtual filesystem, containing information related to hardware and the operating system. On BSD systems, commonly a symlink to the kernel sources in /usr/src/sys.
/tmp	A place for temporary files not expected to survive a reboot. Many systems clear this directory upon startup or use tmpfs to implement it.
/unix	The Unix kernel in Research Unix and System V. With the addition of virtual memory support to 3BSD, this got renamed /vmunix.

/usr	The "user file system": originally the directory holding user home directories, but already by the Third Edition of Research Unix, ca. 1973, reused to split the operating system's programs over two disks (one of them a 256K fixed-head drive) so that basic commands would either appear in /bin or /usr/bin. It now holds executables, libraries, and shared resources that are not system critical, like the X Window System, KDE, Perl, etc. In older Unix systems, user home directories might still appear in /usr alongside directories containing programs, although by 1984 this depended on *local customs*.
/include	Stores the development headers used throughout the system. Header files are mostly used by the #include directive in C language, which historically is how the name of this directory was chosen.
/lib	Stores the needed libraries and data files for programs stored within /usr or elsewhere.
/libexec	Holds programs meant to be executed by other programs rather than by users directly. E.g., the Sendmail executable may be found in this directory. Not present in the FHS until 2011; Linux distributions have traditionally moved the contents of this directory into /usr/lib, where they also resided in 4.3BSD.
/local	Resembles /usr in structure, but its subdirectories are used for additions not part of the operating system distribution, such as custom programs or files from a BSD Ports collection. Usually has subdirectories such as /usr/local/lib or /usr/local/bin.
/share	Architecture-independent program data. On Linux and modern BSD derivatives, this directory has subdirectories such as man for manpages, that used to appear directly under /usr in older versions.
/var	Stands for *variable*. A place for files that may change often - especially in size, for example e-mail sent to users on the system, or process-ID lock files.
/log	Contains system log files.
/mail	The place where all incoming mails are stored. Users (other than root) can access their own mail only. Often, this directory is a symbolic link to /var/spool/mail.
/spool	Spool directory. Contains print jobs, mail spools and other queued tasks.
/tmp	The /var/tmp directory is a place for temporary files which should be preserved between system reboots.

Virtual Networks

- Consider a two-node system with one incoming and one outgoing queue on each node

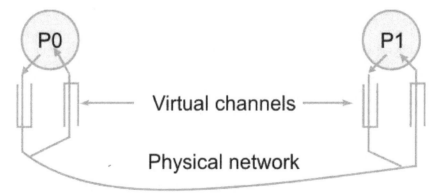

- Single queue is not enough to avoid deadlock
  - Single queue forms a single virtual network
- Similar deadlock issues as multi-level caches

- o An incoming message may generate another message e.g., request generates reply, ReadX generates reply and invalidation requests, request may generate intervention request

- o Memory controller refuses to schedule a message if the outgoing queue is full

- o Same situation may happen on all nodes: deadlock

- o One incoming and one outgoing queue is not enough

- o What if we have two in each direction?: one for request and one for reply

- o Replies can usually sink

- o Requests generating requests?

- What is the length of the longest transaction in terms of number of messages?

  - o This decides the number of queues needed in each direction (Origin 2000 uses a different scheme)

  - o One type of message is usually assigned to a queue

  - o One queue type connected across the system forms a virtual network of that type e.g. request network, reply network, third party request (invalidations and interventions) network

  - o Virtual networks are multiplexed over a physical network

- Sink message type must get scheduled eventually

  - o Resources should be sized properly so that scheduling of these messages does not depend on anything

  - o Avoid buffer shortage (and deadlock) by keeping reserved buffer for the sink queue

Three-lane Protocols

- Quite popular due to its simplicity

  - o Let the request network be R, reply network Y, intervention/invalidation network be RR

  - o Network dependence (aka lane dependence) graph looks something like this

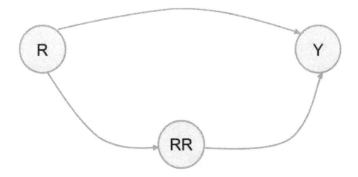

Performance Issues

- Latency optimizations

    o Reduce transactions on critical path: 3-hop vs. 4-hop

    o Overlap activities: protocol processing and data access, invalidations, invalidation acknowledgments

    o Make critical path fast: directory cache, integrated memory controller, smart protocol

    o Reduce occupancy of protocol engine

- Throughput optimizations

    o Pipeline the protocol processing

    o Multiple coherence engines

    o Protocol decisions: where to collect invalidation acknowledgments, existence of clean replacement hints

SGI Origin 2000

- Similar to Stanford DASH

- Flat memory-based directory organization

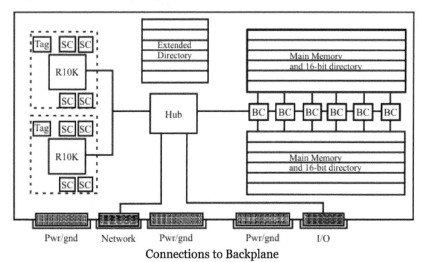

Connections to Backplane

- Directory state in separate DRAMs, accessed in parallel with data

- Up to 512 nodes (1024 processors)

- 195 MHz MIPS R10k (peak 390 MFLOPS and 780 MIPS per processor)

- Peak SysADBus (64 bits) bandwidth is 780 MB/s; same for hub-memory

- Hub to router and Xbow (I/O processor) is 1.56 GB/s

- Hub is 500 K gates in 0.5 micron CMOS

- Outstanding transaction buffer (aka CRB): 4 per processor

- Two processors per node are not snoop-coherent

Origin 2000 Network

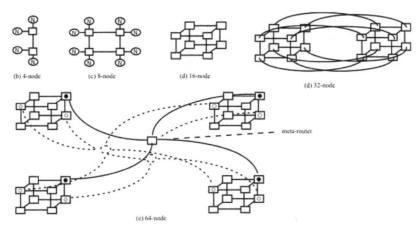

- Each router has six pairs of 1.56 GB/s unidirectional links; two to nodes (bristled), four to other routers

- 41 ns pin to pin latency

- Four virtual networks: request, reply, priority, I/O

Origin 2000 I/O

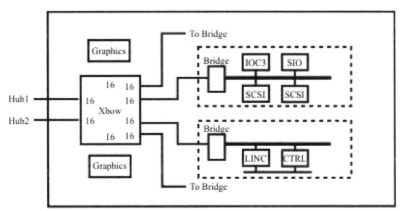

- Any processor can access I/O device either through uncached ops or through coherent DMA

- Any I/O device can access any data through router/hub

Origin Directory

- Directory formats

  - If exclusive in a cache, entry contains processor number (not node number)

- If shared, entry is a bitvector of sharers where each corresponds to a node (not a processor)

  ◊ Invalidations sent to a node is broadcast to both processors by hub

- Two sizes

  ◊ 16-bit format (up to 32 processors), kept in DRAM

  ◊ 64-bit format (up to 128 processors), kept in extension DRAM

  ◊ For machine sizes larger than 128 processors the protocol is coarse-vector (each bit is for 8 nodes)

  ◊ Machine can switch between BV and CV dynamically

Cache and Dir. States

- Cache states: MESI

- Six directory states (may not be six bits)

  o Unowned (I): no cache has a copy, memory copy is valid

  o Shared (S): one or more caches have copies, memory copy is valid

  o Dirty exclusive (M or DEX): exactly one cache has block in M or E state

    ◊ Directory cannot distinguish between M and E

  o Two pending or busy or transient states (PSH and PDEX): a transaction for the cache block is in progress; home cannot accept any new request

  o Poisoned state: used for efficient page migration

Handling A Read Miss

- Origin protocol does not assume anything about ordering of messages in the network

- At requesting hub

  o Address is decoded and home is located

  o Request forwarded to home if home is remote

- At home

  o Directory lookup and data lookup are initiated in parallel

  o Directory banks are designed to be slightly faster than other banks

  o The directory entry may reveal several possible states

    ◊ Actions taken depends on this

- Directory state lookup

  - Unowned: mark directory to point to requester, state becomes M, send cache line

  - Shared: mark directory bit, send cache line

  - Busy: send NACK to requester

  - Modified: if owner is not home, forward to owner

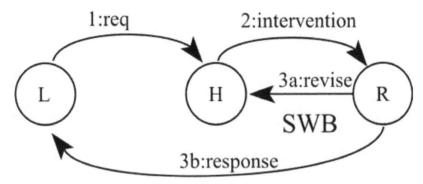

  - 3-hop vs. 4-hop reply?

  - Origin has only two virtual networks available to protocol

    ◊ How to handle interventions?

- Directory state M

  - Actions at home: set PSH state, set the vector with two sharers, NACK all subsequent requests until state is S

  - Actions at owner: if cache state is M send reply to requester (how to know who the requester is?) and send sharing writeback (SWB) to home; if cache state is E send completion messages to requester and home (no data is sent); in all cases cache state becomes S

  - Sharing writeback or completion message, on arrival at home, changes directory state to S

  - If the owner state is E, how does the requester get the data?

    ◊ The famous speculative reply of Origin 2000

    ◊ Note how processor design (in this case MIPS R10k) influences protocol decisions

Handling a Write Miss

- Request opcode could be upgrade or read exclusive

  - State busy: send NACK

  - State unowned: if ReadX send cache block, change state to M, mark owner in vector; if upgrade what do you do?

- o State shared: send reply (upgrade ack or ReadX reply) with number of sharers, send invalidations to sharers, change state to M, mark owner in vector; sharers send invalidation acknowledgments to requester directly

  - ◊ What if outgoing request network queue fills up before all invalidations are sent?

- o State M: same as read miss except directory remains in PDEX state until completion message (no data) is received from owner; directory remains in M state, only the owner changes; how do you handle upgrades here?

Serializing Requests

- The tricky situation is collection of invalidation acknowledgments

  - o Note from previous slides that even before all acknowledgments are collected at the requester, the directory at home goes to M state with the new owner marked

  - o A subsequent request will get forwarded to the new owner (at this point directory goes to PSH or PDEX state)

  - o The owner is responsible for serializing the new request with the previous write

    - ◊ The write is not complete until all invalidation acknowledgments are collected

    - ◊ OTT (aka CRB) of the owner is equipped to block any incoming request until all the acknowledgments and the reply from home are collected (early interventions)

  - o Note that there is no completion message back to home

Handling Writebacks

- Valid directory states: M or busy; cannot be S or I

- State M

  - o Just clear directory entry, write block to memory

  - o Need to send writeback acknowledgment to the evicting processor (explanation coming up)

- State busy

  - o How can this happen? (Late intervention race)

  - o Can NACK writeback? What support needed for this?

  - o Better solution: writeback forwarding

  - o Any special consideration at the evicting node?

    - ◊ Drop intervention (how?)

  - o How does the directory state change in this case?

Replacement of S Blocks

- Send notification to directory?
    - Can save a future invalidation
    - Does it reduce overall traffic?
- Origin 2000 does not use replacement hints
    - No notification to directory
    - Why?
- Replacements of E blocks are hinted and require acknowledgments also (why?)
- Summary of transaction types
    - Coherence: 9 request transaction types, 6 invalidation/intervention, 39 reply types
    - Non-coherent (I/O, synch, special): 19 requests, 14 replies

Serialization

- Home is used to serialize requests
    - The order determined by the home is final
    - No node should violate this order
    - Example: read-invalidate races
        - ◊ P0, P1, and P2 are trying to access a cache block
        - ◊ P0 and P2 want to read while P1 wants to write
        - ◊ The requests from P0 and P2 reach home first, home replies and marks both in sharer vector; but the reply message to P0 gets delayed in the network
        - ◊ P1's write causes home to send out invalidation to P0 and P2; P0's inv. reaches P0 before the read reply
        - ◊ P0's hub sends acknowledgment to P1 and also forwards the invalidation to P0's processor cache
        - ◊ What happens when P0's reply arrives? Can the data be used?
- Requester's viewpoint
    - When a read reply arrives it finds the OTT entry has the "inv" bit set
    - Under what conditions can it happen?
    - Can replacement hints help?

- What about upgrade-invalidation races?

- What about readX-invalidation races?

VN Deadlock

- Origin 2000 has only two virtual networks, but has three-hop transactions

  o Resorts to back-off invalidate or intervention to fall back to strict request-reply

  o Does it really solve the problem or just move the problem elsewhere?

- Stanford DASH has same problems

  o Uses NACKs after a time-out period if the outgoing network doesn't free up

  o Worse compared to Origin because NACKs inflate total traffic and may lead to livelock

  o DASH avoids livelocks by sizing the queues according to the machine size (not a scalable solution)

Starvation

- NACKs can cause starvation

  o Build a FIFO list of waiters either in home memory (Chaudhuri and Heinrich, 2004) or use a distributed linked list (IEEE Scalable Coherent Interface)

    ◊ Former imposes large occupancy on home, yet offers better performance by read combining

    ◊ Latter is an extremely complex protocol with a large number of transient states and 29 stable states, but does distribute the occupancy across the system

  o Origin 2000 devotes extra bits in the directory to raise priority of requests NACKed too many times (above a threshold)

  o Use delay between retries

  o Use Alpha GS320 protocol (will discuss later)

Overflow Schemes

- How to make the directory size independent of the number of processors

  o Basic idea is to have a bit vector scheme until the total number of sharers is not more than the directory entry width

  o When the number of sharers overflows the hardware resorts to an "overflow scheme"

    ◊ Dir_iB: i sharer bits, broadcast invalidation on overflow

    ◊ Dir_iNB: pick one sharer and invalidate it

- o Dir$_i$CV: assign one bit to a group of nodes of size P/i; broadcast invalidations to that group on a write

  - ◊ May generate useless invalidations

- Dir$_i$DP (Stanford FLASH)

  - o DP stands for dynamic pointer

  - o Allocate directory entries from a free list pool maintained in memory

  - o Need replacement hints

  - o Still may run into reclamation mode if free list pool is not sized properly at boot time

    - ◊ How do you size it?

  - o If replacement hints are not supported, assume k sharers on average per cache block (k=8 is found to be good)

  - o Reclamation algorithms?

    - ◊ Pick a random cache line and invalidate it

- Dir$_i$SW (MIT Alewife)

  - o Trap to software on overflow

  - o Software maintains the information about overflown sharers

  - o MIT Alewife has directory entry of five pointers and a local bit (i.e. overflow threshold is five or six)

    - ◊ Remote read before overflow takes 40 cycles and after overflow takes 425 cycles

    - ◊ Five invalidations take 84 cycles while six invalidations take 707 cycles

Sparse Directory

- How to reduce the height of the directory?

  - o Observation: total number of cache blocks in all processors is far less than total number of memory blocks

    - ◊ Assume a 32 MB L3 cache and 4 GB memory: less than 1% of directory entries are active at any point in time

  - o Idea is to organize directory as a highly associative cache

  - o On a directory entry "eviction" send invalidations to all sharers or retrieve line if dirty

Remote Access Cache

- Essentially a large tertiary cache

- o Captures remote cache blocks evicted from local cache hierarchy

- o Also visible to the coherence protocol: so inclusion must be maintained with processor caches

- o Must be highly associative and larger than the outermost level of cache

- o Usually part of DRAM is reserved for RAC

- o For multiprocessor nodes, requests from different processors to the same cache block can be merged together; also there is a prefetching effect

- o Used in Stanford DASH

- o Disadvantage: latency and space

COMA

- • Cache-only memory architecture

  - o Solves the space problem of RAC

  - o Home node only maintains the directory entries, but may not have the cache block in memory

  - o A node requesting a cache block brings it to its local memory and local cache as usual

  - o Entire memory is treated as a large tertiary cache

    - ◊ Known as the attraction memory (AM)

  - o Home as well as any node having a cache block maintain a directory entry for the cache block

  - o A request first looks up AM directory state and, if unowned, gets forwarded to home which, in turn, forwards it to one of the sharers

- • Cache-only memory architecture

  - o To start with home has the cache blocks

  - o It retains a cache block until it is replaced by some other migration

  - o There is always a master copy of each cache block

    - ◊ The last valid copy

  - o What happens on a replacement of the master copy?

    - ◊ Swap with source of migrating cache block

  - o Latency problem remains at the requester

  - o Inclusion problems between AM and processor cache hierarchy

    - ◊ Complicates the protocol

Latency Tolerance

- Page placement

  - Application-directed page placement is used in many cases to minimize the number of remote misses

  - The application provides the kernel (via system call) the starting address and ending address of a chunk of memory (multiple of pages) and also the node number where to map these pages

  - Thus an application writer can specify (based on sharing pattern) which shared pages he/she wants to map in a node's local memory (private pages and stack pages are mapped on local memory by default)

  - The page fault handler of a NUMA kernel is normally equipped with some default policies e.g., round robin mapping or first-touch mapping

  - Examples: matrix-vector multiplication, matrix transpose

- Software prefetching

  - Even after rigorous analysis of a parallel application it may not be possible to map all pages used by a node on its local memory: the same page may be used by multiple nodes at different times (example: matrix-vector multiplication)

  - Two options are available: dynamic page migration (very costly; coming next, stay tuned) or software prefetching

  - Today, most microprocessors support prefetch and prefetch exclusive instructions: use prefetch to initiate a cache line read miss long before application actually accesses it; use prefetch exclusive if you know for sure that you will write to the line and no one else will need the line before you write to it

  - Prefetches must be used carefully

    ◊ Swap with source of migrating cache block

    ◊ Early prefetches may evict useful cache blocks and itself may get evicted before use; may generate extra invalidations or interventions in multiprocessors

    ◊ Late prefetches may not be fully effective, but at least less harmful than early prefetches

    ◊ Wrong prefetches are most dangerous: these bring in cache blocks that may not be used at all in near-future; in multiprocessors this can severely hurt performance by generating extra invalidations and interventions

    ◊ Wrong prefetches waste bandwidth and pollute cache

  - Software prefetching usually offers better control than hardware prefetching

- Software prefetching vs. hardware prefetching

    o Software prefetching requires close analysis of program; profile information may help

    o Hardware prefetching tries to detect patterns in accessed addresses and using the detected patterns predicts future addresses

        ◊ AMD Athlon has a simple next line prefetcher (works perfectly for most numerical applications)

        ◊ Intel Pentium 4 has a very sophisticated stream prefetcher

Page Migration

- Page migration changes the existing VA to PA mapping of the migrated page

    o Requires notifying all TLBs caching the old mapping

    o Introduces a TLB coherence problem

- Origin 2000 uses a smart page migration algorithm: allows the page copy and TLB shootdown to proceed in parallel

    o Array of 64 page reference counters per directory entry to decide whether to migrate a page or not: compare requester's counter against home's and send an interrupt to home if migration is required

- What does the interrupt handler do?

    o Access all directory entries of the lines belonging to the to-be migrated page

    o Send invalidations to sharers or interventions to owners; at the end all cache lines of that page must be in memory

    o Set the poison bits in the directory entries of all the cache lines of the page

    o Start a block transfer of the page from home to requester at this point (30 μs to copy 16 KB)

- An access to a poisoned cache line from a node results in a bus error which invalidates the TLB entry for that page in the requesting node (avoids broadcast shootdown)

- Until the page is completely migrated and is assigned a physical page frame on target node, all nodes accessing a poisoned line wait in a pending queue

- After the page copy is completed the waiting nodes are served one by one; however, the directory entries and the page itself are moved to a "poisoned list" and are not yet freed at the home (i.e. you still cannot use that physical page frame)

- On every scheduler tick the kernel invalidates one TLB entry per processor

- After a time equal to TLB entries per processor multiplied by scheduling quantum the page frame is marked free and is removed from the poisoned list

- Major advantage: requesting nodes only see the page copy latency including invalidation and interventions in critical path, but not the TLB shootdown latency

Queue Lock in Hardware

- Stanford DASH
  - Memory controller recognizes lock accesses
    - ◊ Requires changes in compiler and instruction set
  - Marks the directory entry with contenders
  - On unlock a contender is chosen and lock is granted to that node
  - Unlock is forced to generate a notification message to home
    - ◊ Possibly requires special cache state for lock variables or special uncached instructions for unlock if lock variables are not allowed to be cached

AlphaServer GS320

- Recall that SGI Origin 2000 eliminates NACKs related to late and early interventions
  - Late interventions are replied by home via writeback forwarding
  - Early interventions are buffered at writer until write is completed
- Origin 2000 still uses NACKs if directory state is busy
- GS320 eliminates all NACKs
  - Simply doesn't have busy states
  - How do you serialize transactions?
- Eliminating PSH: dirty sharing
  - Same as a standard MOESI protocol, but state change in directory is immediate
  - Suppose node P0 is caching a block in M state
  - Node P1 issues a read request to home
  - Home forwards it to P0, changes directory state to clean, and marks P0 as the owner (need an owner field in directory)
  - P0 supplies data to P1 and moves to O state
    - ◊ P1 could also become O (is it better or worse?)
  - All subsequent requests are forwarded to P0 by home
  - P0 must serialize them properly
    - ◊ Philosophy: keep home free, serialize in the periphery

- Dirty sharing

  - Problem arises if owner evicts the cache block

  - Now home cannot figure out what to do

    ◊ Directory only specifies the sharers and the owner

    ◊ Home does not know exactly which sharers did not get the cache block from Po

    ◊ Home only writes the block back to memory, marks that there is no owner for this block, and sends a writeback acknowledgment to owner

  - Owner in all cases must source the cache block until the writeback is acknowledged

    ◊ Must hold evicted cache blocks in a writeback buffer

  - More problems: what if a request arrives at home before the WB, but reaches owner after the WB ACK?

- Dirty sharing

  - GS320 maintains total order in the network

    ◊ Needed by other optimizations related to invalidation acknowledgments also

  - What if the protocol allows the ownership to move along the sharer chain?

    ◊ New problem: writeback ordering

    ◊ Easy to resolve at home: only accept data from owner marked in the directory entry

    ◊ Always acknowledge writebacks

    ◊ Still need to rely on network order? No, if there are two types of writeback acknowledgments

- Eliminating the PDEX state: write forwarding

  - Same as read case with ownership changing along a chain

- Performance considerations

  - How will a migratory sharing pattern perform on GS320?

  - How will a large-scale producer-consumer pattern perform on GS320?

  - Any special considerations for LL/SC locks?

    ◊ Note that lock acquire is essentially a large-scale producer-consumer pattern with the number of consumers decreasing from P-1 to zero

Virtual Network: Case Studies

- Each virtual network consists of an NI queue in each direction connected to the corresponding queue or group of queues in the router

- SGI Origin 2000

  - Two virtual networks; uses back-off intervention and invalidation to avoid cycles in the network dependence graph

- Stanford DASH

  - Two virtual networks; in case an incoming request needs space in outgoing request network and outgoing request queue is full, it waits for a pre-defined number of cycles and then if still full, sends a NACK to the requester

- AlphaServer GS320

  - Three virtual networks; longest transaction is 3-hop

- Stanford FLASH

  - Four virtual networks; longest transaction is 4-hop (special case of reply generating a reply)

- Alpha 21364 router

  - 19 virtual channels (essentially queues) in each direction per port: 3 channels per virtual network, six coherence message types, one extra channel forms the seventh virtual network to carry some special coherence control messages (3 channels within a network are used for adaptive routing)

Coherence Controller Occupancy

- How long does it take to service a message on average?

  - If you imagine the coherence controller as a centralized server in a queuing model, occupancy is just the reciprocal of service rate

  - Occupancy of servicing a message induces a waiting time on the subsequent messages (shows up as a contention component in the total end-to-end latency)

    - ◊ Queuing analysis and simulation show that contention grows faster than quadratic in occupancy (Chaudhuri et al, 2003); later empirically confirmed by other researchers that it is likely to be sub-cubic

    - ◊ Goal should be to design low-occupancy protocols

Protocol Occupancy

- Goal is to design low-occupancy protocol

  - Doesn't mean cannot do smart things

  - A high-occupancy protocol can still perform well if it can reduce the message count accordingly

- o   Latency tolerating techniques such as prefetching usually puts more pressure on the coherence controller (why?)

  - ◊   Leads to an increased average protocol occupancy

- o   Some bad protocol decisions

  - ◊   Invalidation acknowledgments at home

  - ◊   Replacement hints

  - ◊   NACKs

- o   Final design is usually influenced by directory organization and coherence controller microarchitecture

Directory Controllers

- Two main designs

  - o   Hardwired finite state machines (fixed protocol)

  - o   Software protocol running on embedded protocol processor in memory controller (suited for off-chip memory controllers) or protocol thread in main processor (suited for multi-threaded processors) or protocol core in main processor (suited for multi-core processors)

- Hardwired FSM

  - o   Low occupancy (all-hardware)

  - o   Protocol must be simple enough to be able to design and verify in hardware

  - o   Possible to pipeline various stages of protocol processing

  - o   Cannot afford late-binding or flexibility in the choice of protocol

  - o   SGI Origin 2000, MIT Alewife, Stanford DASH

Flexible Protocol Engine

- Software protocol

  - o   Executes short sequences of instructions or micro-code known as protocol handlers on a processor

  - o   Each message type has a separate handler

  - o   Can make the protocol complicated

  - o   Allows late-binding of protocol, can choose appropriate protocol, easier verification path

  - o   Normally higher occupancy than hardwired controllers if controller clock is slow

- o Protocol processor may use separate protocol data and code caches to speed up protocol processing

- • Four existing designs

  - o Customized coprocessor embedded in memory controller

    - ◊ ISA designed to include bit field operations: helpful for directory manipulation (bit clear, bit set, branch on bit clear, branch on bit set, find first set bit, etc.)

    - ◊ Processor is normally simple e.g. short pipeline, in-order, no fp unit or mult/div

    - ◊ Example: Stanford FLASH, Sun S3.mp, Alpha Piranha CMP, Sequent STiNG, Sequent NUMA-Q

- • Four existing designs

  - o General purpose processor embedded in memory controller

    - ◊ Uses commodity processor cores

    - ◊ May be wasteful of resources

    - ◊ Normally higher occupancy than customized coprocessor if memory clock is slow

    - ◊ Example: Wisconsin Typhoon

- • Four existing designs

  - o Execute on main processor

    - ◊ Interrupt the main processor to execute coherence protocol on cache miss or network message arrival

    - ◊ Needs an extremely low overhead interrupt mechanism to be competitive

    - ◊ Grahn and Stenstrom (1995)

- • Four existing designs

  - o Execute on spare hardware thread context of multi-threaded (or hyper-threaded) processors

    - ◊ No interrupt overhead

    - ◊ Reserve a protocol thread context

    - ◊ Application and protocol threads co-exist in the processor (no context switch needed)

    - ◊ Chaudhuri and Heinrich (2004)

    - ◊ Can't discuss in detail before talking about SMT/HT

- Possible future design

  - Devote a core to protocol processing in multi-core architectures (Kalamkar, Chaudhuri, and Heinrich, 2007)

  - Increasingly attractive as number of cores increases

Sequent NUMA-Q

- Implements the IEEE SCI directory protocol

  - One node is an Intel Pentium Pro quad SMP

  - The IQ-Link board connects to the system bus and implements the directory protocol

    - ◊ Also contains a 32 MB 4-way set associative RAC

  - Processors within a node are kept coherent via a MESI snoop-based protocol already implemented in Pentium Pro quad

  - The SCI protocol keeps the RACs coherent across nodes

  - The RAC maintains inclusion with the processor caches

SCi Protocol

- Directory structure

  - Home contains the id of the most recently queued sharer or the owner (6 bits)

- Sharing list

  - A sharer contains the id of the next sharer and the previous sharer

  - The last sharer contains the id of home node and previous sharer

  - A circular doubly linked list

- Three major states in directory

  - Home: remotely unowned, but may be in local quad

  - Fresh: same as shared

  - Gone: some node has exclusive ownership; memory stale

- Cache states

  - Processor cache: MESI

  - RAC: 29 stable states and many transient states

    - ◊ 7 bits for representing RAC state

◊ Two-part naming of RAC state: first part says the location of the block in the list (ONLY, HEAD, TAIL, MID), second part mentions the actual state (modified, exclusive, fresh, copy, ...)

◊ We will use some of these to understand the basics of SCI (full description available from IEEE standards)

- HEAD_DIRTY, TAIL_CLEAN, etc

- Three major operations on the list

    o List construction: involves adding a new sharer to the list

    o Rollout: remove a sharer from the list; must synchronize with immediate neighbors

    o Purge/invalidate: head node always has write permission and so it can purge the entire list before writing; naturally, only the head node has the privilege of doing this

- Three classes of protocol

    o Minimal SCI: sharing not allowed

    o Typical SCI (will discuss this): all supports that a normal human being can imagine

    o Full SCI: lot of optimizations including hardware support for synchronization

Directory Overhead

- Directory overhead

    o Need 6 bits to maintain the head node id

        ◊ NUMA-Q scales up to 64 nodes

    o Need 2 bits for encoding three states: HOME, FRESH, GONE

    o A system with P nodes, M bytes of memory, and cache block size of B bytes has M/B cache blocks per node

        ◊ $2 + \log(P)$ bits needed for directory entry per cache block

        ◊ Total overhead = $(M/B)^*(\log(P) + O(1))^*P$

- $O(P^*\log(P))$

Cache Overhead

- Extended RAC tags for storing upstream and downstream pointers

    o $2^*\log(P)$ per cache block

    o Total increased tag DRAM area is $O(P^*\log(P))$

Handling Read Miss

- Requester on missing the RAC as well as quad snoop sends a read request to home

  o Allocates a block in RAC and marks its state PENDING

  o CASE A: directory is HOME state

    ◊ Change directory state to FRESH

    ◊ Change head pointer to requester id

    ◊ Send reply to requester

    ◊ Requester fills cache block in RAC, forwards it to requesting processor, changes RAC block state to ONLY_FRESH

  o CASE B: directory state is FRESH

    ◊ Home changes head pointer to requester id

    ◊ Sends reply with data read from memory and the old head node id

    ◊ Requester sends a request to the previous head expressing intention to become the new head

    ◊ Old head changes its upstream pointer to point to the requester and the RAC state to MID_VALID or TAIL_VALID; sends an acknowledgment to requester

    ◊ Requester changes its downstream pointer to old head and upstream pointer to home; also changes RAC line state to HEAD_FRESH

    ◊ Observe the strict request-reply nature of the protocol

  o CASE C: directory state is GONE

    ◊ Means head node has an exclusive copy of the cache line

    ◊ Home replies to the requester with the head node id, but does not change the state of the directory

    ◊ Requester sets RAC line state to PENDING and sends a data request to the head node

    ◊ Old head changes RAC line state to TAIL_VALID, sets its upstream pointer to the requester, and sends data to requester

    ◊ Requester sets RAC line state to HEAD_DIRTY, sets its upstream pointer to home and downstream pointer to old head

    ◊ Note that directory remains in GONE state and memory is not updated (similar to an M to O transition)

- Handling races

  - Suppose when the requester's (say A) message reaches the old head (say B) the RAC line is in PENDING state

  - SCI doesn't have any pending state in directory or doesn't use NACKs (actually uses, but small in number)

  - B does become the new head (has to because the home has already updated the directory), but inherits the PENDING state from A

  - Any subsequent request will come to B and will become the new pending head

  - Ultimately the PENDING state is resolved along the chain starting from A upstream

  - FIFO nature of the pending list guarantees fairness

  - Also, no problem related to sizing the buffers for holding pending requests (no extra space needed

Handling Write Miss

- CASE A: requester is in HEAD_DIRTY state already

  - Directory must be in GONE state

  - Only need to invalidate sharers

  - Requester sends an invalidation to the next sharer

  - A sharer upon receiving an invalidation sends a roll-out request to its next sharer (unless TAIL); the receiving node sets its upstream pointer properly and sends a roll-out acknowledgment

  - Eventually roll-out request is acknowledged, the sharer invalidates its RAC line and sends a reply back to head with the id of the next sharer

  - Head moves on to purge the sharer with received id

  - During the entire process requester's RAC line remains in PENDING state

  - Note that home is not at all involved here

- CASE B: requester is in ONLY_DIRTY state

  - No transaction needed

- CASE C: requester is in HEAD_FRESH state

  - Send state change request to home (FRESH to GONE)

  - Once acknowledgment from home is received list purging can be started

  - What if the home is in a state different from FRESH with a different head node?

    - ◊ The only case in SCI when a NACK is generated

◊   The requester on receiving the NACK changes its state to PENDING and initiates a new write request to home for transitioning to ONLY_DIRTY

- CASE D: requester in MID_FRESH or TAIL_FRESH state

  o   First it must roll out from the list and attach itself to the head in HEAD_FRESH state (recall that only the head node can write)

  o   This roll-out may require acknowledgments from upstream and downstream neighbors (if MID) or just the upstream neighbor (if TAIL)

  o   Follow CASE C

- CASE E: requester not a sharer

  o   First get the block in HEAD_DIRTY state

  o   Follow CASE A

Handling Writebacks

- Requires the evicting node to roll out

- Same for clean replacements also

- Dirty eviction (requiring a data transaction to home) can happen only from the head node

  o   Requires the head node to roll out

  o   Clean eviction can happen from any node in the list

    ◊   Does not require a transaction to home unless its state is ONLY_FRESH or HEAD_FRESH

    ◊   ONLY_FRESH eviction changes directory state from FRESH to HOME (i.e. no sharer)

    ◊   HEAD_FRESH eviction must update the head pointer in directory (directory state remains unchanged)

  o   Dirty eviction is completed first before initiating the miss generating the eviction

    ◊   Rationale is low complexity, and RAC eviction is rare

Roll-out Protocol

- Some details about the roll-out mechanism

  o   CASE A: rolling out from the middle of the list

    ◊   Request-acknowledgment protocol between the victim and its upstream and downstream neighbors

◊ If one of the neighbors is in PENDING state it can NACK the roll-out request; the requester must retry

◊ Problem arises when two adjacent nodes try to roll out simultaneously (nothing stops both nodes to replace the same cache line at the same time)

- Both will keep on NACKing each other leading to a livelock

- To break this cycle the node closer to tail is given priority (how do you know who is closer to tail?)

o Neighbors may need to change RAC state depending on situation (HEAD_DIRTY to ONLY_DIRTY or HEAD_FRESH to ONLY_FRESH)

- CASE B: Roll-out from head of the list

o Neighbor must update RAC state to reflect the fact that it is the new head

o Home also should be notified about the new head (directory state may not always change)

o Problem arises when the head change message reaching the home finds a totally new head already registered

◊ Means some other node is in the process of attaching itself to the head

◊ Home NACKs the roll-out

◊ Rolling out node remains in PENDING state and keeps on retrying until the request from the new would-be head arrives

◊ At this point the list goes back to stable state and the roll-out can complete

Snoop Interaction

- Interesting design problems arise due to limitations of the Pentium Pro quad

o The biggest problem is that the MESI protocol is designed for in-order response (so what?)

o Had to use the deferred response signal for remote requests

◊ Lesson learned: for hierarchical protocols bus must be split-transaction with out-of-order response (what happens otherwise?)

o Snoop response is available after four cycles earliest

◊ Stall wire may be asserted by any processor unable to meet this four-cycle limit

◊ Bus controller samples the stall wire every two cycles

o RAC and directory (for local requests) are also looked up in parallel

Protocol Processor

- NUMA-Q runs protocols in microcode

    o The protocol processor is customized with bit-field operations and is a three-stage dual issue pipeline

    o Has dedicated cache for holding recently accessed directory entries and RAC tags

    o Protocol processor also contains three counters for monitoring performance

        ◊ These counters can be programmed through protocol code (i.e. read and written to)

Non-uniform Memory Access

Non-uniform memory access (NUMA) is a computer memory design used in multiprocessing, where the memory access time depends on the memory location relative to the processor. Under NUMA, a processor can access its own local memory faster than non-local memory (memory local to another processor or memory shared between processors). The benefits of NUMA are limited to particular workloads, notably on servers where the data is often associated strongly with certain tasks or users.

NUMA architectures logically follow in scaling from symmetric multiprocessing (SMP) architectures. They were developed commercially during the 1990s by Burroughs (later Unisys), Convex Computer (later Hewlett-Packard), Honeywell Information Systems Italy (HISI) (later Groupe Bull), Silicon Graphics (later Silicon Graphics International), Sequent Computer Systems (later IBM), Data General (later EMC), and Digital (later Compaq, then HP, now HPE). Techniques developed by these companies later featured in a variety of Unix-like operating systems, and to an extent in Windows NT.

The first commercial implementation of a NUMA-based Unix system was the Symmetrical Multi Processing XPS-100 family of servers, designed by Dan Gielan of VAST Corporation for Honeywell Information Systems Italy.

Basic Concept

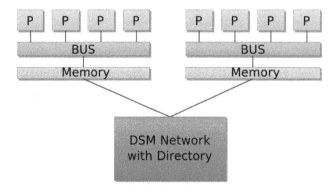

One possible architecture of a NUMA system. The processors connect to the bus or crossbar by connections of varying thickness/number. This shows that different CPUs have different access priorities to memory based on their relative location.

Modern CPUs operate considerably faster than the main memory they use. In the early days of computing and data processing, the CPU generally ran slower than its own memory. The performance lines of processors and memory crossed in the 1960s with the advent of the first supercomputers. Since then, CPUs increasingly have found themselves "starved for data" and having to stall while waiting for data to arrive from memory. Many supercomputer designs of the 1980s and 1990s focused on providing high-speed memory access as opposed to faster processors, allowing the computers to work on large data sets at speeds other systems could not approach.

Limiting the number of memory accesses provided the key to extracting high performance from a modern computer. For commodity processors, this meant installing an ever-increasing amount of high-speed cache memory and using increasingly sophisticated algorithms to avoid cache misses. But the dramatic increase in size of the operating systems and of the applications run on them has generally overwhelmed these cache-processing improvements. Multi-processor systems without NUMA make the problem considerably worse. Now a system can starve several processors at the same time, notably because only one processor can access the computer's memory at a time.

NUMA attempts to address this problem by providing separate memory for each processor, avoiding the performance hit when several processors attempt to address the same memory. For problems involving spread data (common for servers and similar applications), NUMA can improve the performance over a single shared memory by a factor of roughly the number of processors (or separate memory banks). Another approach to addressing this problem, used mainly in non-NUMA systems, is the multi-channel memory architecture, in which a linear increase in the number of memory channels increases the memory access concurrency linearly.

Of course, not all data ends up confined to a single task, which means that more than one processor may require the same data. To handle these cases, NUMA systems include additional hardware or software to move data between memory banks. This operation slows the processors attached to those banks, so the overall speed increase due to NUMA depends heavily on the nature of the running tasks.

AMD implemented NUMA with its Opteron processor (2003), using HyperTransport. Intel announced NUMA compatibility for its x86 and Itanium servers in late 2007 with its Nehalem and Tukwila CPUs. Both CPU families share a common chipset; the interconnection is called Intel Quick Path Interconnect (QPI).

Cache Coherent NUMA (ccNUMA)

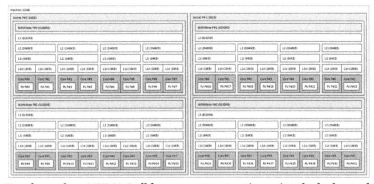

Topology of a ccNUMA Bulldozer server extracting using the hwloc tool.

Nearly all CPU architectures use a small amount of very fast non-shared memory known as cache to exploit locality of reference in memory accesses. With NUMA, maintaining cache coherence across shared memory has a significant overhead. Although simpler to design and build, non-cache-coherent NUMA systems become prohibitively complex to program in the standard von Neumann architecture programming model.

Typically, ccNUMA uses inter-processor communication between cache controllers to keep a consistent memory image when more than one cache stores the same memory location. For this reason, ccNUMA may perform poorly when multiple processors attempt to access the same memory area in rapid succession. Support for NUMA in operating systems attempts to reduce the frequency of this kind of access by allocating processors and memory in NUMA-friendly ways and by avoiding scheduling and locking algorithms that make NUMA-unfriendly accesses necessary.

Alternatively, cache coherency protocols such as the MESIF protocol attempt to reduce the communication required to maintain cache coherency. Scalable Coherent Interface (SCI) is an IEEE standard defining a directory-based cache coherency protocol to avoid scalability limitations found in earlier multiprocessor systems. For example, SCI is used as the basis for the NumaConnect technology.

As of 2011, ccNUMA systems are multiprocessor systems based on the AMD Opteron processor, which can be implemented without external logic, and the Intel Itanium processor, which requires the chipset to support NUMA. Examples of ccNUMA-enabled chipsets are the SGI Shub (Super hub), the Intel E8870, the HP sx2000 (used in the Integrity and Superdome servers), and those found in NEC Itanium-based systems. Earlier ccNUMA systems such as those from Silicon Graphics were based on MIPS processors and the DEC Alpha 21364 (EV7) processor.

NUMA vs. Cluster Computing

One can view NUMA as a tightly coupled form of cluster computing. The addition of virtual memory paging to a cluster architecture can allow the implementation of NUMA entirely in software. However, the inter-node latency of software-based NUMA remains several orders of magnitude greater (slower) than that of hardware-based NUMA.

Software Support

Since NUMA largely influences memory access performance, certain software optimizations are needed to allow scheduling threads and processes close to their in-memory data.

- Microsoft Windows 7 and Windows Server 2008 R2 added support for NUMA architecture over 64 logical cores.

- Java 7 added support for NUMA-aware memory allocator and garbage collector.

- Version 2.5 of the Linux kernel already contained basic NUMA support, which was further improved in subsequent kernel releases. Version 3.8 of the Linux kernel brought a new NUMA foundation that allowed development of more efficient NUMA policies in later kernel releases. Version 3.13 of the Linux kernel brought numerous policies that aim at putting a process near its memory, together with the handling of cases such as having memory pages shared between processes, or the use of transparent huge pages; new sysctl settings allow NUMA balancing to be enabled or disabled, as well as the configuration of various NUMA memory balancing parameters.

- OpenSolaris models NUMA architecture with lgroups.

- FreeBSD added Initial NUMA affinity and policy configuration in version 11.0

References

- Leffler, Samuel J.; McKusick, Marshall Kirk; Karels, Michael J.; Quarterman, John S. (Oc-tober 1989). The Design and Implementation of the 4.3BSD UNIX Operating System. Ad-dison-Wesley. ISBN 0-201-06196-1

- Nakul Manchanda; Karan Anand (2010-05-04). "Non-Uniform Memory Access (NUMA)" (PDF). New York University. Retrieved 2014-01-27

- Barnard III, G. A.; Fein, L. (1958). "Organization and Retrieval of Records Generated in a Large-Scale Engineering Project". Proceedings of the Eastern Joint Computer Conference: 59–63. doi:10.1109/AFIPS.1958.75

- Sergey Blagodurov; Sergey Zhuravlev; Mohammad Dashti; Alexandra Fedorov (2011-05-02). "A Case for NUMA-aware Contention Management on Multicore Systems" (PDF). Si-mon Fraser University. Retrieved 2014-01-27

- George Kraft IV (1 November 2000). "Where to Install My Products on Linux?". Linux Journal. Retrieved 13 November 2014

- Ritchie, D.M.; Thompson, K. (July 1978). "The UNIX Time-Sharing System". Bell System Tech. J. USA: AT&T. 57 (6): 1905–1929. doi:10.1002/j.1538-7305.1978.tb02136.x. Ar-chived from the original on 19 January 2013

- "Linux kernel 3.13, Section 1.6. Improved performance in NUMA systems". kernelnewbies. org. 2014-01-19. Retrieved 2014-02-06

Parallel Computing: A Comprehensive Study

Parallel computing ensures various computer processes can be run concurrently. There are various forms of parallel computing. Some of these are bit-level, task parallelism and instruction level. The chapter on parallel computing offers an insightful focus, keeping in mind the complex subject matter.

Parallel Computing

Parallel computing is a type of computation in which many calculations or the execution of processes are carried out simultaneously. Large problems can often be divided into smaller ones, which can then be solved at the same time. There are several different forms of parallel computing: bit-level, instruction-level, data, and task parallelism. Parallelism has been employed for many years, mainly in high-performance computing, but interest in it has grown lately due to the physical constraints preventing frequency scaling. As power consumption (and consequently heat generation) by computers has become a concern in recent years, parallel computing has become the dominant paradigm in computer architecture, mainly in the form of multi-core processors.

IBM's Blue Gene/P massively parallel supercomputer.

Parallel computing is closely related to concurrent computing—they are frequently used together, and often conflated, though the two are distinct: it is possible to have parallelism without concurrency (such as bit-level parallelism), and concurrency without parallelism (such as multitasking by time-sharing on a single-core CPU). In parallel computing, a computational task is typically broken down in several, often many, very similar subtasks that can be processed independently and whose results are combined afterwards, upon completion. In contrast, in concurrent computing, the various processes often do not address related tasks; when they do, as is typical in distributed computing, the separate tasks may have a varied nature and often require some inter-process communication during execution.

Parallel computers can be roughly classified according to the level at which the hardware supports parallelism, with multi-core and multi-processor computers having multiple processing elements within a single machine, while clusters, MPPs, and grids use multiple computers to work on the same task. Specialized parallel computer architectures are sometimes used alongside traditional processors, for accelerating specific tasks.

In some cases parallelism is transparent to the programmer, such as in bit-level or instruction-level parallelism, but explicitly parallel algorithms, particularly those that use concurrency, are more difficult to write than sequential ones, because concurrency introduces several new classes of potential software bugs, of which race conditions are the most common. Communication and synchronization between the different subtasks are typically some of the greatest obstacles to getting good parallel program performance.

A theoretical upper bound on the speed-up of a single program as a result of parallelization is given by Amdahl's law.

Background

Traditionally, computer software has been written for serial computation. To solve a problem, an algorithm is constructed and implemented as a serial stream of instructions. These instructions are executed on a central processing unit on one computer. Only one instruction may execute at a time—after that instruction is finished, the next one is executed.

Parallel computing, on the other hand, uses multiple processing elements simultaneously to solve a problem. This is accomplished by breaking the problem into independent parts so that each processing element can execute its part of the algorithm simultaneously with the others. The processing elements can be diverse and include resources such as a single computer with multiple processors, several networked computers, specialized hardware, or any combination of the above.

Frequency scaling was the dominant reason for improvements in computer performance from the mid-1980s until 2004. The runtime of a program is equal to the number of instructions multiplied by the average time per instruction. Maintaining everything else constant, increasing the clock frequency decreases the average time it takes to execute an instruction. An increase in frequency thus decreases runtime for all compute-bound programs.

However, power consumption P by a chip is given by the equation $P = C \times V^2 \times F$, where C is the capacitance being switched per clock cycle (proportional to the number of transistors whose inputs change), V is voltage, and F is the processor frequency (cycles per second). Increases in frequency increase the amount of power used in a processor. Increasing processor power consumption led ultimately to Intel's May 8, 2004 cancellation of its Tejas and Jayhawk processors, which is generally cited as the end of frequency scaling as the dominant computer architecture paradigm.

Moore's law is the empirical observation that the number of transistors in a microprocessor doubles every 18 to 24 months. Despite power consumption issues, and repeated predictions of its end, Moore's law is still in effect. With the end of frequency scaling, these additional transistors (which are no longer used for frequency scaling) can be used to add extra hardware for parallel computing.

Amdahl's Law and Gustafson's Law

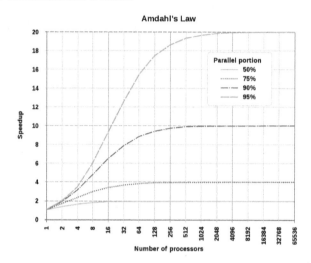

A graphical representation of Amdahl's law. The speedup of a program from parallelization is limited by how much of the program can be parallelized. For example, if 90% of the program can be parallelized, the theoretical maximum speedup using parallel computing would be 10 times no matter how many prozcessors are used.

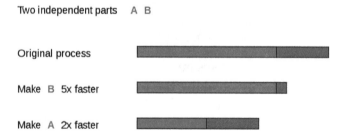

Assume that a task has two independent parts, *A* and *B*. Part *B* takes roughly 25% of the time of the whole computation. By working very hard, one may be able to make this part 5 times faster, but this only reduces the time for the whole computation by a little. In contrast, one may need to perform less work to make part *A* be twice as fast. This will make the computation much faster than by optimizing part *B*, even though part *B*'s speedup is greater by ratio, (5 times versus 2 times).

Optimally, the speedup from parallelization would be linear—doubling the number of processing elements should halve the runtime, and doubling it a second time should again halve the runtime. However, very few parallel algorithms achieve optimal speedup. Most of them have a near-linear speedup for small numbers of processing elements, which flattens out into a constant value for large numbers of processing elements.

The potential speedup of an algorithm on a parallel computing platform is given by Amdahl's law

$$S_{latency}(s) = \frac{1}{1 - p + \dfrac{p}{s}},$$

where

$S_{latency}$ is the potential speedup in latency of the execution of the whole task;

s is the speedup in latency of the execution of the parallelizable part of the task;

p is the percentage of the execution time of the whole task concerning the parallelizable part of the task *before parallelization.*

Since $S_{latency} < 1/(1 - p)$, it shows that a small part of the program which cannot be parallelized will limit the overall speedup available from parallelization. A program solving a large mathematical or engineering problem will typically consist of several parallelizable parts and several non-parallelizable (serial) parts. If the non-parallelizable part of a program accounts for 10% of the runtime ($p = 0.9$), we can get no more than a 10 times speedup, regardless of how many processors are added. This puts an upper limit on the usefulness of adding more parallel execution units. "When a task cannot be partitioned because of sequential constraints, the application of more effort has no effect on the schedule. The bearing of a child takes nine months, no matter how many women are assigned."

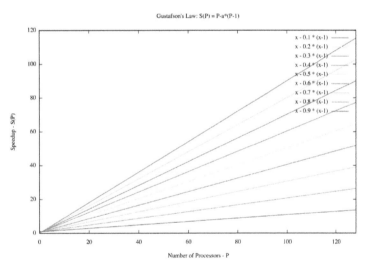

A graphical representation of Gustafson's law.

Amdahl's law only applies to cases where the problem size is fixed. In practice, as more computing resources become available, they tend to get used on larger problems (larger datasets), and the time spent in the parallelizable part often grows much faster than the inherently serial work. In this case, Gustafson's law gives a less pessimistic and more realistic assessment of parallel performance:

$$S_{latency}(s) = 1 - p + sp.$$

Both Amdahl's law and Gustafson's law assume that the running time of the serial part of the program is independent of the number of processors. Amdahl's law assumes that the entire problem is of fixed size so that the total amount of work to be done in parallel is also *independent of the number of processors,* whereas Gustafson's law assumes that the total amount of work to be done in parallel *varies linearly with the number of processors.*

Dependencies

Understanding data dependencies is fundamental in implementing parallel algorithms. No program can run more quickly than the longest chain of dependent calculations (known as the critical path), since calculations that depend upon prior calculations in the chain must be executed in order. However, most algorithms do not consist of just a long chain of dependent calculations; there are usually opportunities to execute independent calculations in parallel.

Let P_i and P_j be two program segments. Bernstein's conditions describe when the two are independent and can be executed in parallel. For P_i, let I_i be all of the input variables and O_i the output variables, and likewise for P_j. P_i and P_j are independent if they satisfy

$$I_j \cap O_i = \varnothing,$$
$$I_i \cap O_j = \varnothing,$$
$$O_i \cap O_j = \varnothing.$$

Violation of the first condition introduces a flow dependency, corresponding to the first segment producing a result used by the second segment. The second condition represents an anti-dependency, when the second segment produces a variable needed by the first segment. The third and final condition represents an output dependency: when two segments write to the same location, the result comes from the logically last executed segment.

Consider the following functions, which demonstrate several kinds of dependencies:

    1: function Dep(a, b)

    2: c := a * b

    3: d := 3 * c

    4: end function

In this example, instruction 3 cannot be executed before (or even in parallel with) instruction 2, because instruction 3 uses a result from instruction 2. It violates condition 1, and thus introduces a flow dependency.

    1: function NoDep(a, b)

    2: c := a * b

    3: d := 3 * b

    4: e := a + b

    5: end function

In this example, there are no dependencies between the instructions, so they can all be run in parallel.

Bernstein's conditions do not allow memory to be shared between different processes. For that, some means of enforcing an ordering between accesses is necessary, such as semaphores, barriers or some other synchronization method.

Race Conditions, Mutual Exclusion, Synchronization, and Parallel Slowdown

Subtasks in a parallel program are often called threads. Some parallel computer architectures use smaller, lightweight versions of threads known as fibers, while others use bigger versions known as processes. However, "threads" is generally accepted as a generic term for subtasks. Threads will often need to update some variable that is shared between them. The instructions between the two programs may be interleaved in any order. For example, consider the following program:

Thread A	Thread B
1A: Read variable V	1B: Read variable V
2A: Add 1 to variable V	2B: Add 1 to variable V
3A: Write back to variable V	3B: Write back to variable V

If instruction 1B is executed between 1A and 3A, or if instruction 1A is executed between 1B and 3B, the program will produce incorrect data. This is known as a race condition. The programmer must use a lock to provide mutual exclusion. A lock is a programming language construct that allows one thread to take control of a variable and prevent other threads from reading or writing it, until that variable is unlocked. The thread holding the lock is free to execute its critical section (the section of a program that requires exclusive access to some variable), and to unlock the data when it is finished. Therefore, to guarantee correct program execution, the above program can be rewritten to use locks:

Thread A	Thread B
1A: Lock variable V	1B: Lock variable V
2A: Read variable V	2B: Read variable V
3A: Add 1 to variable V	3B: Add 1 to variable V
4A: Write back to variable V	4B: Write back to variable V
5A: Unlock variable V	5B: Unlock variable V

One thread will successfully lock variable V, while the other thread will be locked out—unable to proceed until V is unlocked again. This guarantees correct execution of the program. Locks, while necessary to ensure correct program execution, can greatly slow a program.

Locking multiple variables using non-atomic locks introduces the possibility of program deadlock. An atomic lock locks multiple variables all at once. If it cannot lock all of them, it does not lock any of them. If two threads each need to lock the same two variables using non-atomic locks, it is possible that one thread will lock one of them and the second thread will lock the second variable. In such a case, neither thread can complete, and deadlock results.

Many parallel programs require that their subtasks act in synchrony. This requires the use of a barrier. Barriers are typically implemented using a software lock. One class of algorithms, known as lock-free and wait-free algorithms, altogether avoids the use of locks and barriers. However, this approach is generally difficult to implement and requires correctly designed data structures.

Not all parallelization results in speed-up. Generally, as a task is split up into more and more threads, those threads spend an ever-increasing portion of their time communicating with each other. Eventually, the overhead from communication dominates the time spent solving the problem, and further parallelization (that is, splitting the workload over even more threads) increases rather than decreases the amount of time required to finish. This is known as parallel slowdown.

Fine-grained, Coarse-grained, and Embarrassing Parallelism

Applications are often classified according to how often their subtasks need to synchronize or communicate with each other. An application exhibits fine-grained parallelism if its subtasks must communicate many times per second; it exhibits coarse-grained parallelism if they do not communicate many times per second, and it exhibits embarrassing parallelism if they rarely or never have to communicate. Embarrassingly parallel applications are considered the easiest to parallelize.

Consistency Models

Parallel programming languages and parallel computers must have a consistency model (also known as a memory model). The consistency model defines rules for how operations on computer memory occur and how results are produced.

One of the first consistency models was Leslie Lamport's sequential consistency model. Sequential consistency is the property of a parallel program that its parallel execution produces the same results as a sequential program. Specifically, a program is sequentially consistent if "... the results of any execution is the same as if the operations of all the processors were executed in some sequential order, and the operations of each individual processor appear in this sequence in the order specified by its program".

Software transactional memory is a common type of consistency model. Software transactional memory borrows from database theory the concept of atomic transactions and applies them to memory accesses.

Mathematically, these models can be represented in several ways. Petri nets, which were introduced in Carl Adam Petri's 1962 doctoral thesis, were an early attempt to codify the rules of consistency models. Dataflow theory later built upon these, and Dataflow architectures were created to physically implement the ideas of dataflow theory. Beginning in the late 1970s, process calculi such as Calculus of Communicating Systems and Communicating Sequential Processes were developed to permit algebraic reasoning about systems composed of interacting components. More recent additions to the process calculus family, such as the π-calculus, have added the capability for reasoning about dynamic topologies. Logics such as Lamport's TLA+, and mathematical models such as traces and Actor event diagrams, have also been developed to describe the behavior of concurrent systems.

Flynn's Taxonomy

Michael J. Flynn created one of the earliest classification systems for parallel (and sequential) computers and programs, now known as Flynn's taxonomy. Flynn classified programs and computers by whether they were operating using a single set or multiple sets of instructions, and whether or not those instructions were using a single set or multiple sets of data.

The single-instruction-single-data (SISD) classification is equivalent to an entirely sequential program. The single-instruction-multiple-data (SIMD) classification is analogous to doing the same operation repeatedly over a large data set. This is commonly done in signal processing applications. Multiple-instruction-single-data (MISD) is a rarely used classification. While computer architectures to deal with this were devised (such as systolic arrays), few applications that fit this class materialized. Multiple-instruction-multiple-data (MIMD) programs are by far the most common type of parallel programs.

According to David A. Patterson and John L. Hennessy, "Some machines are hybrids of these categories, of course, but this classic model has survived because it is simple, easy to understand, and gives a good first approximation. It is also—perhaps because of its understandability—the most widely used scheme."

Types of Parallelism

Bit-level Parallelism

From the advent of very-large-scale integration (VLSI) computer-chip fabrication technology in the 1970s until about 1986, speed-up in computer architecture was driven by doubling computer word size—the amount of information the processor can manipulate per cycle. Increasing the word size reduces the number of instructions the processor must execute to perform an operation on variables whose sizes are greater than the length of the word. For example, where an 8-bit processor must add two 16-bit integers, the processor must first add the 8 lower-order bits from each integer using the standard addition instruction, then add the 8 higher-order bits using an add-with-carry instruction and the carry bit from the lower order addition; thus, an 8-bit processor requires two instructions to complete a single operation, where a 16-bit processor would be able to complete the operation with a single instruction.

Historically, 4-bit microprocessors were replaced with 8-bit, then 16-bit, then 32-bit microprocessors. This trend generally came to an end with the introduction of 32-bit processors, which has been a standard in general-purpose computing for two decades. Not until the early twothousands, with the advent of x86-64 architectures, did 64-bit processors become commonplace.

Instruction-level Parallelism

A canonical processor without pipeline. It takes five clock cycles to complete one instruction and thus the processor can issue subscalar performance (IPC = 0.2 < 1).

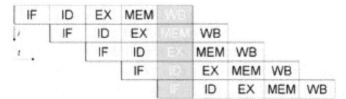

A canonical five-stage pipelined processor. In the best case scenario, it takes one clock cycle to complete one instruction and thus the processor can issue scalar performance (IPC = 1).

A computer program is, in essence, a stream of instructions executed by a processor. Without instruction-level parallelism, a processor can only issue less than one instruction per clock cycle (IPC < 1). These processors are known as *subscalar* processors. These instructions can be re-ordered and combined into groups which are then executed in parallel without changing the result of the program. This is known as instruction-level parallelism. Advances in instruction-level parallelism dominated computer architecture from the mid-1980s until the mid-1990s.

All modern processors have multi-stage instruction pipelines. Each stage in the pipeline corresponds to a different action the processor performs on that instruction in that stage; a processor with an N-stage pipeline can have up to N different instructions at different stages of completion and thus can issue one instruction per clock cycle (IPC = 1). These processors are known as *scalar* processors. The canonical example of a pipelined processor is a RISC processor, with five stages: instruction fetch (IF), instruction decode (ID), execute (EX), memory access (MEM), and register write back (WB). The Pentium 4 processor had a 35-stage pipeline.

IF	ID	EX	MEM	WB				
IF	ID	EX	MEM	WB				
	IF	ID	EX	MEM	WB			
	IF	ID	EX	MEM	WB			
		IF	ID	EX	MEM	WB		
		IF	ID	EX	MEM	WB		
			IF	ID	EX	MEM	WB	
			IF	ID	EX	MEM	WB	
				IF	ID	EX	MEM	WB
				IF	ID	EX	MEM	WB

A canonical five-stage pipelined superscalar processor. In the best case scenario, it takes one clock cycle to complete two instructions and thus the processor can issue superscalar performance (IPC = 2 > 1).

Most modern processors also have multiple execution units. They usually combine this feature with pipelining and thus can issue more than one instruction per clock cycle (IPC > 1). These processors are known as *superscalar* processors. Instructions can be grouped together only if there is no data dependency between them. Scoreboarding and the Tomasulo algorithm (which is similar to scoreboarding but makes use of register renaming) are two of the most common techniques for implementing out-of-order execution and instruction-level parallelism.

Task Parallelism

Task parallelisms is the characteristic of a parallel program that "entirely different calculations can be performed on either the same or different sets of data". This contrasts with data parallelism, where the same calculation is performed on the same or different sets of data. Task parallelism involves the decomposition of a task into sub-tasks and then allocating each sub-task to a processor for execution. The processors would then execute these sub-tasks simultaneously and often cooperatively. Task parallelism does not usually scale with the size of a problem.

Hardware

Memory and Communication

Main memory in a parallel computer is either shared memory (shared between all processing elements in a single address space), or distributed memory (in which each processing element has its own local address space). Distributed memory refers to the fact that the memory is logically distributed, but often implies that it is physically distributed as well. Distributed shared memory and memory virtualization combine the two approaches, where the processing element has its own local memory and access to the memory on non-local processors. Accesses to local memory are typically faster than accesses to non-local memory.

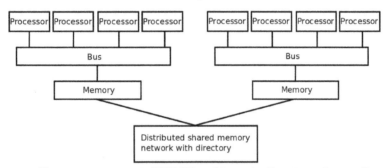

A logical view of a non-uniform memory access (NUMA) architecture. Processors in one directory can access that directory's memory with less latency than they can access memory in the other directory's memory.

Computer architectures in which each element of main memory can be accessed with equal latency and bandwidth are known as uniform memory access (UMA) systems. Typically, that can be achieved only by a shared memory system, in which the memory is not physically distributed. A system that does not have this property is known as a non-uniform memory access (NUMA) architecture. Distributed memory systems have non-uniform memory access.

Computer systems make use of caches—small and fast memories located close to the processor which store temporary copies of memory values (nearby in both the physical and logical sense). Parallel computer systems have difficulties with caches that may store the same value in more than one location, with the possibility of incorrect program execution. These computers require a cache coherency system, which keeps track of cached values and strategically purges them, thus ensuring correct program execution. Bus snooping is one of the most common methods for keeping track of which values are being accessed (and thus should be purged). Designing large, high-performance cache coherence systems is a very difficult problem in computer architecture. As a result, shared memory computer architectures do not scale as well as distributed memory systems do.

Processor–processor and processor–memory communication can be implemented in hardware in several ways, including via shared (either multiported or multiplexed) memory, a crossbar switch, a shared bus or an interconnect network of a myriad of topologies including star, ring, tree, hypercube, fat hypercube (a hypercube with more than one processor at a node), or n-dimensional mesh.

Parallel computers based on interconnected networks need to have some kind of routing to enable the passing of messages between nodes that are not directly connected. The medium used for communication between the processors is likely to be hierarchical in large multiprocessor machines.

Classes of Parallel Computers

Parallel computers can be roughly classified according to the level at which the hardware supports parallelism. This classification is broadly analogous to the distance between basic computing nodes. These are not mutually exclusive; for example, clusters of symmetric multiprocessors are relatively common.

Multi-core Computing

A multi-core processor is a processor that includes multiple processing units (called "cores") on the same chip. This processor differs from a superscalar processor, which includes multiple execution units and can issue multiple instructions per clock cycle from one instruction stream (thread); in contrast, a multi-core processor can issue multiple instructions per clock cycle from multiple instruction streams. IBM's Cell microprocessor, designed for use in the Sony PlayStation 3, is a prominent multi-core processor. Each core in a multi-core processor can potentially be superscalar as well—that is, on every clock cycle, each core can issue multiple instructions from one thread.

Simultaneous multithreading (of which Intel's Hyper-Threading is the best known) was an early form of pseudo-multi-coreism. A processor capable of simultaneous multithreading includes multiple execution units in the same processing unit—that is it has a superscalar architecture—and can issue multiple instructions per clock cycle from *multiple* threads. Temporal multithreading on the other hand includes a single execution unit in the same processing unit and can issue one instruction at a time from *multiple* threads.

Symmetric Multiprocessing

A symmetric multiprocessor (SMP) is a computer system with multiple identical processors that share memory and connect via a bus. Bus contention prevents bus architectures from scaling. As a result, SMPs generally do not comprise more than 32 processors. Because of the small size of the processors and the significant reduction in the requirements for bus bandwidth achieved by large caches, such symmetric multiprocessors are extremely cost-effective, provided that a sufficient amount of memory bandwidth exists.

Distributed Computing

A distributed computer (also known as a distributed memory multiprocessor) is a distributed memory computer system in which the processing elements are connected by a network. Distributed computers are highly scalable.

Cluster Computing

A cluster is a group of loosely coupled computers that work together closely, so that in some respects they can be regarded as a single computer. Clusters are composed of multiple standalone machines connected by a network. While machines in a cluster do not have to be symmetric, load balancing is more difficult if they are not. The most common type of cluster is the Beowulf cluster, which is a cluster implemented on multiple identical commercial off-the-shelf computers connected with a TCP/IP Ethernet local area network. Beowulf technology was originally developed by Thomas Sterling and Donald Becker. The vast majority of the TOP500 supercomputers are clusters.

A Beowulf cluster.

Because grid computing systems (described below) can easily handle embarrassingly parallel problems, modern clusters are typically designed to handle more difficult problems—problems that require nodes to share intermediate results with each other more often. This requires a high bandwidth and, more importantly, a low-latency interconnection network. Many historic and current supercomputers use customized high-performance network hardware specifically designed for cluster computing, such as the Cray Gemini network. As of 2014, most current supercomputers use some off-the-shelf standard network hardware, often Myrinet, InfiniBand, or Gigabit Ethernet.

Massively Parallel Computing

A cabinet from IBM's Blue Gene/L massively parallel supercomputer.

A massively parallel processor (MPP) is a single computer with many networked processors. MPPs have many of the same characteristics as clusters, but MPPs have specialized interconnect networks (whereas clusters use commodity hardware for networking). MPPs also tend to be larger than clusters, typically having "far more" than 100 processors. In an MPP, "each CPU contains its own memory and copy of the operating system and application. Each subsystem communicates with the others via a high-speed interconnect."

IBM's Blue Gene/L, the fifth fastest supercomputer in the world according to the June 2009 TOP500 ranking, is an MPP.

Grid Computing

Grid computing is the most distributed form of parallel computing. It makes use of computers communicating over the Internet to work on a given problem. Because of the low bandwidth and extremely high latency available on the Internet, distributed computing typically deals only with embarrassingly parallel problems. Many distributed computing applications have been created, of which SETI@home and Folding@home are the best-known examples.

Most grid computing applications use middleware (software that sits between the operating system and the application to manage network resources and standardize the software interface). The most common distributed computing middleware is the Berkeley Open Infrastructure for Network Computing (BOINC). Often, distributed computing software makes use of "spare cycles", performing computations at times when a computer is idling.

Specialized Parallel Computers

Within parallel computing, there are specialized parallel devices that remain niche areas of interest. While not domain-specific, they tend to be applicable to only a few classes of parallel problems.

Reconfigurable Computing with Field-programmable Gate Arrays

Reconfigurable computing is the use of a field-programmable gate array (FPGA) as a co-processor to a general-purpose computer. An FPGA is, in essence, a computer chip that can rewire itself for a given task.

FPGAs can be programmed with hardware description languages such as VHDL or Verilog. However, programming in these languages can be tedious. Several vendors have created C to HDL languages that attempt to emulate the syntax and semantics of the C programming language, with which most programmers are familiar. The best known C to HDL languages are Mitrion-C, Impulse C, DIME-C, and Handel-C. Specific subsets of SystemC based on C++ can also be used for this purpose.

AMD's decision to open its HyperTransport technology to third-party vendors has become the enabling technology for high-performance reconfigurable computing. According to Michael R. D'Amour, Chief Operating Officer of DRC Computer Corporation, "when we first walked into AMD, they called us 'the socket stealers.' Now they call us their partners."

General-purpose Computing on Graphics Processing Units (GPGPU)

General-purpose computing on graphics processing units (GPGPU) is a fairly recent trend in computer engineering research. GPUs are co-processors that have been heavily optimized for computer graphics processing. Computer graphics processing is a field dominated by data parallel operations—particularly linear algebra matrix operations.

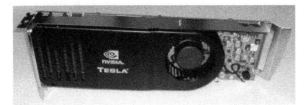

Nvidia's Tesla GPGPU card

In the early days, GPGPU programs used the normal graphics APIs for executing programs. However, several new programming languages and platforms have been built to do general purpose computation on GPUs with both Nvidia and AMD releasing programming environments with CUDA and Stream SDK respectively. Other GPU programming languages include BrookGPU, PeakStream, and RapidMind. Nvidia has also released specific products for computation in their Tesla series. The technology consortium Khronos Group has released the OpenCL specification, which is a framework for writing programs that execute across platforms consisting of CPUs and GPUs. AMD, Apple, Intel, Nvidia and others are supporting OpenCL.

Application-specific Integrated Circuits

Several application-specific integrated circuit (ASIC) approaches have been devised for dealing with parallel applications.

Because an ASIC is (by definition) specific to a given application, it can be fully optimized for that application. As a result, for a given application, an ASIC tends to outperform a general-purpose computer. However, ASICs are created by UV photolithography. This process requires a mask set, which can be extremely expensive. A mask set can cost over a million US dollars. (The smaller the transistors required for the chip, the more expensive the mask will be.) Meanwhile, performance increases in general-purpose computing over time (as described by Moore's law) tend to wipe out these gains in only one or two chip generations. High initial cost, and the tendency to be overtaken by Moore's-law-driven general-purpose computing, has rendered ASICs unfeasible for most parallel computing applications. However, some have been built. One example is the PFLOPS RIKEN MDGRAPE-3 machine which uses custom ASICs for molecular dynamics simulation.

Vector Processors

The Cray-1 is a vector processor.

A vector processor is a CPU or computer system that can execute the same instruction on large sets of data. Vector processors have high-level operations that work on linear arrays of numbers or vectors. An example vector operation is $A = B \times C$, where A, B, and C are each 64-element vectors of 64-bit floating-point numbers. They are closely related to Flynn's SIMD classification.

Cray computers became famous for their vector-processing computers in the 1970s and 1980s. However, vector processors—both as CPUs and as full computer systems—have generally disappeared. Modern processor instruction sets do include some vector processing instructions, such as with Freescale Semiconductor's AltiVec and Intel's Streaming SIMD Extensions (SSE).

Software

Parallel Programming Languages

Concurrent programming languages, libraries, APIs, and parallel programming models (such as algorithmic skeletons) have been created for programming parallel computers. These can generally be divided into classes based on the assumptions they make about the underlying memory architecture—shared memory, distributed memory, or shared distributed memory. Shared memory programming languages communicate by manipulating shared memory variables. Distributed memory uses message passing. POSIX Threads and OpenMP are two of the most widely used shared memory APIs, whereas Message Passing Interface (MPI) is the most widely used message-passing system API. One concept used in programming parallel programs is the future concept, where one part of a program promises to deliver a required datum to another part of a program at some future time.

CAPS entreprise and Pathscale are also coordinating their effort to make hybrid multi-core parallel programming (HMPP) directives an open standard called OpenHMPP. The OpenHMPP directive-based programming model offers a syntax to efficiently offload computations on hardware accelerators and to optimize data movement to/from the hardware memory. OpenHMPP directives describe remote procedure call (RPC) on an accelerator device (e.g. GPU) or more generally a set of cores. The directives annotate C or Fortran codes to describe two sets of functionalities: the offloading of procedures (denoted codelets) onto a remote device and the optimization of data transfers between the CPU main memory and the accelerator memory.

The rise of consumer GPUs has led to support for compute kernels, either in graphics APIs (referred to as compute shaders), in dedicated APIs (such as OpenCL), or in other language extensions.

Automatic Parallelization

Automatic parallelization of a sequential program by a compiler is the holy grail of parallel computing. Despite decades of work by compiler researchers, automatic parallelization has had only limited success.

Mainstream parallel programming languages remain either explicitly parallel or (at best) partially implicit, in which a programmer gives the compiler directives for parallelization. A few fully implicit parallel programming languages exist—SISAL, Parallel Haskell, SequenceL, System C (for FPGAs), Mitrion-C, VHDL, and Verilog.

Application Checkpointing

As a computer system grows in complexity, the mean time between failures usually decreases. Application checkpointing is a technique whereby the computer system takes a "snapshot" of the application—a record of all current resource allocations and variable states, akin to a core dump—; this information can be used to restore the program if the computer should fail. Application checkpointing means that the program has to restart from only its last checkpoint rather than the beginning. While checkpointing provides benefits in a variety of situations, it is especially useful in highly parallel systems with a large number of processors used in high performance computing.

Algorithmic Methods

As parallel computers become larger and faster, it becomes feasible to solve problems that previously took too long to run. Parallel computing is used in a wide range of fields, from bioinformatics (protein folding and sequence analysis) to economics (mathematical finance). Common types of problems found in parallel computing applications are:

- dense linear algebra;

- sparse linear algebra;

- spectral methods (such as Cooley–Tukey fast Fourier transform)

- N-body problems (such as Barnes–Hut simulation);

- structured grid problems (such as Lattice Boltzmann methods);

- unstructured grid problems (such as found in finite element analysis);

- Monte Carlo method;

- combinational logic (such as brute-force cryptographic techniques);

- graph traversal (such as sorting algorithms);

- dynamic programming;

- branch and bound methods;

- graphical models (such as detecting hidden Markov models and constructing Bayesian networks);

- finite-state machine simulation.

Fault-tolerance

Parallel computing can also be applied to the design of fault-tolerant computer systems, particularly via lockstep systems performing the same operation in parallel. This provides redundancy in case one component should fail, and also allows automatic error detection and error correction if the results differ. These methods can be used to help prevent single event upsets caused by transient errors. Although additional measures may be required in embedded or specialized systems, this method can provide a cost effective approach to achieve n-modular redundancy in commercial off-the-shelf systems.

History

ILLIAC IV, "the most infamous of supercomputers".

The origins of true (MIMD) parallelism go back to Luigi Federico Menabrea and his *Sketch of the Analytic Engine Invented by Charles Babbage.*

In April 1958, S. Gill (Ferranti) discussed parallel programming and the need for branching and waiting. Also in 1958, IBM researchers John Cocke and Daniel Slotnick discussed the use of parallelism in numerical calculations for the first time. Burroughs Corporation introduced the D825 in 1962, a four-processor computer that accessed up to 16 memory modules through a crossbar switch. In 1967, Amdahl and Slotnick published a debate about the feasibility of parallel processing at American Federation of Information Processing Societies Conference. It was during this debate that Amdahl's law was coined to define the limit of speed-up due to parallelism.

In 1969, company Honeywell introduced its first Multics system, a symmetric multiprocessor system capable of running up to eight processors in parallel. C.mmp, a 1970s multi-processor project at Carnegie Mellon University, was among the first multiprocessors with more than a few processors. The first bus-connected multiprocessor with snooping caches was the Synapse N+1 in 1984."

SIMD parallel computers can be traced back to the 1970s. The motivation behind early SIMD computers was to amortize the gate delay of the processor's control unit over multiple instructions. In 1964, Slotnick had proposed building a massively parallel computer for the Lawrence Livermore National Laboratory. His design was funded by the US Air Force, which was the earliest SIMD parallel-computing effort, ILLIAC IV. The key to its design was a fairly high parallelism, with up to 256 processors, which allowed the machine to work on large datasets in what would later be known as vector processing. However, ILLIAC IV was called "the most infamous of supercomputers", because the project was only one fourth completed, but took 11 years and cost almost four times the original estimate. When it was finally ready to run its first real application in 1976, it was outperformed by existing commercial supercomputers such as the Cray-1.

Consistency Model

In computer science, Consistency models are used in distributed systems like distributed shared memory systems or distributed data stores (such as a filesystems, databases, optimistic replication systems or Web caching). The system is said to support a given model if operations on memory follow specific rules. The data consistency model specifies a contract between programmer and system, wherein the system guarantees that if the programmer follows the rules, memory will be consistent and the results of memory operations will be predictable. This is different from Cache coherence, an issue that occurs in systems that are cached or cache-less is consistency of data with respect to all processors. This is not handled by Coherence as coherence deals with maintaining a global order in which writes only to a single location or a single variable are seen by all processors. Consistency deals with the ordering of operations to multiple locations with respect to all processors.

High level languages, such as C++ and Java, partially maintain the contract by translating memory operations into low-level operations in a way that preserves memory semantics. To hold to the contract, compilers may reorder some memory instructions, and library calls such as pthread_mutex_lock() encapsulate required synchronization.

Verifying sequential consistency through model checking is undecidable in general, even for finite-state cache-coherence protocols.

Consistency models define rules for the apparent order and visibility of updates, and it is a continuum with tradeoffs.

Example

Assume that the following case occurs:

- The row X is replicated on nodes M and N
- The client A writes row X to node N
- After a period of time t, client B reads row X from node M

The consistency model has to determine whether client B sees the write from client A or not.

Types

There are two methods to define and categorize consistency models; issue and view.

Issue: Issue method describes the restrictions that define how a process can issue operations.

View: View method which defines the order of operations visible to processes.

For example, a consistency model can define that a process is not allowed to issue an operation until all previously issued operations are completed. Different consistency models enforce different conditions. One consistency model can be considered stronger than another if it requires all conditions of that model and more. In other words, a model with fewer constraints is considered a weaker consistency model.

These models define how the hardware needs to be laid out and at high-level, how the programmer must code. The chosen model also affects how the compiler can re-order instructions. Generally, if control dependencies between instructions and if writes to same location are ordered, then the compiler can reorder as required. However, with the models described below, some may allow Writes before Loads to be reordered while some may not.

Strict Consistency

Strict consistency is the strongest consistency model. Under this model, a write to a variable by any processor needs to be seen instantaneously by all processors. The Strict model diagram and non-Strict model diagrams describe the time constraint – instantaneous. It can be better understood as though a global clock is present in which every write should be reflected in all processor caches by the end of that clock period. The next operation must happen only in the next clock period.

P_1: $W(x)1$	P_1: $W(x)1$
P_2: $R(x)1$	P_2: $R(x)0$ $R(x)1$
Strict Model	Non-strict Model

This is the most rigid model and is impossible to implement without forgoing performance. In this model, the programmer's expected result will be received every time. It is deterministic. A distributed system with many nodes will take some time to copy information written to one node to all the other nodes responsible for replicating that information. That time can't be zero because it takes time for information to propagate through space, and there is a limit to how fast information can travel through space: the speed of light. Therefore, strict consistency is impossible. The best one can do is design a system where the time-to-replicate approaches the theoretical minimum.

Sequential Consistency

The sequential consistency model is a weaker memory model than strict consistency. A write to a variable does not have to be seen instantaneously, however, writes to variables by different processors have to be seen in the same order by all processors. As defined by Lamport(1979), Sequential Consistency is met if "the result of any execution is the same as if the operations of all the processors were executed in some sequential order, and the operations of each individual processor appear in this sequence in the order specified by its program."

Program order within each processor and sequential ordering of operations between processors should be maintained. In order to preserve sequential order of execution between processors, all operations must appear to execute instantaneously or atomically with respect to every other processor. These operations need only "appear" to be completed because it is physically impossible to send information instantaneously. For instance, once a bus line is posted with information, It is guaranteed that all processors will see the information at the same instant. Thus, passing the information to the bus line completes the execution with respect to all processors and has appeared to have been executed. Cache-less architectures or cached architectures with interconnect networks that are not instantaneous can contain a slow path between processors and memories. These slow paths can result in sequential inconsistency, because some memories receive the broadcast data faster than others.

Sequential consistency can produce non-deterministic results. This is because the sequence of sequential operations between processors can be different during different runs of the program. All memory operations need to happen in the program order.

Linearizability (also known as atomic consistency) can be defined as sequential consistency with the real-time constraint.

Causal Consistency

Causal consistency is a weakening model of sequential consistency by categorizing events into those causally related and those that are not. It defines that only write operations that are causally related need to be seen in the same order by all processes.

This model relaxes Sequential consistency on concurrent writes by a processor and on writes that are not causally related. Two writes can become causally related if one write to a variable is dependent on a previous write to any variable if the processor doing the second write has just read the first write. The two writes could have been done by the same processor or by different processors.

As in sequential consistency, reads do not need to reflect changes instantaneously, however, they need to reflect all changes to a variable sequentially.

$$P1: W_1(x)3$$
$$P2: W_2(x)5 \ R_1(x)3$$

W_1 is not causally related to W_2. R1 would be Sequentially Inconsistent but is Causally consistent.

$P1$:W(x)1		W(x)3	
$P2$:R(x)1	W(x)2		
$P3$:R(x)1		R(x)3	R(x)2
$P4$:R(x)1		R(x)2	R(x)3

W(x)1 and W(x) 2 are causally related due to the read made by P2 to x before W(x)2.

Processor Consistency

In order for consistency in data to be maintained and to attain scalable processor systems where every processor has its own memory, the Processor consistency model was derived. All processors need to be consistent in the order in which they see writes done by one processor and in the way they see writes by different processors to the same location (coherence is maintained). However, they do not need to be consistent when the writes are by different processors to different locations.

Every write operation can be divided into several sub-writes to all memories. A read from one such memory can happen before the write to this memory completes. Therefore, the data read can be stale. Thus, a processor under PC can execute a younger load when an older store needs to be stalled. Read before Write, Read after Read and Write before Write ordering is still preserved in this model.

The processor consistency model is similar to PRAM consistency model with a stronger condition that defines all writes to the same memory location must be seen in the same sequential order by all other processes. Process consistency is weaker than sequential consistency but stronger than PRAM consistency model.

The Stanford DASH multiprocessor system implements a variation of processor consistency which is incomparable (neither weaker nor stronger) to Goodmans definitions. All processors need to be consistent in the order in which they see writes by one processor and in the way they see writes by different processors to the same location. However, they do not need to be consistent when the writes are by different processors to different locations.

PRAM Consistency (Also known as FIFO Consistency)

PRAM consistency (Pipelined RAM) was presented by Lipton and Sandberg in 1988 as one of the first described consistency models. Due to its informal definition, there are in fact at least two subtle different implementations, one by Ahamad et al. and one by Mosberger.

In PRAM consistency, all processes view the operations of a single process in the same order that they were issued by that process, while operations issued by different processes can be viewed in different order from different processes. PRAM consistency is weaker than processor consistency. PRAM relaxes the need to maintain coherence to a location across all its processors. Here, reads to any variable can be executed before writes in a processor. Read before Write, Read after Read and Write before Write ordering is still preserved in this model.

P1:	W(x)1				
P2:		R(x)1	W(x)2		
P3:				R(x)1	R(x)2
P4:				R(x)2	R(x)1

Cache Consistency

Cache consistency requires that all write operations to the same memory location are performed in some sequential order. Cache consistency is weaker than process consistency and incomparable with PRAM consistency.

Slow Consistency

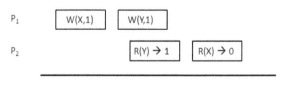

Slow Memory

In slow consistency, if a process reads a value previously written to a memory location, it cannot subsequently read any earlier value from that location. Writes performed by a process are immediately visible to that process. Slow consistency is a weaker model than PRAM and cache consistency.

Example: Slow memory diagram depicts a slow consistency example. The first process writes 1 to the memory location X and then it writes 1 to the memory location Y. The second process reads 1 from Y and it then reads 0 from X even though X was written before Y.

Hutto, Phillip W., and Mustaque Ahamad (1990) illustrate that by appropriate programming, slow memory (consistency) can be expressive and efficient. They mention that slow memory has two valuable properties; locality and supporting reduction from atomic memory. They propose two algorithms to present the expressiveness of slow memory.

The following models require specific synchronization by programmers.

Weak Ordering

Program order and atomicity is maintained only on a group of operations and not on all reads and writes. This was derived from the understanding that certain memory operations – such as those conducted in a critical section - need not be seen by all processors – until after all operations in the critical section are completed for instance. It also exploits the fact that programs written to be executed on a multi-processor system contain the required synchronization to make sure that data races do not occur and SC outcomes are produced always. Thus, in weak ordering, operations other than synchronization operations can be classified as *data* operations.

P1	P2
X = 1;	*fence*
fence	while(!xready) {};
xready =	*fence*
1;	
	y = 2;

Synchronization operations signal the processor to make sure it has completed and seen all previous operations done by all processors. In order to maintain Weak ordering, write operations prior to a synchronization operation must be globally performed before the synchronization operation. Operations present in after a synchronization operation should also be performed only after the synchronization operation completes. Therefore, accesses to synchronization variables is sequentially consistent and any read or write should be performed only after previous synchronization operations have completed. Coherence is not relaxed in this model. Once these requirements are met, all other "data" operations can be reordered.

There is high reliance on explicit synchronization in the program. For weak ordering models, the programmer must use atomic locking instructions such as test-and-set, fetch-and-op, store conditional, load linked or must label synchronization variables or use fences.

Release Consistency

This model relaxes the Weak consistency model by distinguishing the entrance synchronization operation from the exit synchronization operation. Under weak ordering, when a synchronization operation is to be seen, all operations in all processors need to be visible before the Synchronization operation is done and the processor proceeds. However, under Release consistency model, during the entry to a critical section, termed as "acquire", all operations with respect to the local memory variables need to be completed. During the exit, termed as "release", all changes made by the local processor should be propagated to all other processors. Coherence is still maintained.

The acquire operation is a load/read that is performed to access the critical section. A release operation is a store/write performed to allow other processors use the shared variables.

Among synchronization variables, sequential consistency or processor consistency can be maintained. Using SC, all competing synchronization variables should be processed in order. However, with PC, a pair of competing variables need to only follow this order. Younger Acquires can be allowed to happen before older Releases.

Entry Consistency

This is a variant of the Release Consistency model. It also requires the use of Acquire and Release instructions to explicitly state an entry or exit to a critical section. However, under Entry Consistency, every shared variable is assigned a synchronization variable specific to it. This way, only when the Acquire is to variable x, all operations related to x need to be completed with respect to that processor. This allows concurrent operations of different critical sections of different shared variables to occur. Concurrency cannot be seen for critical operations on the same shared variable. Such a consistency model will be useful when different matrix elements can be processed at the same time.

General Consistency

In general consistency, all the copies of a memory location are eventually identical after all processes' writes are completed.

Local Consistency

In local consistency, each process performs its own operations in the order defined by its program. There is no constraint on the ordering in which the write operations of other processes appear to be performed. Local consistency is the weakest consistency model in shared memory systems.

Some other consistency models are as follows:

- Causal+ Consistency
- Delta consistency
- Eventual consistency
- Fork consistency
- One-copy serializability
- Serializability
- Vector-field consistency
- Weak consistency
- Strong consistency

Several other consistency models have been conceived to express restrictions with respect to ordering or visibility of operations, or to deal with specific fault assumptions.

Relaxed Memory Consistency Models

Some different consistency models can be defined by relaxing one or more requirements in sequential consistency called relaxed consistency models. These consistency models do not provide memory consistency at the hardware level. In fact, the programmers are responsible for implementing the memory consistency by applying synchronization techniques. The above models are classified based on four criteria and are detailed further.

There are four comparisons to define the relaxed consistency:

- Relaxation: One way to categorize the relaxed consistency is to define which sequential consistency requirements are relaxed. We can have less strict models by relaxing either program order or write atomicity requirements defined by Adve and Gharachorloo, 1996. Program order guarantees that each process issues a memory request ordered by its program and write atomicity defines that memory requests are serviced based on the order of a single FIFO queue. In relaxing program order, any or all the ordering of operation pairs, write-after-write, read-after-write, or read/write-after-read, can be relaxed. In the relaxed write atomicity model, a process can view its own writes before any other processors.

- Synchronizing vs. Non-Synchronizing: A synchronizing model can be defined by dividing the memory accesses into two groups and assigning different consistency restrictions to each group considering that one group can have a weak consistency model while the other one needs a more restrictive consistency model. In contrast, a non-synchronizing Model assigns the same consistency model to the memory access types.

- Issue vs. View-Based: Issue method provides sequential consistency simulation by defining the restrictions for processes to issue memory operations. Whereas, view method describes the visibility restrictions on the events order for processes.

- Relative Model Strength: Some consistency models are more restrictive than others. In other words, strict consistency models enforce more constraints as consistency requirements. The strength of a model can be defined by the program order or atomicity relaxations and the strength of models can also be compared. Some models are directly related if they apply same relaxations or more. On the other hand, the models that relax different requirements are not directly related.

Sequential consistency has two requirements, program order and write atomicity. Different relaxed consistency models can be obtained by relaxing these requirements. This is done so that, along with relaxed constraints, the performance increases, but the programmer is responsible for implementing the memory consistency by applying synchronisation techniques and must have a good understanding of the hardware.

Potential relaxations:

- Write to Read program order

- Write to Write program order

- Read to Read and Read to Write program orders

Relaxation Models

The following models are some models of relaxed consistency:

Relaxed Write to Read

An approach to improving the performance at the hardware level is by relaxing the PO of a write followed by a read which effectively hides the latency of write operations. The optimisation this type of relaxation relies on is that it allows the subsequent reads to be in a relaxed order with respect to the previous writes from he processor. Because of this relaxation some programs like XXX may fail to give SC results because of this relaxation. Whereas, programs like YYY are still expected to give consistent results because of the enforcement of the remaining program order constraints.

Three models fall under this category. IBM 370 model is the strictest model. A Read can be complete before an earlier write to a different address, but it is prohibited from returning the value of the write unless all the processors have seen the write. The SPARC V8 total store ordering model (TSO) model partially relaxes the IBM 370 Model, it allows a read to return the value of its own processor's write with respect to other writes to the same location i.e. it returns the value of its own write before others see it. Similar to the previous model, this cannot return the value of write unless all the processors have seen the write. The processor consistency model (PC) is the most relaxed of the three models and relaxes both the constraints such that a read can complete before an earlier write even before it is made visible to other processors.

In Example A, the result is possible only in IBM 370 because Read(A) is not issued until the write(A) in that processor is completed. On the other hand, this result is possible in TSO and PC because they allow the reads of the flags before the writes of the flags in a single processor.

In Example B the result is possible only with PC as it allows P2 to return the value of a write even before it is visible to P3. This won't be possible in the other two models.

To ensure sequential consistency in the above models, safety nets or fences are used to manually enforce the constraint. The IBM370 model has some specialised *serialisation instructions* which are manually placed between operations. These instructions can consist of memory instructions such or non-memory instructions such as branches. On the other hand, the TSO and PC models do not provide safety nets, but the programmers can still use read-modify-write operations to make it appear like the program order is still maintained between a write and a following read. In case of TSO, PO appears to be maintained if the R or W which is already a part of a R-modify-W is replaced by a R-modify-W, this requires the W in the R-modify-W is a 'dummy' that returns the read value. Similarly for PC, PO seems to be maintained if the read is replaced by a write or is already a part of R-modify-W.

However, compiler optimisations cannot be done after exercising this relaxation alone. Compiler optimisations require the full flexibility of reordering any two operations in the PO, so the ability to reorder a write with respect to a read is not sufficiently helpful in this case.

```
Example A.

Initially, A=flag1=flag2=0

P1                      P2

flag1=1                 flag2=1

A=1                     A=2

reg1=A                  reg3=A

reg2=flag2              reg4=flag1


Result: reg1=1 ; reg3=2, reg2=reg4=0

Example B. Initially, A=B=0

P1                P2                P3

A=1

                  if(A==1)

                  B=1               if(B==1)

                                    reg1=A


Result: B=1, reg1=0
```

Relaxed Write to Read and Write to Write

Some models relax the program order even further by relaxing even the ordering constraints between writes to different locations. The SPARC V8 Partial Store Ordering model (PSO) is the only example of such a model. The ability to pipeline and overlap writes to different locations from the same processor is the key hardware optimisation enabled by PSO. PSO is similar to TSO in terms of atomicity requirements, in that, it allows a processor to read the value of its own write and preventing other processors from reading another processor's write before the write is visible to all other processors. Program order between two writes is maintained by PSO using an explicit STBAR instruction. The STBAR is inserted in a write buffer in implementations with FIFO write buffers. A counter is used to determine when all the writes before the STBAR instruction have been completed, which triggers a write to the memory system to increment the counter. A write acknowledgement decrements the counter, and when the counter becomes 0, it signifies that all the previous writes are completed.

In the examples A and B, PSO allows both these non-sequentially consistent results. The safety net that PSO provides is similar to TSO's, it imposes program order from a write to a read and enforces write atomicity.

Similar to the previous models, the relaxations allowed by PSO are not sufficiently flexible to be useful for compiler optimisation, which requires a much more flexible optimisation.

Relaxing Read and Read to Write Program Orders

In some models, all operations to different locations are relaxed. A read or write may be reordered with respect a different read or write in a different location. The *weak ordering* may be classified under this category and two types of Release consistency models (RCsc and RCpc) also come under this model. Three commercial architectures are also proposed under this category of relaxation: the Digital Alpha, SPARC V9 relaxed memory order (RMO), and IBM PowerPC models. All these models allow reordering of reads to the same location, except the Digital Alpha. These models violate sequential in examples A and B. An additional relaxation allowed in these models that is absent ninth previous models is that memory operations following a read operation can be overlapped and reordered with respect to the read. All these models, expect the RCpc and PowerPC allow a read to return the value of another processor's early write. From a programmer's perspective all these models must maintain the illusion of write atomicity even though they allow the processor to read its own write early.

These models can be classified into two categories based on the type of safety net provided. Here, the necessity for carefully written programs is seen. The nature of the synchronization helps to categorize between Weak Ordering, RCsc and RCpc models. Where as, The Alpha, RMO and PowerPC models provide fence instructions so that program order can be imposed between different memory operations.

Weak Ordering

An example of a model that relaxes most of the above constraints (except reading others' write early) is Weak Ordering. It classifies memory operations into two categories: *Data operations* and *Synchronization operations*. To enforce program order, a programmer needs to find at least one synchronisation operation in a program. The assumption under which this works is that, reordering memory operations to data regions between synchronisation operations does not affect the outcome of the program. They just act as the safety net for enforcing program order. The way this works is that a counter tracks the number of data operations and until this counter becomes zero, the synchronisation operation isn't issued. Furthermore, no more data operations are issued unless all the previous synchronisation's are completed. Memory operations in between two synchronisation variables can be overlapped and reordered without affecting the correctness of the program. This model ensures that write atomicity is always maintained, therefore no additional safety net is required for Weak Ordering.

Release Consistency (RCsc/RCpc)

More classification is made to memory operations depending on when they occur. Operations are divided into ordinary and special. Special operations are further divided into sync or sync operations. Syncs correspond to synchronisation operations and syncs correspond to data operations or other special operations that aren't used for synchronisation. Sync operations are further divided into acquire or release operations. An acquire is effectively a read memory operation used to obtain access to a certain set of shared locations. Release, on the other hand, is a write operation that is performed for granting permission to access the shared locations.

There are two types of Release consistency, RCsc (Release consistency with Sequential consistency) and RCpc (Release consistency with processor consistency). The first type, RCsc maintains SC among special operations, while RCpc maintains PC among such operations.

For RCsc the constraints are: Acquire->All, All->Release,Special->Special.

For RCpc the write to read program order is relaxed: Acquire->All, All->Release, Special->Special(expect when special write is followed by special read)

NOTE: the above notation A->B, implies that if the operation A precedes B in the program order, then program order is enforced.

Alpha, RMO, and PowerPC

These three commercial architectures exhibit explicit fence instructions as their safety nets. The Alpha model provides two types of fence instructions, Memory barrier(MB) and Write memory barrier(WMB). The MB operation can be used to maintain program order of any memory operation before the MB with a memory operation after the barrier. Similarly, the WMB maintains program order only among writes. The SPARC V9 RMO model provides a MEMBAR instruction which can be customised to order previous reads and writes with respect to future read and write operations. There is no need for using read-modify-writes to achieve this order because the MEMBAR instruction can be used to order a write with respect to a succeeding read. The PowerPC model uses a single fence instruction called the SYNC instruction. It is similar to the MB instruction, but with a little exception that reads can occur out of program order even if a SYNC is placed between two reads to the same location. This model also differs from Alpha and RMO in terms of Atomicity. It allows write to be seen earlier than a read's completion. A combination of read modify write operations may be required to make an illusion of write atomicity.

Transactional Memory Models

Transactional Memory model is the combination of cache coherency and memory consistency models as a communication model for shared memory systems supported by software or hardware; a transactional memory model provides both memory consistency and cache coherency. A transaction is a sequence of operations executed by a process that transforms data from one consistent state to another. A transaction either commits when there is no conflict or aborts. In commits, all changes are visible to all other processes when a transaction is completed, while aborts discard all changes. Compared to relaxed consistency models, a transactional model is easier to use and can provide the higher performance than a sequential consistency model.

Consistency and Replication

Tanenbaum et al., 2007 defines two main reasons for replicating; reliability and performance. Reliability can be achieved in a replicated file system by switching to another replica in the case of the current replica failure. The replication also protects data from being corrupted by providing multiple copies of data on different replicas. It also improves the performance by dividing the work. While replication can improve performance and reliability, it can cause consistency problems between multiple copies of data. The multiple copies are consistent if a read operation returns the same value from all copies and a write operation as a single atomic operation (transaction) updates all copies before any other operation takes place. Tanenbaum, Andrew, & Maarten Van Steen, 2007 refer to this type of consistency as tight consistency provided by synchronous replication. However, applying global synchronizations to keep all copies consistent is costly. One way to decrease the cost of global synchronization and improve the performance can be weakening the consistency restrictions.

Data-centric Consistency Models

Tanenbaum et al., 2007 defines the consistency model as a contract between the software (processes) and memory implementation (data store). This model guarantees that if the software follows certain rules, the memory works correctly. Since, in a system without a global clock, defining the last operation writes is difficult, some restrictions can be applied on the values that can be returned by a read operation.

Consistent Ordering of Operations

Some consistency models such as sequential and also causal consistency models deal with the order of operations on shared replicated data in order to provide consistency. In this models, all replicas must agree on a consistent global ordering of updates.

Sequential Consistency

The goal of data-centric consistency models is to provide a consistent view on a data store where processes may carry out concurrent updates. One important data-centric consistency model is sequential consistency defined by Lamport (1979). Tanenbaum et al., 2007 defines sequential consistency under following condition:

"The result of any execution is the same as if the (read and write) operations by all processes on the data store were executed in some sequential order and the operations of each individual process appear in this sequence in the order specified by its program."

Adve and Gharachorloo, 1996 define two requirements to implement the sequential consistency; program order and write atomicity.

- Program order: Program order guarantees that each process issues a memory request ordered by its program.

- Write atomicity: Write atomicity defines that memory requests are serviced based on the order of a single FIFO queue.

In sequential consistency, there is no notion of time or most recent write operations. There are some operations interleaving that is same for all processes. A process can see the write operations of all processes but it can just see its own read operations.

Linearizability (Atomic memory) can be defined as a sequential consistency with real time constraint by considering a begin time and end time for each operation. An execution is linearizable if each operation taking place in linearizable order by placing a point between its begin time and its end time and guarantees sequential consistency.

Causal Consistency

The causal consistency defined by Hutto and Ahamad, 1990 is a weaker consistency model than sequential consistency by making the distinction between causally related operations and those that are not related. For example, if an event b takes effect from an earlier event a, the causal consistency guarantees that all processes see event b after event a.

Tanenbaum et al., 2007 defines that a data store is considered causal consistent under the following condition:

"Writes that are potentially causally related must be seen by all processes in the same order. Concurrent writes may be seen in a different order on different machines."

Grouping Operations

In grouping operation, accesses to the synchronization variables are sequentially consistent. A process is allowed to access a synchronization variable that all previous writes have been completed. In other words, accesses to synchronization variables are not permitted until all operations on the synchronization variables are completely performed.

Continuous Consistency

The continuous consistency is defined later in the consistency protocol section.

Client-centric Consistency Models

In distributed systems, maintaining sequential consistency in order to control the concurrent operations is essential. In some special data stores without simultaneous updates, client-centric consistency models can deal with inconsistencies in a less costly way. The following models are some client-centric consistency models:

Eventual Consistency

An eventual consistency is a weak consistency model in the system with the lack of simultaneous updates. It defines that if no update takes a very long time, all replicas eventually become consistent.

Monotonic Read Consistency

Tanenbaum et al., 2007 defines monotonic read consistency as follows:

"If a process reads the value of a data item x, any successive read operation on x by that process will always return that same value or a more recent value."

Monotonic read consistency guarantees that after a process reads a value of data item x at time t, it will never see the older value of that data item.

Monotonic Write Consistency

Monotonic write consistency condition is defined by Tanenbaum et al., 2007 as follows:

"A write operation by a process on a data item X is completed before any successive write operation on X by the same process."

Read-your-writes Consistency

A value written by a process on a data item X will be always available to a successive read operation performed by the same process on data item X.

Writes-follows-reads Consistency

In Writes-follow-reads consistency, updates are propagated after performing the previous read operations. Tanenbaum et al., 2007 defines the following condition for Writes-follow-reads consistency:

"A write operation by a process on a data item x following a previous read operation on x by the same process is guaranteed to take place on the same or a more recent value of x that was read."

Consistency Protocols

The implementation of a consistency model is defined by a consistency protocol. Tanenbaum et al., 2007 illustrates some consistency protocols for data-centric models.

Continuous Consistency

Continuous consistency introduced by Yu and Vahdat (2000). In this model, consistency semantic of an application is described by using conits in the application. Since the consistency requirements can differ based on application semantics, Yu and Vahdat (2000) believe that a predefined uniform consistency model may not be an appropriate approach. The application should specify the consistency requirements that satisfy the application semantic. In this model, an application specifies each consistency requirements as a conits (abbreviation of consistency units). A conit can be a physical or logical consistency and is used to measure the consistency. Tanenbaum et al., 2007 describes the notion of a conit by giving an example. There are three inconsistencies that can be tolerated by applications.

- Deviation in numerical values Numerical deviation bounds the difference between the conit value and relative value of last update. A weight can be assigned to the writes which defines the importance of the writes in a specific application. The total weights of unseen writes for a conit can be defined as a numerical deviation in an application. There are two different types of numerical deviation; absolute and relative numerical deviation.

- Deviation in ordering Ordering deviation is the discrepancy between the local order of writes in a replica and their relative ordering in the eventual final image.

- Deviation in staleness between replicas Staleness deviation defines the validity of the oldest write by bounding the difference between the current time and the time of oldest write on a conit not seen locally. Each server has a local queue of uncertain write that is required an actual order to be determined and applied on a conit. The maximal length of uncertain writes queue is the bound of ordering deviation. When the number of writes exceeds the limit, instead of accepting new submitted write, the server will attempt to commit uncertain writes by communicating with other servers based on the order that writes should be executed.

If all three deviation bounds set to zero, the continuous consistency model is the strong consistency.

Primary-based Protocols

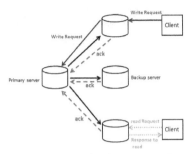

Primary backup protocol

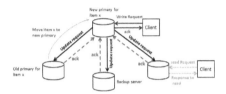

Primary-backup protocol (local-write)

Primary-based protocols can be considered as a class of consistency protocols that are simpler to implement. For instance, sequential ordering is a popular consistency model when consistent ordering of operations is considered. The sequential ordering can be determined as primary-based protocol. In these protocols, there is an associated primary for each data item in a data store to coordinate write operations on that data item.

Remote-write Protocols

In the simplest primary-based protocol that supports replication, also known as primary-backup protocol, write operations are forwarded to a single server and read operations can be performed locally.

> Example: Tanenbaum et al., 2007 gives an example of a primary-backup protocol. The diagram of primary-backup protocol shows an example of this protocol. When a client requests a write, the write request is forwarded to a primary server. The primary server sends request to backups to perform the update. The server then receives the update acknowledgement from all backups and sends the acknowledgement of completion of writes to the client. Any client can read the last available update locally. The trade-off of this protocol is that a client who sends the update request might have to wait so long to get the acknowledgement in order to continue. This problem can be solved by performing the updates locally, and then ask other backups perform their updates. The non-blocking primary-backup protocol does not guarantee the consistency of update on all backup servers. However, it improves the performance. In the primary-backup protocol, all processes will see the same order of write operations since this protocol orders all incoming writes based on a globally unique time. Blocking protocols guarantee that processes view the result of the last write operation.

Local-write Protocols

In primary-based local-write protocols, primary copy moves between processes willing to perform an update. To update a data item, a process first moves it to its location. As a result, in this approach, successive write operations can be performed locally while each process can read their local copy of data items. After the primary finishes its update, the update is forwarded to other replicas and all perform the update locally. This non-blocking approach can lead to an improvement. The diagram of the local-write protocol depicts the local-write approach in primary-based protocols. A process requests a write operation in a data item x. The current server is considered as the new primary for a data item x. The write operation is performed and when the request is finished, the primary sends an update request to other backup servers. Each backup sends an acknowledgment to the primary after finishing the update operation.

Replicated-write Protocols

In Replicated-write protocols, unlike the primary-based protocol, all updates are carried out to all replicas.

Active Replication

In active replication, there is a process associated to each replica to perform the write operation. In other words, updates are sent to each replica in the form of an operation in order to be executed. All updates need to be performed in the same order in all replicas. As a result, a totally-ordered multicast mechanism is required. There is a scalability issue in implementing such a multicasting mechanism in large distributed systems. There is another approach in which each operation is sent to a central coordinator (sequencer). The coordinator first assigns a sequence number to each operation and then forwards the operation to all replicas. Second approach cannot also solve the scalability problem.

Quorum-based Protocols

Voting can be another approach in replicated-write protocols. In this approach, a client requests and receives permission from multiple servers in order to read and write a replicated data. As an example, suppose in a distributed file system, a file is replicated on N servers. To update a file, a client must send a request to at least $N/2+1$ in order to make their agreement to perform an update. After the agreement, changes are applied on the file and a new version number is assigned to the updated file. Similarly, for reading replicated file, a client sends a request to $N/2+1$ servers in order to receive the associated version number from those servers. Read operation is completed if all received version numbers are the most recent version.

Cache-coherence Protocols

In a replicated file system, a cache-coherence protocol provides the cache consistency while caches are generally controlled by clients. In many approaches, cache consistency is provided by the underlying hardware. Some other approaches in middleware-based distributed systems apply software-based solutions to provide the cache consistency. Cache consistency models can differ in their coherence detection strategies that define when inconsistencies occur. There are two approaches to detect the inconsistency; static and dynamic solutions. In the static solution, a compiler determines which variables can cause the cache inconsistency. So, the compiler enforces an instruction in order to avoid the inconsistency problem. In the dynamic solution, the server checks for inconsistencies at run time to control the consistency of the cached data that has changed after it was cached. The coherence enforcement strategy is another cache-coherence protocol. It defines that *how* to provide the consistency in caches by using the copies located on the server. One way to keep the data consistent is to never cache the shared data. A server can keep the data and apply some consistency protocol such as primary-based protocols to ensure the consistency of shared data. In this solution, only private data can be cached by clients. In the case that shared data are cached, there are two approaches in order to enforce the cache coherence. In first approach, when a shared data is updated, the server forwards invalidation to all caches. In second approach, an update is propagated. Most caching systems apply these two approaches or dynamically choose between them.

Ocean Current Simulation

- Regular structure, scientific computing, important for weather forecast
- Want to simulate the eddy current along the walls of ocean basin over a period of time
  - Discretize the 3-D basin into 2-D horizontal grids
  - Discretize each 2-D grid into points
  - One time step involves solving the equation of motion for each grid point
  - Enough concurrency within and across grids
  - After each time step synchronize the processors

Galaxy Simulation

- Simulate the interaction of many stars evolving over time
- Want to compute force between every pair of stars for each time step
  - Essentially $O(n^2)$ computations (massive parallelism)
- Hierarchical methods take advantage of square law
  - If a group of stars is far enough it is possible to approximate the group entirely by a single star at the center of mass
  - Essentially four subparts in each step: divide the galaxy into zones until further division does not improve accuracy, compute center of mass for each zone, compute force, update star position based on force
- Lot of concurrency across stars

Ray Tracing

- Want to render a scene using ray tracing

- Generate rays through pixels in the image plane
- The rays bounce from objects following reflection/refraction laws
  - New rays get generated: tree of rays from a root ray
- Need to correctly simulate paths of all rays
- The outcome is color and opacity of the objects in the scene: thus you render a scene
- Concurrency across ray trees and subtrees

Writing a Parallel Program

- Start from a sequential description
- Identify work that can be done in parallel
- Partition work and/or data among threads or processes
  - Decomposition and assignment
- Add necessary communication and synchronization
  - Orchestration
- Map threads to processors (Mapping)
- How good is the parallel program?
- Measure speedup = sequential execution time/parallel execution time = number of processors ideally

Some Definitions

- Task
  - Arbitrary piece of sequential work
  - Concurrency is only across tasks
  - Fine-grained task vs. coarse-grained task: controls granularity of parallelism (spectrum of grain: one instruction to the whole sequential program)
- Process/thread
  - Logical entity that performs a task
  - Communication and synchronization happen between threads
- Processors
  - Physical entity on which one or more processes execute

Decomposition of Iterative Equation Solver

- Find concurrent tasks and divide the program into tasks

  o Level or grain of concurrency needs to be decided here

  o Too many tasks: may lead to too much of overhead communicating and synchronizing between tasks

  o Too few tasks: may lead to idle processors

  o Goal: Just enough tasks to keep the processors busy

- Number of tasks may vary dynamically

  o New tasks may get created as the computation proceeds: new rays in ray tracing

  o Number of available tasks at any point in time is an upper bound on the achievable speedup

Static Assignment

- Given a decomposition it is possible to assign tasks statically

  o For example, some computation on an array of size N can be decomposed statically by assigning a range of indices to each process: for k processes P_0 operates on indices 0 to $(N/k)-1$, P_1 operates on N/k to $(2N/k)-1$,..., P_{k-1} operates on $(k-1)N/k$ to N-1

  o For regular computations this works great: simple and low-overhead

- What if the nature computation depends on the index?

  o For certain index ranges you do some heavy-weight computation while for others you do something simple

  o Is there a problem?

Dynamic Assignment

- Static assignment may lead to load imbalance depending on how irregular the application is

- Dynamic decomposition/assignment solves this issue by allowing a process to dynamically choose any available task whenever it is done with its previous task

  o Normally in this case you decompose the program in such a way that the number of available tasks is larger than the number of processes

  o Same example: divide the array into portions each with 10 indices; so you have N/10 tasks

  o An idle process grabs the next available task

- o   Provides better load balance since longer tasks can execute concurrently with the smaller ones

- Dynamic assignment comes with its own overhead

  - o   Now you need to maintain a shared count of the number of available tasks

  - o   The update of this variable must be protected by a lock

  - o   Need to be careful so that this lock contention does not outweigh the benefits of dynamic decomposition

- More complicated applications where a task may not just operate on an index range, but could manipulate a subtree or a complex data structure

  - o   Normally a dynamic task queue is maintained where each task is probably a pointer to the data

  - o   The task queue gets populated as new tasks are discovered

Decomposition Types

- Decomposition by data

  - o   The most commonly found decomposition technique

  - o   The data set is partitioned into several subsets and each subset is assigned to a process

  - o   The type of computation may or may not be identical on each subset

  - o   Very easy to program and manage

- Computational decomposition

  - o   Not so popular: tricky to program and manage

  - o   All processes operate on the same data, but probably carry out different kinds of computation

  - o   More common in systolic arrays, pipelined graphics processor units (GPUs) etc.

Orchestration

- Involves structuring communication and synchronization among processes, organizing data structures to improve locality, and scheduling tasks

  - o   This step normally depends on the programming model and the underlying architecture

- Goal is to

  - o   Reduce communication and synchronization costs

○   Maximize locality of data reference

○   Schedule tasks to maximize concurrency: do not schedule dependent tasks in parallel

○   Reduce overhead of parallelization and concurrency management (e.g., management of the task queue, overhead of initiating a task etc.)

Mapping

- At this point you have a parallel program

    ○   Just need to decide which and how many processes go to each processor of the parallel machine

- Could be specified by the program

    ○   Pin particular processes to a particular processor for the whole life of the program; the processes cannot migrate to other processors

- Could be controlled entirely by the OS

    ○   Schedule processes on idle processors

    ○   Various scheduling algorithms are possible e.g., round robin: process#k goes to processor#k

    ○   NUMA-aware OS normally takes into account multiprocessor-specific metrics in scheduling

- How many processes per processor? Most common is one-to-one

An Example

- Iterative equation solver

    ○   Main kernel in Ocean simulation

    ○   Update each 2-D grid point via Gauss-Seidel iterations

    ○   A[i,j] = 0.2(A[i,j]+A[i,j+1]+A[i,j-1]+A[i+1,j]+A[i-1,j])

    ○   Pad the n by n grid to (n+2) by (n+2) to avoid corner problems

    ○   Update only interior n by n grid

    ○   One iteration consists of updating all n2 points in-place and accumulating the difference from the previous value at each point

    ○   If the difference is less than a threshold, the solver is said to have converged to a stable grid equilibrium

Sequential Program

```
int n;                                                begin Solve (A)
```

```
float **A, diff;                          int i, j, done = 0;

                                            float temp;

                                            while (!done)
begin main()                               diff = 0.0;

  read (n);    /* size of grid */       for i = 0 to n-1

  Allocate (A);                                          for
j = 0 to n-1

  Initialize (A);                                      temp =
A[i,j];

  Solve (A);                                           A[i,j]
= 0.2(A[i,j]+A[i,j+1]+A[i,j-1]+A[i-

end main                                     1,j]+A[i+1,j]);

                                                       diff
+= fabs (A[i,j] - temp);

                                                       end-
for

                                                      endfor

                                                        if
(diff/(n*n) < TOL) then done = 1;

                                                    endwhile
                                                  end Solve
```

Decomposition of Iterative Equation Solver

- Look for concurrency in loop iterations
  - In this case iterations are really dependent
  - Iteration (i, j) depends on iterations (i, j-1) and (i-1, j)

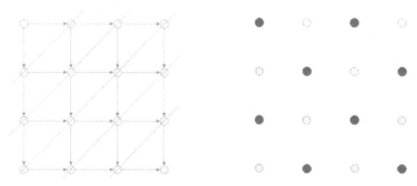

  - Each anti-diagonal can be computed in parallel

- o   Must synchronize after each anti-diagonal (or pt-to-pt)

- o   Alternative: red-black ordering (different update pattern)

- Can update all red points first, synchronize globally with a barrier and then update all black points

  - o   May converge faster or slower compared to sequential program

  - o   Converged equilibrium may also be different if there are multiple solutions

  - o   Ocean simulation uses this decomposition

- We will ignore the loop-carried dependence and go ahead with a straight-forward loop decomposition

  - o   Allow updates to all points in parallel

  - o   This is yet another different update order and may affect convergence

  - o   Update to a point may or may not see the new updates to the nearest neighbors (this parallel algorithm is non-deterministic)

```
while (!done)

   diff = 0.0;

   for_all i = 0 to n-1

      for_all j = 0 to n-1

         temp = A[i, j];

       A[i, j] = 0.2(A[i, j]+A[i, j+1]+A[i, j-1]+A[i-1, j]+A[i+1, j]);

            diff += fabs (A[i, j] - temp);

         end for_all

      end for_all

      if (diff/(n*n) < TOL) then done = 1;

   end while
```

- Offers concurrency across elements: degree of concurrency is n^2

- Make the j loop sequential to have row-wise decomposition: degree n concurrency

Assignment

- Possible static assignment: block row decomposition

  - o   Process 0 gets rows 0 to (n/p)-1, process 1 gets rows n/p to (2n/p)-1 etc.

- Another static assignment: cyclic row decomposition

  o Process 0 gets rows 0, p, 2p,...; process 1 gets rows 1, p+1, 2p+1,....

- Dynamic assignment

  o Grab next available row, work on that, grab a new row,...

- Static block row assignment minimizes nearest neighbor communication by assigning contiguous rows to the same process

Shared memory version

```
/* include files */
MAIN_ENV;
int P, n;
void Solve ();
struct gm_t {
   LOCKDEC (diff_lock);
   BARDEC (barrier);
   float **A, diff;
} *gm;
int main (char **argv, int argc)
{
   int i;
   MAIN_INITENV;
   gm = (struct gm_t*) G_MALLOC (sizeof (struct gm_t));
   LOCKINIT (gm->diff_lock);
BARINIT (gm->barrier);
   n = atoi (argv);
   P = atoi (argv);
   gm->A = (float**) G_MALLOC ((n+2)*sizeof (float*));
   for (i = 0; i < n+2; i++) {
      gm->A[i] = (float*) G_MALLOC ((n+2)*sizeof (float));
   }
   Initialize (gm->A);
   for (i = 1; i < P; i++) {   /* starts at 1 */
      CREATE (Solve);
   }
   Solve ();
```

```
    WAIT_FOR_END (P-1);

    MAIN_END;

}

void Solve (void)

{

    int i, j, pid, done = 0;

    float temp, local_diff;

    GET_PID (pid);

    while (!done) {

        local_diff = 0.0;

        if (!pid) gm->diff = 0.0;

        BARRIER (gm->barrier, P);/*why?*/

        for (i = pid*(n/P); i < (pid+1)*(n/P); i++) {

            for (j = 0; j < n; j++) {

                temp = gm->A[i] [j];

                gm->A[i] [j] = 0.2*(gm->A[i] [j] + gm->A[i] [j-1] + gm->A[i] [j+1] +
gm->A[i+1] [j] + gm->A[i-1] [j]);

local_diff += fabs (gm->A[i] [j] - temp);

            }   /* end for */

        }   /* end for */

        LOCK (gm->diff_lock);

        gm->diff += local_diff;

        UNLOCK (gm->diff_lock);

        BARRIER (gm->barrier, P);

        if (gm->diff/(n*n) < TOL) done = 1;

        BARRIER (gm->barrier, P); /* why? */

    }   /* end while */

}
```

Mutual Exclusion

- Use LOCK/UNLOCK around critical sections
    - Updates to shared variable diff must be sequential
    - Heavily contended locks may degrade performance

o   Try to minimize the use of critical sections: they are sequential anyway and will limit speedup

o   This is the reason for using a local_diff instead of accessing gm->diff every time

o   Also, minimize the size of critical section because the longer you hold the lock, longer will be the waiting time for other processors at lock acquire

LOCK Optimization

- Suppose each processor updates a shared variable holding a global cost value, only if its local cost is less than the global cost: found frequently in minimization problems

```
LOCK (gm->cost_lock);

if (my_cost < gm->cost) {

gm->cost = my_cost;

}

UNLOCK (gm->cost_lock);

/* May lead to heavy lock contention if everyone tries to update at the
same time */

if (my_cost < gm->cost) {

LOCK (gm->cost_lock);

if (my_cost < gm->cost)

{ /* make sure*/

gm->cost = my_cost;

}

UNLOCK (gm->cost_lock);

} /* this works because gm->cost is monotonically decreasing */
```

More Synchronization

- Global synchronization
  o   Through barriers
  o   Often used to separate computation phases
- Point-to-point synchronization
  o   A process directly notifies another about a certain event on which the latter was waiting
  o   Producer-consumer communication pattern
  o   Semaphores are used for concurrent programming on uniprocessor through P and V functions

- o   Normally implemented through flags on shared memory multiprocessors (busy wait or spin)

P_0: A = 1; flag = 1;

P_1: while (!flag); use (A);

Message Passing

- What is different from shared memory?

  - o   No shared variable: expose communication through send/receive

  - o   No lock or barrier primitive

  - o   Must implement synchronization through send/receive

- Grid solver example

  - o P_0 allocates and initializes matrix A in its local memory

  - o   Then it sends the block rows, n, P to each processor i.e. P_1 waits to receive rows n/P to 2n/P-1 etc. (this is one-time)

  - o   Within the while loop the first thing that every processor does is to send its first and last rows to the upper and the lower processors (corner cases need to be handled)

  - o   Then each processor waits to receive the neighboring two rows from the upper and the lower processors

- At the end of the loop each processor sends its local_diff to P_0 and P_0 sends back the done flag

Major Changes

```
/* include files */
MAIN_ENV;
int P, n;
void Solve ();
struct gm_t {
  LOCKDEC (diff_lock);
  BARDEC (barrier);
  float **A, diff;
} *gm;

int main (char **argv, int argc)
{
  int i; int P, n; float **A;
  MAIN_INITENV;
  gm = (struct gm_t*) G_MALLOC
  (sizeof (struct gm_t));
  LOCKINIT (gm->diff_lock);
```

Local Alloc.

```
BARINIT (gm->barrier);
n = atoi (argv[1]);
P = atoi (argv[2]);
gm->A = (float**) G_MALLOC
((n+2)*sizeof (float*));
for (i = 0; i < n+2; i++) {
  gm->A[i] = (float*) G_MALLOC
((n+2)*sizeof (float));
}
Initialize (gm->A);
for (i = 1; i < P; i++) { /* starts at 1 */
  CREATE (Solve);
}
Solve ();
WAIT_FOR_END (P-1);
MAIN_END;
}
```

```
void Solve (void)
{
  int i, j, pid, done = 0;
  float temp, local_diff;
  GET_PID (pid);
  while (!done) {                  —— if (pid) Recv rows, n, P
    local_diff = 0.0;                   Send up/down
    if (!pid) gm->diff = 0.0;       Recv up/down
    BARRIER (gm->barrier, P);/*why?*/
    for (i = pid*(n/P); i < (pid+1)*(n/P);
    I++) {
      for (j = 0; j < n; j++) {
        temp = gm->A[i] [j];
        gm->A[i] [j] = 0.2*(gm->A[i] [j] +
        gm->A[i] [j-1] + gm->A[i] [j+1] + gm-
        >A[i+1] [j] + gm->A[i-1] [j];
```

```
        local_diff += fabs (gm->A[i] [j] –
temp);
      } /* end for */
    } /* end for */
    LOCK (gm->diff_lock);      Send local diff
    gm->diff += local_diff;      to P0
    UNLOCK (gm->diff_lock);   Recv diff
    BARRIER (gm->barrier, P);
    if (gm->diff/(n*n) < TOL) done = 1;
    BARRIER (gm->barrier, P); /* why? */
  } /* end while */
}
```

Message Passing

- This algorithm is deterministic

- May converge to a different solution compared to the shared memory version if there are multiple solutions: why?

  o There is a fixed specific point in the program (at the beginning of each iteration) when the neighboring rows are communicated

  o This is not true for shared memory

Message Passing Grid Solver

MPI-like Environment

- MPI stands for Message Passing Interface

  o A C library that provides a set of message passing primitives (e.g., send, receive, broadcast etc.) to the user

- PVM (Parallel Virtual Machine) is another well-known platform for message passing programming

- Only need to know

  o When you start an MPI program every thread runs the same main function

  o We will assume that we pin one thread to one processor just as we did in shared memory

- Instead of using the exact MPI syntax we will use some macros that call the MPI functions

```
MAIN_ENV;
```

```
/* define message tags */
 #define ROW 99
#define DIFF 98
#define DONE 97
int main(int argc, char **argv)
{
    int pid, P, done, i, j, N;
    float tempdiff, local_diff, temp, **A;
    MAIN_INITENV;
    GET_PID(pid);
    GET_NUMPROCS(P);
    N = atoi(argv);
    tempdiff = 0.0;
    done = 0;
    A = (double **) malloc ((N/P+2) * sizeof(float *));
    for (i=0; i < N/P+2; i++) {
        A[i] = (float *) malloc (sizeof(float) * (N+2));
    }
    initialize(A);
while (!done) {
    local_diff = 0.0;
    /* MPI_CHAR means raw byte format */
    if (pid) {   /* send my first row up */
        SEND(&A, N*sizeof(float), MPI_CHAR, pid-1, ROW);
    }
    if (pid != P-1) {   /* recv last row */
        RECV(&A[N/P+1], N*sizeof(float), MPI_CHAR, pid+1, ROW);
    }
    if (pid != P-1) {   /* send last row down */
        SEND(&A[N/P], N*sizeof(float), MPI_CHAR, pid+1, ROW);
```

```
    }

    if (pid) {   /* recv first row from above */

       RECV(&A, N*sizeof(float), MPI_CHAR, pid-1, ROW);

    }

    for (i=1; i <= N/P; i++) for (j=1; j <= N; j++) {

         temp = A[i][j];

         A[i][j] = 0.2 * (A[i][j] + A[i][j-1] +          A[i-1][j] + A[i]
[j+1] + A[i+1][j]);

         local_diff += fabs(A[i][j] - temp);

         }

if (pid) {   /* tell P0 my diff */

     SEND(&local_diff, sizeof(float),    MPI_CHAR, 0, DIFF);

      RECV(&done, sizeof(int), MPI_CHAR, 0, DONE);

    }

    else {   /* recv from all and add up */

      for (i=1; i < P; i++) {

        RECV(&tempdiff, sizeof(float), MPI_CHAR, MPI_ANY_SOURCE, DIFF);

        local_diff += tempdiff;

      }

      if (local_diff/(N*N) < TOL) done=1;

      for (i=1; i < P; i++) {

        /* tell all if done */

        SEND(&done, sizeof(int), MPI_CHAR, i, DONE);

      }

    }

}  /* end while */

MAIN_END;

}  /* end main */
```

- Note the matching tags in SEND and RECV
- Macros used in this program

- o GET_PID

- o GET_NUMPROCS

- o SEND

- o RECV

- These will get expanded into specific MPI library calls

- Syntax of SEND/RECV

  - o Starting address, how many elements, type of each element (we have used byte only), source/dest, message tag

Bit-level Parallelism

Bit-level parallelism is a form of parallel computing based on increasing processor word size. Increasing the word size reduces the number of instructions the processor must execute in order to perform an operation on variables whose sizes are greater than the length of the word. (For example, consider a case where an 8-bit processor must add two 16-bit integers. The processor must first add the 8 lower-order bits from each integer, then add the 8 higher-order bits, requiring two instructions to complete a single operation. A 16-bit processor would be able to complete the operation with single instruction.)

Originally, all electronic computers were serial (single-bit) computers. The first electronic computer that was not a serial computer—the first bit-parallel computer—was the 16-bit Whirlwind from 1951.

From the advent of very-large-scale integration (VLSI) computer chip fabrication technology in the 1970s until about 1986, advancements in computer architecture were done by increasing bit-level parallelism, as 4-bit microprocessors were replaced by 8-bit, then 16-bit, then 32-bit microprocessors. This trend generally came to an end with the introduction of 32-bit processors, which have been a standard in general purpose computing for two decades. Only recently, with the advent of x86-64 architectures, have 64-bit processors become commonplace.

On 32-bit processors, external data bus width continues to increase. For example, DDR1 SDRAM transfers 128 bits per clock cycle. DDR2 SDRAM transfers a minimum of 256 bits per burst.

Instruction-level Parallelism

Instruction-level parallelism (ILP) is a measure of how many of the instructions in a computer program can be executed simultaneously.

There are two approaches to instruction level parallelism:

- Hardware

- Software

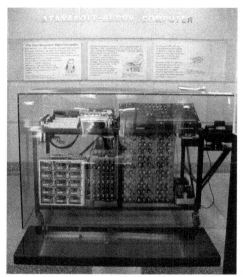

Atanasoff–Berry computer, the first computer with parallel processing

Hardware level works upon dynamic parallelism whereas, the software level works on static parallelism. Dynamic parallelism means the processor decides at run time which instructions to execute in parallel, whereas static parallelism means the compiler decides which instructions to execute in parallel. The Pentium processor works on the dynamic sequence of parallel execution but the Itanium processor works on the static level parallelism.

Consider the following program:

1. e = a + b

2. f = c + d

3. m = e * f

Operation 3 depends on the results of operations 1 and 2, so it cannot be calculated until both of them are completed. However, operations 1 and 2 do not depend on any other operation, so they can be calculated simultaneously. If we assume that each operation can be completed in one unit of time then these three instructions can be completed in a total of two units of time, giving an ILP of 3/2.

A goal of compiler and processor designers is to identify and take advantage of as much ILP as possible. Ordinary programs are typically written under a sequential execution model where instructions execute one after the other and in the order specified by the programmer. ILP allows the compiler and the processor to overlap the execution of multiple instructions or even to change the order in which instructions are executed.

How much ILP exists in programs is very application specific. In certain fields, such as graphics and scientific computing the amount can be very large. However, workloads such as cryptography may exhibit much less parallelism.

Micro-architectural techniques that are used to exploit ILP include:

- Instruction pipelining where the execution of multiple instructions can be partially over-lapped.

- Superscalar execution, VLIW, and the closely related explicitly parallel instruction computing concepts, in which multiple execution units are used to execute multiple instructions in parallel.

- Out-of-order execution where instructions execute in any order that does not violate data dependencies. Note that this technique is independent of both pipelining and superscalar. Current implementations of out-of-order execution dynamically (i.e., while the program is executing and without any help from the compiler) extract ILP from ordinary programs. An alternative is to extract this parallelism at compile time and somehow convey this information to the hardware. Due to the complexity of scaling the out-of-order execution technique, the industry has re-examined instruction sets which explicitly encode multiple independent operations per instruction.

- Register renaming which refers to a technique used to avoid unnecessary serialization of program operations imposed by the reuse of registers by those operations, used to enable out-of-order execution.

- Speculative execution which allow the execution of complete instructions or parts of instructions before being certain whether this execution should take place. A commonly used form of speculative execution is control flow speculation where instructions past a control flow instruction (e.g., a branch) are executed before the target of the control flow instruction is determined. Several other forms of speculative execution have been proposed and are in use including speculative execution driven by value prediction, memory dependence prediction and cache latency prediction.

- Branch prediction which is used to avoid stalling for control dependencies to be resolved. Branch prediction is used with speculative execution.

It is known that the ILP is exploited by both the compiler and hardware support but the compiler also provides inherit and implicit ILP in programs to hardware by compilation optimization. Some optimization techniques for extracting available ILP in programs would include scheduling, register allocation/renaming, and memory access optimization.

Dataflow architectures are another class of architectures where ILP is explicitly specified.

Some limits to ILP are compiler sophistication and hardware sophistication. To overcome these limits, new and different hardware techniques may be able to overcome limitations. However, unlikely such advances when coupled with realistic hardware will overcome these limits in the near future.

In recent years, ILP techniques have been used to provide performance improvements in spite of the growing disparity between processor operating frequencies and memory access times (early ILP designs such as the IBM System/360 Model 91 used ILP techniques to overcome the limitations imposed by a relatively small register file). Presently, a cache miss penalty to main memory costs several hundreds of CPU cycles. While in principle it is possible to use ILP to tolerate even such memory latencies the associated resource and power dissipation costs are disproportionate. Moreover, the complexity and often the latency of the underlying hardware structures results in reduced operating frequency further reducing any benefits. Hence, the aforementioned techniques prove inadequate to keep the CPU from stalling for the off-chip data. Instead, the industry is heading towards exploiting higher levels of parallelism that can be exploited through techniques such as multiprocessing and multithreading.

Task Parallelism

Task parallelism (also known as function parallelism and control parallelism) is a form of parallelization of computer code across multiple processors in parallel computing environments. Task parallelism focuses on distributing tasks—concurrently performed by processes or threads—across different processors. In contrast to data parallelism which involves running the same task on different components of data, task parallelism is distinguished by running many different tasks at the same time on the same data. A common type of task parallelism is pipelining which consists of moving a single set of data through a series of separate tasks where each task can execute independently of the others.

Description

In a multiprocessor system, task parallelism is achieved when each processor executes a different thread (or process) on the same or different data. The threads may execute the same or different code. In the general case, different execution threads communicate with one another as they work, but is not a requirement. Communication usually takes place by passing data from one thread to the next as part of a workflow.

As a simple example, if a system is running code on a 2-processor system (CPUs "a" & "b") in a parallel environment and we wish to do tasks "A" and "B", it is possible to tell CPU "a" to do task "A" and CPU "b" to do task "B" simultaneously, thereby reducing the run time of the execution. The tasks can be assigned using conditional statements as described below.

Task parallelism emphasizes the distributed (parallelized) nature of the processing (i.e. threads), as opposed to the data (data parallelism). Most real programs fall somewhere on a continuum between task parallelism and data parallelism.

Thread-level parallelism (TLP) is the parallelism inherent in an application that runs multiple threads at once. This type of parallelism is found largely in applications written for commercial servers such as databases. By running many threads at once, these applications are able to tolerate the high amounts of I/O and memory system latency their workloads can incur - while one thread is delayed waiting for a memory or disk access, other threads can do useful work.

The exploitation of thread-level parallelism has also begun to make inroads into the desktop market with the advent of multi-core microprocessors. This has occurred because, for various reasons, it has become increasingly impractical to increase either the clock speed or instructions per clock of a single core. If this trend continues, new applications will have to be designed to utilize multiple threads in order to benefit from the increase in potential computing power. This contrasts with previous microprocessor innovations in which existing code was automatically sped up by running it on a newer/faster computer.

Example

The pseudocode below illustrates task parallelism:

```
program:

...

if CPU="a" then

    do task "A"

else if CPU="b" then

    do task "B"

end if

...

end program
```

The goal of the program is to do some net total task ("A+B"). If we write the code as above and launch it on a 2-processor system, then the runtime environment will execute it as follows.

- In an SPMD system, both CPUs will execute the code.

- In a parallel environment, both will have access to the same data.

- The "if" clause differentiates between the CPUs. CPU "a" will read true on the "if" and CPU "b" will read true on the "else if", thus having their own task.

- Now, both CPU's execute separate code blocks simultaneously, performing different tasks simultaneously.

Code executed by CPU "a":

```
program:

...

do task "A"

...

end program
```

Code executed by CPU "b":

```
program:
```

```
...

do task "B"

...

end program
```

This concept can now be generalized to any number of processors.

Language Support

Task parallelism can be supported in general-purposes languages either built-in facilities or libraries. Notable examples include:

- C++ (Intel): Threading Building Blocks

- C++ (Open Source/Apache 2.0): RaftLib

- C, C++, Objective-C (Apple): Grand Central Dispatch

- D: tasks and fibers

- Go: goroutines

- Java: Java concurrency

- .NET: Task Parallel Library

Examples of fine-grained task-parallel languages can be found in the realm of Hardware Description Languages like Verilog and VHDL.

References

- Paolo Viotti; Marko Vukolic (2016). "Consistency in Non-Transactional Distributed Stor-age Systems". ACM Computer Surveys. 49 (1): 19:1––19:34. doi:10.1145/2926965

- David E. Culler, Jaswinder Pal Singh, Anoop Gupta. Parallel Computer Architecture - A Hardware/Software Approach. Morgan Kaufmann Publishers, 1999. ISBN 1-55860-343-3, pg 15

- Hicks, Michael. "Concurrency Basics" (PDF). University of Maryland: Department of Com-puter Science. Retrieved 8 May 2017

- Steinke, Robert C.; Gary J. Nutt (2004). "A unified theory of shared memory consistency.". Journal of the ACM (JACM). 51 (5): 800–849. doi:10.1145/1017460.1017464

- Hutto, Phillip W.; Mustaque Ahamad (1990). "Slow memory: Weakening consistency to enhance concurrency in distributed shared memories.". IEEE: 302–309. doi:10.1109/ICDCS.1990.89297

- Quinn, Michael J. (2007). Parallel programming in C with MPI and openMP (Tata McGraw-Hill ed. ed.). New Delhi: Tata McGraw-Hill Pub. ISBN 0070582017

- Sarita V. Adve; Kourosh Gharachorloo (December 1996). "Shared Memory Consistency Models: A Tutorial" (PDF). IEEE Computer. 29 (12): 66–76. doi:10.1109/2.546611. Re-trieved 2008-05-28

- Lamport, Leslie (Sep 1979). "How to make a multiprocessor computer that correctly executes multiprocess programs.". Computers, IEEE Transactions. C–28 (9): 690–691. doi:10.1109/TC.1979.1675439

Permissions

All chapters in this book are published with permission under the Creative Commons Attribution Share Alike License or equivalent. Every chapter published in this book has been scrutinized by our experts. Their significance has been extensively debated. The topics covered herein carry significant information for a comprehensive understanding. They may even be implemented as practical applications or may be referred to as a beginning point for further studies.

We would like to thank the editorial team for lending their expertise to make the book truly unique. They have played a crucial role in the development of this book. Without their invaluable contributions this book wouldn't have been possible. They have made vital efforts to compile up to date information on the varied aspects of this subject to make this book a valuable addition to the collection of many professionals and students.

This book was conceptualized with the vision of imparting up-to-date and integrated information in this field. To ensure the same, a matchless editorial board was set up. Every individual on the board went through rigorous rounds of assessment to prove their worth. After which they invested a large part of their time researching and compiling the most relevant data for our readers.

The editorial board has been involved in producing this book since its inception. They have spent rigorous hours researching and exploring the diverse topics which have resulted in the successful publishing of this book. They have passed on their knowledge of decades through this book. To expedite this challenging task, the publisher supported the team at every step. A small team of assistant editors was also appointed to further simplify the editing procedure and attain best results for the readers.

Apart from the editorial board, the designing team has also invested a significant amount of their time in understanding the subject and creating the most relevant covers. They scrutinized every image to scout for the most suitable representation of the subject and create an appropriate cover for the book.

The publishing team has been an ardent support to the editorial, designing and production team. Their endless efforts to recruit the best for this project, has resulted in the accomplishment of this book. They are a veteran in the field of academics and their pool of knowledge is as vast as their experience in printing. Their expertise and guidance has proved useful at every step. Their uncompromising quality standards have made this book an exceptional effort. Their encouragement from time to time has been an inspiration for everyone.

The publisher and the editorial board hope that this book will prove to be a valuable piece of knowledge for students, practitioners and scholars across the globe.

Index

9 781682 854808